Boarding School Syndrome

The psychological trauma of the 'privileged' child

Joy Schaverien

Routledge
Taylor & Francis Group
LONDON AND NEW YORK

First published 2015
by Routledge
27 Church Road, Hove, East Sussex, BN3 2FA

And by Routledge
711 Third Avenue, New York, NY 10017

Routledge is an imprint of the Taylor & Francis Group, an informa business

© 2015 Joy Schaverien

The right of Joy Schaverien to be identified as author of this work has been asserted by her in accordance with sections 77 and 78 of the Copyright, Designs and Patents Act 1988.

All rights reserved. No part of this book may be reprinted or reproduced or utilised in any form or by any electronic, mechanical, or other means, now known or hereafter invented, including photocopying and recording, or in any information storage or retrieval system, without permission in writing from the publishers.

Trademark notice: Product or corporate names may be trademarks or registered trademarks, and are used only for identification and explanation without intent to infringe.

British Library Cataloguing-in-Publication Data
A catalogue record for this book is available from the British Library

Library of Congress Cataloging-in-Publication Data
Schaverien, Joy, 1943–
   Boarding school syndrome : the psychological trauma of the 'privileged' child / Joy Schaverien.
      pages cm
   1. Boarding school students—Great Britain—Psychology. 2. Boarding schools—Great Britain. 3. Elite (Social sciences)—Education—Great Britain 4. Upper class—Education—Great Britain. I. Title.
   LC53.G7S35 2015
   373.22'20941—dc23
   2014046521

ISBN: 978-0-415-69002-7 (hbk)
ISBN: 978-0-415-69003-4 (pbk)
ISBN: 978-1-315-71630-5 (ebk)

Typeset in Times
by Apex CoVantage, LLC

Printed and bound in Great Britain by
TJ International Ltd, Padstow, Cornwall

Boarding School Syndrome

Boarding School Syndrome is an analysis of the trauma of the 'privileged' child sent to boarding school at a young age. Joy Schaverien offers an innovative and challenging psychological analysis of the long-established British and colonial preparatory and public boarding school tradition. Richly illustrated with pictures and the narratives of adult ex-boarders the book demonstrates how some forms of enduring distress in adult life may be traced back to the early losses of home and family. Developed from clinical research and informed by attachment and child development theories, *Boarding School Syndrome* offers a theoretical framework on which the psychotherapeutic treatment of ex-boarders may build.

Divided into four parts – 'History: In the name of privilege'; 'Exile and healing'; 'Broken attachments: A hidden trauma'; and 'The boarding school body' – the book includes vivid case studies of ex-boarders in psychotherapy. Their accounts reveal details of the suffering endured: loss, bereavement and captivity are sometimes compounded by physical, sexual and psychological abuse. Here, Joy Schaverien shows how many boarders adopt unconscious coping strategies, including dissociative amnesia resulting in a psychological split between the 'home self' and the 'boarding school self'. This pattern may continue into adult life, causing difficulties in intimate relationships, generalised depression and separation anxiety amongst other forms of psychological distress.

Boarding School Syndrome demonstrates how boarding school may damage those whom it is meant to reward and discusses the wider implications of this tradition. It will be essential reading for psychoanalysts, Jungian analysts, psychotherapists, art psychotherapists, counsellors and others interested in the psychological, political, cultural and international legacy of this tradition, including ex-boarders and their partners.

Joy Schaverien, Ph.D., is a Jungian psychoanalyst, a training analyst of the Society of Analytical Psychology (London). She is a member of the IAAP and Visiting Professor at the Northern Programme for Art Psychotherapy. Her many publications include *Gender, Countertransference and the Erotic Transference* (Routledge, 2006).

For
Alice Krystal, Arlo Louis, Misty Georgia and Coco Joy
With love

Contents

List of illustrations ix
Preface xi
Acknowledgements xiii
Definition of terms xv

1 Boarding School Syndrome: An introduction   1

PART I
History: In the name of privilege   15

2 Man and boy: A brief history of boarding schools   17
3 All girls together: A brief history of boarding schools   32

PART II
Exile and healing   47

4 Developmental trauma (case study part 1)   49
5 Mapping the psyche (case study part 2)   60
6 The distortion of a boy (case study part 3)   80
7 The return: Trauma and the developing brain
   (case study part 4)   94

PART III
Broken attachments: A hidden trauma — 111

8 A hidden trauma: Amnesia — 113
9 Broken attachments: The bereaved child — 125
10 The captive child: Abandonment — 137
11 Children of Empire — 151
12 Homesickness: Eating and sleeping — 164

PART IV
The boarding school body — 177

13 The armoured self: Masculinity, leathers and the lash — 179
14 The hidden self: Girls and the tyranny of the dinner table — 192
15 Puberty in girls' schools: Love and homosexuality — 205
16 Boys' sexual activity and sexual abuse: Its lasting impact — 215
17 Boarding School Syndrome: Towards a theory — 227

Bibliography — 233
Index — 241

List of illustrations

Chapter 5

5.1	Map 1, 18 November, Year 1	62
5.2	The Headmaster, 18 November, Year 1	63
5.3	The Headmaster's Wife, November Year 1	64
5.4	Map 2, 23 November, Year 1	66
5.5	Shadows, 23 November, Year 1	67
5.6	The Ammonite Priests, 22–24 February, Year 2	68
5.7	Food 1, 23 November, Year 1	70
5.8	Food 2, 10 February, Year 2	72
5.9	The Cricket Bat, 2 December, Year 1	74
5.10	Soul Murder, 2 December, Year 1	75
5.11	A Moment of Kindness, 14 December, Year 1	76
5.12	Asthma Agony, 14 December, Year 1	77
5.13	Oh God Help Me, 16 February, Year 2	78

Chapter 6

6.1	The Wall, 1 March, Year 1	82
6.2	The Tortoise, 31 March, Year 1	84
6.3	Our Garden in Spring, 21 April, Year 1	85
6.4	The Boy, 5 May, Year 1	86
6.5	The Fight, 12 May, Year 1	87
6.6	You Are Safe With Me, 14 July, Year 2	88
6.7	Lonely, 14 July, Year 2	89
6.8	Toads, 15 June, Year 2	92

Chapter 7

7.1	The Cellar 1, 6 July, Year 2	95
7.2	The Split, 24 November, Year 1	97
7.3	The Controller, 30 March, Year 2	100
7.4	The Cellar 2, 11 & 13 June, Year 3	106

Chapter 10

| 10.1 | The Police Cell | 145 |
| 10.2 | The Attic Room | 148 |

Preface

> We cannot be certain that school, at any rate boarding school is not still for many children as dreadful . . . as it used to be. Take away God, Latin, the cane, class distinctions and the sexual taboos, and the fear, the hatred, the snobbery and the misunderstanding might still all be there.
>
> George Orwell[1]

This book has developed out of my practice as a Jungian psychoanalyst. It was in 1990 that I began to notice the negative impact that early boarding had had on many of those who consulted me for psychotherapy. I turned to the psychoanalytic and psychotherapy literature for the road map and found there was little there to inform my practice. Reflecting on this, I came to realise that there is a cultural taboo on noticing that there is a problem with this socially condoned abandonment of the very young. This book breaks a cultural taboo and tells stories that many of my clients have feared that, if voiced, would not be believed. It will hopefully inform psychoanalysts, psychotherapists and counsellors in considering the approach they take with those who have attended boarding schools.

My interest in the topic is not based on my own experience; I did not attend a boarding school. It was my patients who drew my attention to the trauma of early boarding. However, as analysts we always question our personal motivation, and I do have a personal association. My father went to a preparatory boarding school at the age of 6 in 1916. (This was just a few years later than George Orwell, who went in 1911, when he was 8.) It was not a family tradition. This anecdote, written for his family seventy years later, gives a sense of my father's first day at school:

> I was sent from home to a prep boarding school in Sussex Square, in Brighton, at the age of six. Not only was I devastated at this but my Mother added insult to injury by sending me in short trousers and wearing a velour hat with elastic under the chin. If I was so precious that she dressed me in this way, why then did she part with me? I was the youngest boy in the school and was greeted with derisive jeers and laughter by a howling mob in long formal grey striped trousers and short Eton jackets with overlapping wide starched

collars. They all wore bowler hats when outside the school. They bullied me unmercifully and all I learnt the whole time I was there was aggressiveness and bad language.

Hymie Schaverien, July 1986

The query raised here is a central one: 'If I was so precious, why then did she part with me?' This question could be asked by any one of the many people, from different generations devastated in the same way, with whose stories this book is illustrated. Mostly it is a rhetorical question and rarely satisfactorily answered.

The book has educational, social and political implications as well as psychological ones. It is hoped that all who are interested in this British tradition will find something of interest, whether from a cultural or historical perspective, as well as those who come into contact with present-day boarders or ex-boarders. Men and women who attended boarding schools may find that it elucidates some of their emotional experience. It may offer clarification for partners who are sometimes puzzled by the ex-boarders' apparently inexplicable behaviours with regard to intimacy. Thinking about this afresh may create dialogue between members of a couple and between siblings separated by boarding school. Ex-boarders may find it opens up potential discourse with their parents. Last, but certainly not least, parents who may be contemplating boarding schools for their young children may pause to consider the potential emotional impact of the separation from home and loved ones.

Joy Schaverien
South Luffenham, Rutland, August 2014

Note

1 Orwell, G. (1947/2003) *Such, Such Were the Joys*, London: Penguin, p. 54.

Acknowledgements

Most of the stories told in this book are those of men and women who have come to me in distress, only partly believing that they could have been adversely affected by their 'privileged' upbringing in boarding schools. Permission to share the accounts of their childhood suffering was given in the hope that people will listen, believe and act in the interests of future children. I am deeply indebted to them and, especially, to the person I call 'Theo'. His pictures demonstrate the magnitude of his childhood trauma in a way words could not have conveyed. Along with the others whose stories illustrate the theory, he must, for the sake of confidentiality, remain anonymous. Many people not in analysis with me kindly gave their time to discuss their boarding school experiences, some in person and others by email. I am grateful to them because even when their accounts are not directly included, they have helped to build a picture of the extent of this trauma.

Friends and colleagues have contributed in various ways. My grateful thanks are due to Danielle Bradley, Andrew Colman, Nick Duffell, Michael Miller, Hilary Simon, James Taylor and Catriona Wrottesley. At the Society of Analytical Psychology the insightful discourse and peer exchange with colleagues has enriched the clinical work, and so thank you to Catherine Crowther, Lucinda Hawkins, Penny Pickles, Oliver McShane, Jean Thomson and Bob Withers. A special debt of gratitude is owed to Caroline Case, Ann Oakley, Helen Odell Miller, Jane Schaverien and Peter Wilson, who generously read and commented on the whole manuscript. Their observations, pertinent suggestions of reading material and their friendship, throughout, have enhanced the book, as well as the experience of writing it. Damien Wilson, Galia Wilson, Becky Seager and Oliver John have been immensely encouraging, often corroborating my findings with their own observations. The depth of my gratitude to Peter Wilson is, as always immeasurable: his support, encouragement and understanding have been invaluable.

My thanks to Andrew Russell, the librarian at the Society of Analytical Psychology, and James Foucar of Boarding Concern, who have both helped in tracing references and to Kirsten Buchanan at Routledge for her careful editorial attention at every stage of the process.

Although the book has been greatly enhanced by these contributions no one else is in any way responsible and any omissions or errors remain entirely my own.

I am grateful to the following for permission to quote:

Stephen Fry and Random House for permission to quote from *Moab Is My Washpot*, Arrow Books (2004).
Andrew Motion and Faber & Faber Ltd, to quote from *In the Blood: A Memoir of my Childhood*, Faber & Faber (2006).
Quotes from *Half to Remember* by D. R. West (1985), reprinted with permission of Christ's Hospital.
Such, Such Were the Joys by George Orwell (Copyright © George Orwell, 1952) reprinted by permission of Bill Hamilton as the Literary Executor of the Estate of the Late Sonia Brownell Orwell.
Electronic license: 354 words from *George Orwell: Essays* by George Orwell with an introduction by Bernard Crick (first published as *The Collected Essays, Journalism, and Letters of George Orwell*, volumes 1–4, Martin Secker and Warburg 1968, this edition Penguin Books, 2000). Copyright © the Estate of Sonia Brownell Orwell, 1984. Introduction copyright © Bernard Crick, 1994.

Excerpts from *Such, Such Were the Joys* by George Orwell, Copyright © 1953 by Sonia Brownell Orwell and renewed 1981 by Mrs George K. Perutz, Mrs Miriam Gross, and Dr Michael Dickson, Executors of the Estate of Sonia Brownell Orwell. Reprinted by permission of Houghton Mifflin Harcourt Publishing Company. All rights reserved.

Definition of terms

The terms *psychoanalysis* and *psychotherapy* are used interchangeably. The distinction may sometimes reflect the frequency of sessions and sometimes the depth of the work. The related designations *analyst* and *psychotherapist* are similarly used interchangeably.

> *Patient* and *client* are also both used. I tend to favour the term patient as it reflects the suffering involved in this work.
> *He* and *she* are used interchangeably. This may reflect the topic of a particular chapter, where the experiences of either men or women dominate. At other times it is because gender is not the main focus of a chapter.
> *Names*: In the interests of confidentiality all names of patients and informants have been changed to pseudonyms.

Chapter 1

Boarding School Syndrome
An introduction

This book is an in-depth analysis of some of the enduring psychological effects of boarding schools on men and women who, as children, lived in them for lengthy periods of time. In this introduction the main themes of the book are presented. The content of the four sections, each with an explanatory title is outlined, as well as the evolution of the term *Boarding School Syndrome*. The culmination of twenty years' research, this term was first proposed in a pilot study that was published in *The British Journal of Psychotherapy* in 2011.[1]

The hypothesis, initially derived from observations from psychoanalytic practice, was that sending children away from home to boarding schools, whilst considered to be a privilege, is also psychologically damaging. As a result there might be an identifiable cluster of symptoms in the presentation of adult analytic patients who had attended a boarding school as children. Understanding this would help in identifying and treating ex-boarders. The term *Boarding School Syndrome* was tentatively proposed.

A more rigorous inquiry than had previously been undertaken was required in order to interrogate this hypothesis and to analyse the nature of its origins. Investigation of the literature revealed relatively little published material on the psychological impact of boarding schools. Thus a gap in the existing literature to which this book might contribute was identified. Two areas for investigation emerged. First, it became evident that the existing texts centred on the history and social impact of boarding schools, whilst the psychological impact was relatively little explored. Second, it emerged that men were the focus of most of the literature and relatively little had been written about women's experiences. Two main areas for further inquiry were thus identified. This is, as far as I know, the first full-length, research-based, psychological analysis of the lasting effects of boarding schools. It is also the first that includes examination of the impact on women. Their stories are interwoven with those of men and there are also separate chapters in which distinct gendered experiences are examined.

Boarding School Syndrome – the hypothesis

Syndrome is a term usually applied to a collection of symptoms related to disease, but it is also a combination of opinions, emotions or behaviours. The *Oxford Dictionary* offers the following definitions:

Syndrome: **1.** A group of symptoms which consistently occur together or a condition characterised by a set of associated symptoms . . .
2. A characteristic combination of opinions, emotions or behaviour.[2]

Boarding School Syndrome is not a medical category. However, it is proposed that there is an identifiable cluster of learned behaviours and emotional states that may follow growing up in a boarding school. It is not my intention to pathologise everyone who attended a boarding school. The aim in naming this syndrome is to alert practitioners to common, identifiable, elements in the presentation of those for whom early boarding ruptured their primary attachments. These women and men, as children, had to adapt to growing up in an inflexible system and learn to hide their emotions. However, it would be a misunderstanding to limit any one person to specific symptoms. Its manifestation in each case is different, as we shall see as the book progresses. It is the *pattern* that is discernible.

This pattern may replay in a number of subtle ways, including the re-enactment in a marriage or life partnership of the boarding school/parent dynamic. The difficulty in identifying this syndrome is that it is rarely the presenting problem. Ex-boarders might present with a generalised sense of depression, a history of broken relationships, marital or work-related problems. They may only gradually become aware that aspects of their distress originate in the losses and broken attachments of their early childhood.

It is proposed that the learned behaviours and discontents that result in Boarding School Syndrome revolve around problems with intimacy. Whilst appearing socially confident, the ex-boarder may find intimate engagement difficult. This is a pattern observed in couples' psychotherapy where one partner – often the man – attended boarding school and is unable to talk about his feelings. It is common for the ex-boarder to make deeply dependent relationships and then suddenly emotionally, or actually, abandon the loved person. This cutting off from emotional need may be experienced by the partner as a violent attack or abrupt rejection. In analysis this pattern may replay in the therapeutic relationship and may lead to sudden termination when the rage associated with dependency begins to surface.[3]

Research method

The starting point for this study was observations from clinical practice. Analysis of case histories constitutes an established form of research in the field of psychoanalysis. As a method of investigation it can be traced back to Freud's early writings. Since then case studies have been the evidence on which numerous psychotherapy studies have been based.[4][5] The research method itself has been at the centre of a number of publications.[6][7][8] In this tradition, my inquiry began with questions raised by working with ex-boarders in analysis. Adult ex-boarders, from different generations, have consulted me over the years. Some had been boarders as far back as the 1950s, others in all the decades to the 1990s. Occasionally a general practitioner or counsellor refers children who are currently boarding. Whilst clinical case studies are useful research data, they alone were insufficient evidence on which to base what was turning into serious criticism of a long-established educational practice.

In order to question the observations and substantiate any consequent theoretical conclusions, they needed to be tested with a cluster of informants beyond analytic patients. To this end interviews were conducted with ex-boarders who were not my patients. They were recruited from amongst acquaintances and, as word spread, friends of friends volunteered. Added to this demographic were some people who, having heard me speak at conferences, volunteered to be interviewed. Thus the group of informants widened and a purposive sample was built up of informed consenting participants. Initially the inquiry began with a questionnaire followed by semi-structured interviews. However, as each interview evolved I found respondents were eager to recount their own unique experiences. These took unforeseen directions and, in most cases, the questionnaire became redundant and an emergent thematic process ensued.

An additional source of information came from unsolicited testimony. Over the past ten years I have published preliminary findings in articles in professional journals.[9][10][11] These were taken up by journalists in the national press in 2011,[12] 2012[13] and 2013.[14] Since then, people have written to me to confirm the findings. Some of these informants were 70 or 80 years old, others were still at school or had recently left, but the majority were in their middle years. These witness accounts – from Africa, Australia, India, New Zealand and the USA, as well as Britain – contribute to the evidence of the enduring suffering caused to children by the rupture from their families at an early age. Thus this book is based on a large sample of adults who as children attended boarding schools in Britain and abroad. Even when their testimony is not quoted directly they have all contributed to the wider picture. I am indebted to each one of them for their anonymous contributions.

Discourse with colleagues, many of whom work with ex-boarders, has been invaluable. These included psychoanalysts, psychotherapists, arts therapists and counsellors; some were ex-boarders and others, like myself, non-boarders. They were consulted in peer supervision, professional meetings, conferences and informal discussions. I am also informed by supervising colleagues who work as counsellors and psychotherapists in present-day boarding schools. This evidence from other psychotherapy professionals supplements my own findings. At times it challenges and leads me to question assumptions but it also verifies and supports many of the conclusions.

Boarders in the population

The Independent Schools Council (ICS) report for 2013 compares the numbers of boarders to day pupils in schools in the independent sector. A total of 66,776 pupils board at ISC schools, which makes up 13.1 per cent of the total pupil numbers. They report that of those schools completing census returns in both 2012 and 2013, the number of pupils boarding fell by 1.4 per cent. This is in line with the percentages reported since 1987 when boarders were 25 per cent of the total of pupils in these schools. It has now fallen to 15 per cent.[15] There are around 465 independent boarding schools in the UK and these accept children of any nationality. There are also 35 State boarding schools, which accept only UK pupils or those from the European Economic Area.[16] What is so extraordinary about the statistics is that those attending boarding schools are a minority – yet in government most of the policy makers are ex-boarders. They are also represented in all the major institutions in Britain.

Those who enjoyed boarding

Most of the accounts in this book tell of those who suffered in their schools. It is important therefore to acknowledge that some respondents have positive memories of their boarding schools. These go beyond the rather defensive comment, commonly heard, that 'it never did me any harm.' Some of my respondents made it clear that the education, sense of fair play and altruism engendered in the best of the public schools, stays with them as a positive attitude all their lives. For some, the love of sport, music, art or drama acquired in their schools has greatly enriched their lives. Others remember an inspiring or motivational teacher who made a lasting impression. In my experience these are a minority, but I am aware that this may be because these people are less likely to seek psychotherapy. Many of the people who enjoyed boarding were those who first boarded when they were 13 or over. Those who first go at 16 very often enjoy the social as well as the educational aspects.

The ambivalence of some informants was evident: gratitude to their boarding schools was tempered by the upset caused by loss of attachment figures. Many who went to prep school at an early age suffered from living without their families and without love. However, there were others who felt boarding school was preferable to their homes. Some of my informants considered that they were saved by boarding school from neglectful, intolerably chaotic or abusive family situations. These people benefitted from the order and care provided in their schools, as well as the educational opportunities. These included those with a parent who suffered from severe mental illness or whose background was very unstable; they relished the stability provided by the school.

One man told how, on the train journey to school, he was relieved to be leaving home, where he suffered emotional abuse. Whilst the others in his peer group were miserable to be returning to school he just felt relief. His school was no soft option, with bullying and beatings a regular part of life there. Even so, at the end of term, whilst the others were excited to be going home, he would dread it. Thus he felt isolated and separated from his peers. A woman, who began boarding at 8, was relieved to live in that structured environment rather than her unstable home. Another woman who went at 13 chose boarding and thoroughly enjoyed it. Her mother moved away from the area where they were living and she chose to stay with her friends. Perhaps these redress the balance a little. The point is that the suffering I have observed is common but not universal. For some, boarding schools provide the stability and predictability that is lacking in their homes. Others seem to enjoy the large sibling group.

Review of the literature

This book differs from previous inquiries into boarding schools because the method is primarily psychoanalytic. Research-based publications on the psychological impact of boarding schools are few and were mostly written in the 1960s by sociologists. Notable is the investigation conducted by Royston Lambert and his team of young researchers, who lived in sixty-six boarding schools for a week at a time and, in some cases, for several weeks. Their remit was to encourage the children to keep diaries, reflecting their views of school life. In some cases, staff members were also asked to contribute. Thus a picture, from the perspective of students and staff, of the 1960s emerged.[17] The study is in many ways outdated but it is relevant to today's clinical practice because some present-day adult patients were the boarding school children of that time. Thus to read Lambert is to be informed of the ethos in which some of our clients lived.

John Wakeford's sociological analysis was published the following year. It investigated boys' schools as residential organisations, comparing the structure with those of other institutions such as prisons.[18] Walford's research was conducted in 1981 and 1982 in two schools. His interest was in the experiences of the teaching staff as well as the pupils. The schools were both boys' schools but one admitted girls to the sixth form.[19] Alisdare Hickson investigated the different attitudes to sex and sexual experiences in boys' public schools. He conducted interviews with ex-boarders, which revealed fierce taboos in some schools and a permissive attitude in others.[20] (This topic will be developed in Chapter 16.) Mallory Wober extended Lambert's research, conducting a similar project in six girl's schools.[21] As a man conducting research in female establishments, his observations are tempered by the outsider's view. Judith Okely, a social anthropologist, gives an insider's view. Okely used her own experience retrospectively, exposing life in a girls' boarding school from the inside. In 1978 this was published as two articles in *New Society* and later developed in a book, *Own and Other Culture*.[22]

The research conducted by historians has been central in informing Part 1. Jonathan Gathorne-Hardy[23] gives an overview of the scale and the timeline of boarding schools, exposing the history of their brutal origins and the reforms that gradually took place. Limiting his remit to the boys' boarding schools of the nineteenth century, John Chandos[24] gives a detailed account of the chaos and barbarity engaged in by boys left to their own devices in this era. To build their historical pictures, both Gathorne-Hardy and Chandos had access to the extensive archives kept in some of the oldest public schools. Vyvyen Brendon, who found in the archives numerous letters written from children to their parents, traced the links to Empire. Through these documents she tracked children of the Raj in their – often unaccompanied – travels across the world.[25] Then, in her second book, she turned her attention to the history of prep school children across two centuries.[26] The letters provide poignant testimony from numerous young children exiled from their homes and their parents. Many of these young correspondents were destined to become famous men, whilst others endured the suffering only to die young, sometimes whilst still at school. (The experiences of children from abroad will be discussed in Chapter 11.)

The first psychologically informed book on children who attended boarding school was by Nick Duffell.[27] Duffell identified the significant emotional suffering of some children. His book is based on the testimony of numerous men who took part in the annual weekend workshops he runs for those whom he called 'boarding school survivors'. These workshops have been running since October 1990; workshops for women were instated in 1998 by Duffell working with Helena Lovendal-Duffell. In 1994, inspired by the workshops, Colin Luke made a BBC television film, *The Making of Them*,[28] the title later used by Duffell for his book. First screened in 1994, the film movingly documents young children's progress as they enter the boarding school system.

My interest in the psychological damage of boarding schools was evoked around the same time. It was in 1990, when working with a certain psychoanalytic patient, that I began to notice the psychological distress caused by early boarding. This later became the subject of my book, *The Dying Patient in Psychotherapy*.[29] When Luke's film was first shown, it affirmed my observations and alerted me when a new patient mentioned, usually in passing, that he or she had attended boarding school. I realised that the experience needed closer psychological attention than it was usually accorded. Later I met with Duffell, and in 2005, we collaborated in offering a post-graduate training for psychotherapists working with ex-boarders. In 2011, along with Helena Lovendal-Duffell, this was developed into a series of Continuing Professional Development days for experienced practitioners.

As already stated, a number of published articles prefigured this book. In the *Journal of Analytical Psychology* in 2004, I suggested that boarding school is a particularly 'British form of child abuse and social control', and substantiated that claim with clinical examples.[30] In the *British Journal of Psychotherapy* in 2011 I introduced the term *Boarding School Syndrome*.[31] Then in 'Lost for words', an article in *Therapy Today*[32] published alongside one by Duffell,[33] I suggested that the experience for the child sent to boarding school at a young age could be literally unspeakable. This is because without adult guidance the child lacks the language to describe emotional experience. These articles have drawn attention to this as a wider issue, worthy of psychoanalytic consideration. Since then a number of articles have appeared and Francis Grier has contributed a chapter in a book on trauma.[34] In the journal *Attachment* a psychoanalytically informed personal account by Simon Partridge was published, followed by a response from an attachment perspective by Anne Power.[35] An article by Mary Stack appeared the following year[36] and in 2013 a further two articles by Power and Partridge were published in the same journal.[37][38] Thus the research base is gradually building.

Looked after children

The suffering we are considering is often hidden behind a veneer of social polish learned at school and reinforced, in some cases, by inherited wealth and position. Despite this, a number of people from apparently privileged backgrounds were, in effect, 'looked after children'. The term *looked after* here has a double meaning. Children whose families break down are sometimes taken into foster care: in the social care system in Britain, these are called 'looked after children'. The National Society for the Prevention of Cruelty to Children (NSPCC) defines the term in the following way:

Definition of 'looked after children'

The term 'looked after children and young people' is generally used to mean those looked after by the state . . .

The term is also used to describe 'accommodated' children and young people who are looked after on a voluntary basis at the request of, or by agreement with, their parents. We refer to these children as 'children in care'.[39]

The definition of 'children in care' seems to fit the child in boarding school. There are of course some evident differences; children in care are usually from economically deprived backgrounds. Children's homes and special schools are also sometimes residential. They play a necessary role, often as a last resort for desperate parents and for children with behaviour problems or special educational needs. In them there is usually a high staff/student ratio with attention to the needs of the individual child.

The initial impression would be that there is little comparison with the child from an affluent home. However, a child living in boarding school is also a 'looked after' child. They spend many of their formative years in institutional care and are, in effect, fostered with strangers. The attitude of the parents is significant for the child's understanding of what is happening to them. The parents of children in the social care system are often reluctant to let their children go (this is evident from the much-publicised custody battles in the press, as well as observations from clinical practice). The pain for the boarder is that their parents choose this form of care for them and pay a great deal of money for it. The similarity is that, in both situations, the child experiences loss of attachment figures and the distress of being 'looked after' by strangers.

Boarders cannot console themselves with the thought that their parents did not want them to go. They have to try to understand why, if they are loved, this painful experience is good for them. Not all boarders are from wealthy homes: some boarding school places are subsidised by the military, government or other employers. Other parents go to extreme sacrifices to obtain this prized education for their children, as Christine Heward's study of the aspirations of parents for their sons' education revealed.[40] This makes little difference to the child; the separation is still the same. The point is that parents of children who do not need to be 'looked after' are voluntarily delegating childcare to others. This may subject the child to emotional or physical harm and in some cases neglect. Added to this the special education, for which the parents pay, is variable: in some cases it is indisputably excellent, but in others it is far from adequate.

Day schools

In this introduction it is important to make a rather obvious distinction between day and boarding schools. It is not suggested that bullying and abuse are the exclusive territory of boarding school. Many children will suffer upsetting experiences in day schools; some will be ostracised by their friendship group, or experience bullying on the way to or from school; the rules in school may be rigid and the punishments unjust. They too may be singled out in class by a cruel teacher or, in earlier times, be beaten by a sadistic teacher for a misdemeanour. However, when the day school child returns home in the evening, there is a refuge away from the bully and from the system. This is not to idealise homes: children are also beaten and abused in their homes, which is why some are taken into care. However in most homes, even if the child cannot speak of it, a parent might notice and be concerned if the child is apparently upset. For the child living in school the parents have delegated that responsibility to others. There is no respite and no one in whom to confide. The child lives in the school at night and at weekends, for months at a time. Even if the instinct is to tell, there is rarely anyone to listen. When there is, that person is not someone who loves the child. This may compound the sense of having been abandoned and contribute to a devastating realisation of being alone in the world.

Today contact is simpler because children have mobile phones and are freer to communicate with home. Even so there is a difference between telephone contact and living at home. There is now an additional area of potential bullying that is online harassment, which reaches into homes, sometimes beyond the protective barrier of the front door and the parents. This raises the question: how can children be protected from this at school?[41] This is a question beyond the remit of this current work but one that merits future research. I turn now to the way in which the book is organised.

Organisation of the book

As already discussed, Part 1 ('History: In the name of privilege') is made up of two chapters and presents a brief history of boys' and girls' boarding schools respectively. Part 2 is entitled 'Exile and healing'. The four chapters in this section give a detailed case history tracing the story of one man. Three chapters are illustrated with pictures made in analysis. This demonstrates how art offers a unique way of mediating trauma and so has implications for approaches in treatment for those other than the ex-boarder.

Part 3, entitled 'Broken attachments: A hidden trauma', draws on case vignettes and published material to analyse the nature of the broken attachments of the prep school child. Each chapter is devoted to one aspect of the accumulation of linked distressing events. In Chapter 8, the amnesia of dissociation is discussed. There are times when the broken attachments have been so unbearable that they have been repressed and the emotions are beyond conscious recall. In Chapter 9 homesickness is reframed as bereavement. In Chapter 10, the often-humorous comment that boarding school is a form of captivity is taken seriously and illustrated through the experiences of one girl. In Chapter 11, the additional bereavements of children sent to boarding school from abroad are discussed. In Chapter 12 I return to consider homesickness, this time with regard to food, hunger and greed.

The purpose of this book is to differentiate the psychological impact of boarding on children at distinctive developmental stages. The latency child (that is the child from the age of 5 or 6 prior to puberty) has different needs from the adolescent. Thus the final section, Part 4, addresses 'The boarding school body' and is an analysis of some of the physical and emotional privations experienced in some boarding schools. At puberty gender differences become significant and the respective experiences of girls and boys may become more marked. In Chapter 13 I consider how the hardships and beatings in the schools of earlier times have affected men's attitude to their bodies and to masculinity. In girls' schools beatings were rare but other forms of cruelty were inflicted on their bodies, as we see in Chapter 14 and Chapter 15. In Chapter 16, sexuality in boys' schools is considered, distinguishing between sexual activity and sexual abuse.

Psychotherapy and the hidden trauma

There is a very particular form of cultural amnesia associated with the boarding school tradition. It is hardly a secret that boarding school experiences are harsh: since *Tom Brown's School Days*[42] in 1855 and Robert Graves *Goodbye to All That*[43] in 1929, stories of boarding school excesses have permeated society. Why are these pleas for attention largely ignored? Even in psychotherapy the depth of the traumatic nature of these experiences is often missed. In the last twenty years, the worst excesses – such as fagging and beatings – have been curbed, but the trauma that begins with entry to the school continues. It seems that social acceptance, combined with apparent privilege, makes most ex-boarders feel ashamed to complain. This is one reason for naming this trauma and analysing it.

One might speculate that analysts, in common with other members of society, take this damage for granted, as a sort of by-product of a system of privilege in education which is so familiar that it hardly merits comment – this, despite some notable biographies and autobiographies by analysts who themselves attended boarding schools. These commentators include Wilfred Bion,[44] who conveys the bewilderment of a small boy growing up in the lonely and mysterious world of boarding school. John Bowlby's[45] emphasis on the importance of attachment in child development is significant in this context, and he was unambiguous in his repudiation of the tradition of sending children under 13 away to boarding school. He boarded for a brief period himself, at 13.[46] Holmes quotes Bowlby as describing the public school as 'merely the traditional first step in *the time-honoured barbarism required to produce English gentlemen*'.[47] This unequivocal indictment from a distinguished psychoanalyst is greeted, as is usual, with a wry smile and everything continues as it was.

Patrick Casement went to boarding school at 8.[48] It was not until into his adult life that he began to realise how profoundly his early experiences had affected him. He shows how, in the absence of family, places are substituted in the imagination of the lonely child.[49] The attachment to houses, rather than people, is a kind of desperate solution found by the child, whose capacity to love is distorted by the absence of human attachment figures.[50] Casement's first psychotherapy did not address the depth of his early experiences of loss.[51] This was rectified in a later analysis five times a week, as shared in a personal communication. There are many other cases where the depth of the pain associated with early boarding has passed unnoticed in psychotherapy. There are other examples; see my 2011 *British Journal of Psychotherapy* article[52] for a deeper discussion of this. The acquired veneer of confidence may contribute to this formative experience being missed in psychotherapy. In British society the assumption that boarding school is a privilege is a cultural myth, with some justification.

There is huge social pressure not to complain about what is generally seen as a benefit of privilege. It has been notable that the suggestions made respectively and at different times by Okely,[53] Duffell[54,55] and myself[56,57] that boarding school is emotionally damaging have caused a flurry of interest each time. However, the excitement soon dies down and the findings are forgotten. If the damage is acknowledged, it is attributed to those regarded as the most socially vulnerable. It is convenient to dismiss the harm as a sad consequence for those whose suffering leads to symptoms of psychiatric illness. The bravado of the repost 'it never did me any harm' spoken by socially successful men and women may be masking their suffering with good-natured humour. This leaves those who admit to the pain feeling socially isolated, and it can feel humiliating to ask for psychological help.

The social implications of boarding school are based on a patriarchal tradition that runs like a fault line, an unseen influence, in British society. An outcome of early boarding may be that children have to learn to cut themselves off from compassion for their own predicament. It may follow in some cases that empathic understanding may also be lacking. Boarding schools are based on masculine principles. The balance of opposites is skewed by sometimes unsympathetic treatment of children. In the student group in boys' schools, traits of vulnerability and weakness are attributed to the feminine and then repudiated. In girls' schools this is complex: although they are apparently female environments, they are often based on the same masculine principles as the boys' schools. The British establishment is composed largely of men who attended boarding schools from an early age. This raises questions of how this affects their attitude to those on whose behalf policy decisions are made. This is beyond the scope of this book, but in Duffell's most recent book[58] he addresses the role of British boarding schools in the creation of political leaders.

A note on clinical method

The Jungian psychoanalytic and relational approach described in this book has been honed in clinical practice. The book is written for practitioners, but it is hoped that the ex-boarder will also find much of interest in these pages. Most analysts and psychotherapists already know that boarding school is damaging, but it is the *depth* of the trauma that may be missed. Concepts can be problematic in that they fix knowledge that has previously been fluid, but theory can also be helpful. Thus it is hoped that identifying the multiple facets of the presentation of Boarding School Syndrome will aid in recognition of patterns of behaviour that trouble many of our clients.

Throughout the book general points about working with trauma are made. In working with trauma, the analytic approach may at times need to be adapted. The so-called 'blank screen', in which the analyst remains opaque, is often unhelpful and may even serve to re-traumatise the patient. However, analyst disclosure is also unhelpful. To befriend or tell the analyst's personal story, even when it has parallels with that of the client, merely serves to confuse. This may leave some of the more negative emotions unprocessed and the patient may unconsciously feel obliged to monitor disclosures to protect the therapist.

It is hoped that the reader will emerge from this book with an understanding of depth psychology and its potential to heal. Many of the ex-boarders described in these pages have suffered profoundly and as a result they are often fiercely defended. They need an empathic but firm approach to penetrate their emotional armour and to contain the vulnerability that is sometimes exposed. Most of all they need a psychotherapist who *believes* their story – and that is the reason for writing this book. We need to believe the depth of trauma sometimes caused by early boarding.

Notes

1 Schaverien, J. (2011a) 'Boarding School Syndrome: Broken attachments a hidden trauma', *British Journal of Psychotherapy* 17 (2), pp. 138–155.
2 Pearsall, J., & Hanks, P. (eds) (2001) *The New Oxford Dictionary of English*, Oxford: Oxford University Press, p. 1,881.
3 Schaverien, J. (2002) *The Dying Patient in Psychotherapy: Desire, Dreams and Individuation*, New York: Palgrave Macmillan.
4 McLeod, J. (1994) *Doing Counselling Research*, London, Thousand Oaks, California: Sage, p. 103.
5 Roth, A., & Fonagy, P. (1996) *What Works for Whom? A Critical Review of Psychotherapy Research*, London: Guilford, p. 49.
6 Sandler, J., Sandler, A. M., & Davies, R. (2000) *Clinical and Observational Psychoanalytic Research Andre Green and David Stern*, London: Karnac Books.
7 Midgely, N. (2006) 'The "inseparable bond between cure and research": Clinical case study as a method of psychoanalytic inquiry,' *Journal of Child Psychotherapy* 32, pp. 122–147.
8 Hinshelwood, R. D. (2013) *Research on the Couch: Single-Case Studies, Subjectivity and Psychoanalytic Knowledge*, London: Routledge, New Library of Psychoanalysis, 'Beyond the Couch' series.

9 Schaverien, J. (2004) 'Boarding school: the trauma of the "privileged" child', *Journal of Analytical Psychology* 49 (5), pp. 683–705.
10 Schaverien, J. (2011a), op. cit.
11 Schaverien, J. (2011b) 'Lost for words', *Therapy Today* 22 (3), pp. 18–21.
12 Lakani, N. (2011) 'Boarding is as damaging as being taken into care, says therapist', *The Independent on Sunday* (24 April); Leigh, W. (2011) 'Bedlam, bullying and baked beans three times a day', *The Mail* (1 May); Marsh, S. (2011) 'Cold, disengaged, and detached: do you suffer from boarding school syndrome?' *The Times* (23 June); Brown, A. M. (2011) 'Does 'brusque' and 'rude' David Cameron suffer from boarding school syndrome?' (23 June).
13 Monbiot, G. (2012) 'The British boarding school remains a bastion of cruelty', *The Guardian* (17 January) www.theguardian.com/commentisfree/2012/jan/16/boarding-school-bastion-cruelty.
14 E Englhart, K. (2013) 'Brits warned to beware of "boarding school syndrome"', *Macleans* (23 April).
15 Lockhart, R. E., Gilpin, A., & Jasiocha, E. (2013) *ISC Census*, London: Independent Schools Council www.isc.co.uk/Resources/Independent%20Schools%20Council/Research%20Archive/Annual%20Census/2013_annualcensus_isc.pdf.
16 British Council, The UK boarding school system www.educationuk.org/global/articles/uk-boarding-school-system/.
17 Lambert, R. with Millham, S. (1968) *The Hothouse Society*, London: Weidenfeld & Nicolson.
18 Wakeford, J. (1969) *The Cloistered Elite: A Sociological Analysis of the English Public School*, London, New York: Macmillan, pp. 174.
19 Walford, G. (1986) *Life in Public Schools*, London: Methuen.
20 Hickson, A. (1996) *The Poisoned Bowl: Sex and the Public School*, London: Gerald Duckworth, 1996.
21 Wober, M. (1971) *English Girls' Boarding Schools*, London: Allen Lane, the Penguin Press.
22 Okely, J. (1996) *Own and Other Culture*, London: Routledge. (The 1978 article was titled 'The Isle of Wight as a Site for English-British Identity.')
23 Gathorne-Hardy, J. (1977) *The Public School Phenomenon, 597–1977*, London: Hodder & Stoughton.
24 Chandos, J. (1984) *Boys Together: English Public Schools 1800–1864*, London: Yale University Press.
25 Brendon, V. (2005/2006) *Children of the Raj*, Phoenix: Orion.
26 Brendon, V. (2009) *Prep School Children: A Class Apart Over Two Centuries*, London, Continuum, 2009.
27 Duffell, N. (2000) *The Making of Them*, London: Lone Arrow Press.
28 *The Making of Them* (1994). Directed by Colin Luke (film). Broadcast on BBC 4.
29 Schaverien (2002), op. cit.
30 Schaverien (2004), op. cit., p. 683.
31 Schaverien (2011a), op. cit.
32 Schaverien (2011b), op. cit.
33 Duffell, N., (2011) 'The old school ties', *Therapy Today* 22 (3), pp. 11–15.
34 Grier, F. (2013) 'The hidden trauma of the young boarding school child as seen through the lens of adult couple therapy', *Enduring Trauma Through the Life Cycle*, McGinley, E. & Varchevker, A. (eds), London, Karnac Books.
35 Partridge, S. (2007) 'Trauma at the threshold: An eight-year-old goes to boarding school', *Attachment* 1 (3), pp. 310–313; Power, A. (2007) 'Discussion of trauma at the threshold: The impact of boarding school on attachment in young children', *Attachment* 1 (3), pp. 313–320.

36 Stack, M. (2008), 'The making of her: My boarding school experience', *Attachment* 2 (3), pp. 321–328.
37 Power, A. (2013a) 'Early boarding: Rich children in care, their adaptation to loss of attachment', *Attachment* 7 (2), pp. 186–201.
38 Partridge, S. (2013) 'Boarding School Syndrome: Disguised attachment-deficit and dissociation reinforced by institutional neglect and abuse', *Attachment* 7 (2), pp. 202–213.
39 National Society for the Prevention of Cruelty to Children (2015) www.nspcc.org.uk/Inform/resourcesforprofessionals/lookedafterchildren/introduction_wda88884.html.
40 Heward, C. (1988) *Making a Man of Him: Parents and Their Sons' Education at an English Public School 1929–1950*, London: Routledge.
41 Wilson, A.N., 'Scarred for life by the boarding school sadists: How A. N. Wilson was deluged with similar horror stories after revealing his abuse at hands of paedophile head', *Mail Online* (17 May) www.dailymail.co.uk/news/article-2630951/Scarred-life-boarding-school-sadists-How-A-N-Wilson-deluged-similar-horror-stories-revealing-abuse-hands-paedophile-head.html.
42 Hughes, T. (1857/2013) *Tom Brown's School Days*, Burlingame, California: Collins Classics.
43 Graves, R. (1929/1960) *Goodbye to All That*, London: Penguin.
44 Bion, W. R. (1985) *The Long Weekend 1897–1919, Part of a Life*, London: Karnac Books.
45 Bowlby, J. (1969) *Attachment*, Attachment and Loss, vol. 1, London: Hogarth Press; (1973) *Separation: Anxiety and Anger*, Attachment and Loss, vol. 2, London: Hogarth Press; (1980) *Loss: Sadness and Depression*, Attachment and Loss, vol. 3, London: Hogarth Press.
46 Van Dijken, S. (1998) *John Bowlby: His Early Life*, London: Free Association Books.
47 Holmes, J. (1993) *John Bowlby and Attachment Theory*, London: Routledge, p. 17.
48 Casement, P. (2008) *Learning From Life*, London: Routledge.
49 Ibid., p. 29.
50 Schaverien (2002), op. cit., pp. 32–38.
51 Casement (2008) op. cit., pp. 14–15.
52 Schaverien (2011a), op. cit.
53 Okely (1996), op. cit.
54 Duffell, N. (1990) 'The old school', *The Independent* (1 September).
55 Duffell (2000), op. cit.
56 Schaverien (2004), op. cit.
57 Schaverien (2011a), op. cit.
58 Duffell, N. (2014) *Wounded Leaders: British Elitism and the Entitlement Illusion: A Psychohistory*, London: Lone Arrow Press.

Part 1

History

In the name of privilege

Chapter 2

Man and boy
A brief history of boarding schools

A man of 63 lies on my couch and tells me with huge emotion of how he was sent to a school run by Jesuit brothers in the 1950s. He was 13 years of age. He was horrified on his first night when, after some talking took place after lights out, a monk came in the room and beat every one of the boys in the dormitory. This was a terrifying shock. However, it became a regular occurrence to which he soon became accustomed. Very little provocation was needed to merit a beating.

The effects of such acts of institutionalised cruelty are long term and often a factor in the experiences of men who attended boarding school and who later engage in psychotherapy. European legislation on the rights of the child meant that corporal punishment was prohibited in the late twentieth century. In Britain beating was banned in State schools in 1987, but it was 1999 before it was banned in private schools. Thus this time-honoured means of chastising children was finally banned. In psychotherapy we meet many of those who attended boarding schools prior to this legislation and many of them, like the man described above, suffered the indignity and pain of this form of punishment. Today this would be considered physical assault. What is acceptable in one generation may become unacceptable to the next and eventually abhorrent to later generations. The history of the British public school is such a story. However, the legacy of some of the punitive practices, exploitation and neglect, of which we will learn, continued well into the twentieth century and in some cases continues even today. Therefore in this chapter the scene is set through the history of the British public school.

The legacy of the boarding school system is woven into the fabric of British society. It has affected politics, public and economic policy for countless generations. Moreover, many of the apparently arcane traditions, unspoken rules and practices of initiation which can be traced to the earliest forms of these schools continue to permeate the law and systems of government. They are perpetuated by what is known in Britain as the 'old boys' network, the unspoken camaraderie of powerful men who, as boys, attended these elite schools. These same traditions were exported throughout the British Empire. It is not only children growing up in Britain that have been subject to this system but many who were raised in the former British colonies as well. Thus the influence of the British public school is international, affecting those raised in Africa, India, Canada, Australia, New Zealand, and the USA – in fact all the countries to which the British Empire extended.

The old grammar schools

Boarding schools for boys were established when Christianity was first introduced into Britain. The first 'grammar schools' were attached to monasteries. Well-known public schools still in existence often proudly trace their origins to this tradition; for example, St Peter's School, York, was founded in AD 627, and The Kings School, Canterbury, in AD 598.[1] These, like other Church schools, took in boys from poor backgrounds, not as charity but to serve the needs of the Church for choristers and Latin scholars – and so when Winchester was founded in 1382, by William of Wykeham, it was specified that the scholars must be poor. Eton was founded in 1442 by Henry VI, in the Church tradition, with the aim of providing boys to sing masses for the King.[2] The belief was that the younger a child was taken in, the easier they were to train. Children who showed aptitude as choristers or Latin scholars were retained, but others, less talented, were rapidly dropped. It was only later that the aims of the Church schools became charitable.[3]

The new grammar school foundations

The dissolution of the monasteries and the break with Rome during the reign of Henry VIII brought about the closure of many of the early Church grammar schools. During the Reformation, the official religion of Britain was changed from Catholic to Anglican. Church property was seized, and during the mid 1530s many monasteries, friaries and nunneries were destroyed; over a very short time as many as 800 disappeared. Along with the monasteries to which they belonged, Church grammar schools were destroyed. For a time, it seemed that education was in danger of disappearing altogether. However, Henry VIII began a new system with the founding of 'Kings' Schools'; these new grammar schools, now Protestant, were created and old ones re-endowed, often using former monastic and Church (or Catholic) property.[4,5] The English Reformation thus brought about modifications in education, which continued well into the reign of Elizabeth I. So it was that during the sixteenth century a new basis for education was established. Moreover, following the lead of the King, liveried companies endowed new grammar schools. These were merchant, rather than Church schools: Oundle, Blundell's, Greshams, Tonbridge and many more were created under this system.[6] Other schools were founded by wealthy individuals, many of whom also established university colleges, thus providing continuity of education. Pupils would graduate from school to the associated university college. So it was that the rich gradually took over education.[7]

Now education became more sought after and the wealthy began to send their sons to boarding schools. In earlier times the children of the nobility were taught in their own homes or else sent to be educated in the homes of other noblemen, usually at the age of 7 or 8. It seems that the tradition of sending children to boarding schools at such a young age began with this early history and has continued unquestioned to the present day. Preparatory schools for younger children were not introduced until the late eighteenth century and so at first the grammar schools took in the young children as well as the older ones. All the ages mixed together in the same schools, with boys arriving and leaving at different stages. There are reports of infants of 3 and 4 being sent to Dulwich in 1707, whilst others entered school at 13.[8]

It was not generally considered to be necessary or desirable to educate girls. Very few girls were educated at all during these centuries, except for some daughters of the nobility who were taught at home. It was not until the 1830s that girls' schools were established. Because there is a significant difference in their history this is explored in Chapter 3.

The public schools

The endowed schools continued to be known as grammar schools until the eighteenth century, when the term *public school* emerged as a way of differentiating the old grammar schools from the smaller private schools that had by then begun to flourish. The public schools 'were public, in that they were not privately owned, but incorporated under statute at law'.[9]

Latin was used by the Church and the Law, and was deemed the path to employment, therefore it continued to be the main subject taught in grammar schools until the Renaissance, when the curriculum widened to include Classics and Classical Latin. According to Gathorne-Hardy it was illegal to teach other subjects until 1840. The emphasis on the Classics remained until the twentieth century, but some schools had a much wider curriculum. As early as 1587, Uppingham Public School had a wide syllabus that included Italian, Spanish, logic, arithmetic, geometry, music and natural philosophy (science).[10]

Accommodation: Lessons and sleeping arrangements

Many boys travelled long distances by horse-drawn carriages to the schools, sometimes the length and breadth of the country. Others travelled by boat from the far distant reaches of the Empire.[11] Travel was such an obstacle that even boys from Britain stayed at school most of the year, returning home only in the summer for about twenty or thirty days. Brendon gives personal accounts of the journeys undertaken by these, often small, boys from their own testimony. Her researches led to the discovery of numerous letters home from boys, many who were later to become influential men.[12] The vast distances travelled meant that the children needed accommodation and, at first, arrangements were made for them to stay in boarding houses in the nearby towns. Subsequently lodging houses were established, and then the schoolmasters (who were often poorly paid) began to supplement their income by taking the boys into their own homes. By the seventeenth century schoolmasters were running boarding houses for profit and parents were paying for accommodation.[13] So it was that boarding and the house system became established and parents began paying for the education of their children. They paid first for accommodation but then, later, fees for education were introduced.

The classes were huge, with as many as 70 or 100 children in a class with two or three teachers. At Sherborne, in the sixteenth century, 144 boys were taught in two classes divided between the headmaster, who took the top three forms, and the usher, who had the bottom three. There were approximately seventy boys in each of these classes. In 1561 at Shrewsbury three schoolmasters tried to control 266 boys. There was little change in class sizes over the centuries. Keate, the famous headmaster of Eton in the early nineteenth century, taught classes with 200 students.[14] John Betjeman reported a conversation with a man who remembered these large classes. This eyewitness had attended Totnes Grammar School at the end of the nineteenth century and recalled sitting around a huge hall: 'Your education depended on whether or not the master reached you. Sometimes he did not reach you for months.'[15] May gives illustrations showing these vast classrooms.[16] Eventually exams were initiated, primarily to motivate the boys, but also to assess their learning in the chaos of these huge classes. Thus it was that formal competition was introduced.

Brutality

During the early centuries brutality was rife. Although comparison with the schools of that time might seem unpalatable, the legacy of their brutal history ran like a thread through the public schools of the twentieth century. These were attended by many of my patients, such as the man with whose beating this chapter began. Therefore no history of the British public school is complete without attention to the harshness on which many of these schools built their foundations.

With so many boys and so few teachers, discipline was a real problem. During the eighteenth and nineteenth centuries beatings were ubiquitous and institutionalised. This gave license to those teachers who became renowned for their open cruelty. In a close-up account of the period from 1800 to 1864, Chandos gives a sense of the anarchy prevalent in the schools prior to the reforms of the mid-nineteenth century.[17] Like Gathorne-Hardy, he drew on the archives of this period preserved by the schools, which are sometimes very detailed. Both Chandos and Gathorne-Hardy demonstrate the extreme anarchy, neglect and abuse suffered by boys during these centuries, including cruel beatings and sexual misconduct, which were endemic. There were few adults in these communities; the schoolmasters were often dominated by the far more numerous boys. Given the ethos of the time, it was hardly surprising that conditions were tough:

> If you leave a lot of boys to their own devices in a brutal age, themselves brutalised by rude surroundings and rendered aggressive by violent discipline and often harsh childhoods you will get bullying . . . the bullying in these centuries was inevitable, continuous and fiendish.[18]

Charles Dickens gives an account of this with Dotheboys Hall in *Nicholas Nickleby*.[19] His books give a vivid portrait of aspects of the society that these schools served. When considering them we are observing a society different in many ways from that of twenty-first–century Britain. Hardships which seem excessive today were much more prevalent in all walks of life in the eighteenth and early nineteenth centuries.[20] The practices described here were modified following the reforms of the mid-nineteenth century. Even so many of the traditions established during these times lived on into the twentieth century, affecting the physical and psychological well-being of generations of men, as I will show.

Dormitories and brutality

It was not easy to keep discipline with boys scattered in lodging houses, so dormitories gradually replaced them. During the eighteenth and nineteenth centuries it was common for boys to be locked in one long dormitory at eight o'clock in the evening and left, with no adult supervision, until morning. At Westminster forty boys, and at Eton fifty boys between the ages of 9 and 19 were locked up together. Here the younger children suffered multiple torments. The Long Chamber at Eton was notorious for its brutality. This is vividly described by both Gathorne-Hardy[21] and Chandos. Their descriptions evoke something of the atmosphere, so I quote them at length. The first description is from Chandos:

> [The Long Chamber at Eton] became, a 'free', self-contained, self-governing community, with its own class system, moral standards, public opinion and legal code, . . . In this setting nothing changed over the years except the rough beds and blankets deteriorated. Beside each bed was a stand up desk, no chairs were provided.[22]
>
> On a winter night with all its draughts and leaks, lit from top to bottom with fifty 'dips' [candles] and two roaring fires, Long Chamber presented a vital and atmospheric picture. Some boys would be at their desks writing or lying down on their beds, with candles standing up in their own wax; some reading; some walking up and down laughing or in earnest talk; others boxing, or fencing with a single stick.[23]

A description of the same dormitory from Gathorne-Hardy adds to the impression:

> This barn-like room where 52 scholars slept, was 172 feet long and 15 feet high, it was unheated [until] 1784 when two fireplaces were put in; the windows were broken and, in winter, snow drifted in and covered their beds. It was filthy, stinking of corrupting rats corpses, ordure and urine . . . There were not enough of the large oaken beds four feet six inches across, in which the boys slept together for sex or huddled close for warmth and some had to sleep on the floor . . . In 1834 a report stated "that the inmates of a workhouse

or a gaol are better fed and lodged than the scholars of Eton" . . . But it is at night that the accounts read like descriptions of hell out of Dostoevsky. Then great fires were lit . . . sending monstrous shadows dancing up the walls. Rats poured out of the walls and floors to feed on the filth, at which the fags would give chase, stuff them into socks and smash them against the beds . . . Larger boys, inflamed by drink, could become demons.[24]

At this time it was not unusual for children to share beds in their homes, and it was general for working-class children. However, it is evident that in this context the younger children were exposed to the added stresses of sleeping with abusive older boys who could bully them at will. Regular torments endured by the younger boys included scorching in front of the fires or being tossed in blankets. There were 'horrific accounts from all centuries . . . but the eighteenth and early nineteenth centuries marked a climax. Boys killed each other'.[25] This may sound rather dramatic, but given the unsupervised excesses it is unsurprising. In one case a boy was tossed in a blanket and after hitting his head on a bedpost, he was scalped and no one came until the morning.[26] In 1730 a boy at Eton was stabbed with a penknife and died; a boy at Charterhouse, in the late eighteenth century, was roasted before the fire and shut in a trunk filled with sawdust until he nearly suffocated. An eyewitness commented: 'The Charterhouse at that time was a sort of hell upon earth for the younger boys.'[27]

Brutality resulting in death was not limited to the dormitories. A notorious example was a fight which took place at Eton in 1825 between two ill-matched boys, Charles Wood and Francis Ashley.[28] [29] These two boys had a disagreement and then were pitted in battle against one another. Wood was a year older than Ashley and much bigger. Driven on by other boys, they fought for two and a half hours and sixty rounds. Ashley was violently punched and several times fell down but he was given alcohol to fortify him and sent back into the fight. Eventually he collapsed and was carried back, unconscious, to his house by his friends and supporters, including his brothers. His tutor was sought but could not be found, so Ashley was left on his bed and there he died.[30] [31] The fact that he died made this a notorious case but it was far from an isolated incident. It seems that the lack of adult supervision exposed the boys to extremes of unruly behaviour.

This death toll cannot be dismissed as merely historical: many of those whom I have interviewed, whose schooling took place in the 1950s, 1960s and 1970s, recall children who died, either directly at the hands of other boys, or, indirectly, as a result of bullying. Some died when forced to engage in dangerous behaviours, others committed suicide following prolonged episodes of severe bullying and some died from epidemics of contagious illnesses. Looking back on these events, men recall how they became part of the dimly remembered folklore of the school. It is only on deeper reflection, and often as fathers themselves, that they now realise the seriousness of these events. This forms part of the basis for the cut-off feelings of ex-boarders. The emotional implications of such events cannot be processed at the time and so are repressed, often emerging to consciousness only decades later.

Accidents happen in all schools, and indeed homes, but the children in these schools were exposed to excessive danger because of the unsupervised nature of their lives and as a result of the institutionalised bullying condoned through the prefect system and subsequently fagging.

Prefects and fagging

The tradition of fagging evolved from the prefect system. This system was initially established because, with so few schoolmasters, there was a lack of adult supervision. Older boys who were deemed responsible were given the privileged status of prefect and expected to help in maintaining order in the schools. 'If the society of a public school in the eighteenth century were not to dissolve into boiling anarchy, some power had to be allowed to the older and more responsible boys.'[32] Fagging was a progression from this. Although it is likely it started a lot earlier, accounts of fagging begin in the seventeenth century. There was a shortage of servants during the civil war (1642–1651) and so younger boys were enlisted to do the menial chores. Initially this was a symbiotic relationship whereby the fag served the master (the older boy) and in turn the master protected the fag: 'they served each other for the discipline of the community.'[33] However, it soon became an institutionalised form of bullying whereby the older boys forced the smaller ones to be their slaves, beating them up if they refused or did their jobs badly. This system, which began in the distant past, was only gradually abolished in the 1970s.

A fag started working for his master at three or four o'clock in the morning and much of his leisure hours were spent running errands. Sometimes he would have to engage in a fight with another fag on behalf of their masters. The fag would fetch food, clean his master's shoes, make tea and generally be at the beck and call of the older boy at all times of the day or night. In winter, when the weather was icy, smaller boys were woken in the night in order to pour buckets of water down the length of the dormitory for a slide in the morning. 'This was preferable to having a bucket of water poured down ones back, not for any wrong doing, but just on the whim of a senior to toughen up a junior.'[34]

The prime duties of the fag were to make his master's bed, shop for him, run errands and do as he was told. 'Faults were punished by slapping the fag's face till it was "red hot", or by flaking his hands with a wet towel.'[35] If a bed were incorrectly made, the fag would be dragged from his bed by his master accompanied by several older boys who would kick and punch him. The smaller boys had to cut logs for the fire and 'the smaller the boy the larger the log he was given.'[36] The relationship between a junior boy and his master could influence his whole experience of the school for many years. This meant that boys might have significantly different experiences in the same school at the same time.[37] Of course this did not continue throughout school life. As the boys became older, everything changed as they attained senior status. Chandos evokes a sense of this transformation:

> A sudden and dramatic change took place in the condition of these boys . . . They went home at the end of one half, fags and juniors, in some cases harassed and troubled ones; and they returned to find the quality of their lives all at once changed beyond imagining by an elevation of their standing and position . . . they all felt the translation from subordinate to oligarch. They were aware of having entered into possession of the school. The very air they breathed was charged with the scent of inheritance, and more, the process seemed magically curative of the effects of previous hardship.[38]

This may be why some men recall their school days with affection. These hardships were extolled by those who had been through them as a great preparation for the adversities of life. To have suffered and survived made them feel strong. They entered adult life secure in the knowledge that they were unlikely to encounter worse torments than they had already endured. Some, looking back with nostalgia, seemed to have enjoyed their time there.[39] This produced men ready to go out and play their part in building an Empire; fearless and inculcated with the British sense of 'fair play', learned on the sports fields of their public schools.

There were those cultural commentators who objected to fagging at the time. It was described in 1816 by George Lewis in *The Edinburgh Review* as 'the only regular institution of slave labour enforced by brute force which exists in these islands'.[40][41] The Prime Minister, Palmerstone, expressed doubts about the fagging system. He questioned C. J. Vaughan, the respected headmaster of Harrow, and was told that fagging kept the hierarchy in place. Vaughan explained it was not just a method of keeping discipline but also of 'inculcating a system of organised rank' and it was therefore essential.[42]

Rebellion

Because of the lack of staff and indiscipline, rebellion was not uncommon. Boys often ran wild. Evelyn Waugh is quoted as saying: 'Boys . . . roamed the countryside, tippled ale and when they were not roasting fags [boys], roasted, snared pheasants over open fires.'[43] There were uprisings in a number of the schools, culminating in the Marlborough Rebellion in 1851. Gathorne-Hardy gives a sense of the terror and anarchy in the years preceding both this rebellion and the subsequent reforms.

By the 1820s and 1830s the growing awareness of problems in the schools had led to a decrease in numbers. In the hope of attracting students, Marlborough reduced its fees. This led to a rapid expansion: between 1843 and 1848, the number of students increased from 200 to 500. This led to overcrowding, with nine forms all packed into the upper school. The efforts at discipline led to extreme cruelty and violence perpetrated by the schoolmasters. 'Ferocious beatings' took place; 'the masters would openly thrash until screams of pain had been elicited.'[44] This was witnessed by all. One boy was thrashed so badly that strips of his shirt had to be removed from the wounds by a doctor using pincers.

This type of physical violence, combined with overcrowding (the boys were sleeping in the huge dormitories described earlier), made for anarchic behaviour. They ate in one large dining room, but there was so little food that they 'were ravaged by hunger'.[45] It was later observed that the boys at Marlborough were living in conditions similar to those of the prisons. The schoolmasters, who were scared of the boys, refrained from venturing among them except when in class. They attempted to maintain order by withdrawing privileges. On 5 November a planned rebellion took place when the boys let off fireworks in the school grounds. They took over the school, smashing windows. This continued for a week. Unable to stop it, the headmaster eventually capitulated, reinstating the withdrawn privileges. The rebellion ended. There had been riots in other schools, but this was the final one. At last, note was taken – something had to be done to change the system.

These events took place more than 150 years ago and they give a sense of the extreme privations suffered by the boys of that time. However, such license became tradition and influenced the ethos inherited in the schools attended by some of our patients a hundred years later. I have heard personal stories of beatings and hunger in boarding schools in the late twentieth century which, whilst not as extreme as those described here, were not dissimilar. One respondent told me that he was admitted to his public school in South Africa, modelled on the British tradition, in the 1950s. His parents had not thought to put his name down in advance for this much sought-after school. However, there had been riots there the previous year and because of this, many parents had withdrawn their applications for places, leaving a vacancy for him. These riots occurred in the middle of the twentieth century.

Public school reform – the Clarendon commission

Eventually public criticism led to reforms of the schools in the mid-nineteenth century. The nature of the abuses began to come to public attention, with articles in *The Edinburgh Review* leading the way. Through its co-founders Henry Brougham and Sydney Smith, this publication was consistently critical of the British public schools.[46] In its pages George Cornwall Lewis, who as we saw earlier had been critical of fagging, later exposed the pervasiveness of extreme floggings: 'For all offences except the most trivial every boy below the sixth form, whatever his age, is punished by flogging. This is performed on the naked back by the headmaster himself.'[47] So it was that the public started to become aware of the brutal excesses to which boys in these schools were subjected. In addition to this it came to public attention that the education was very poor: 'a boy may leave Eton with credit and be quite unable to pass the common tests of the Civil Service Examination.'[48]

In 1816, the Brougham Committee of the House of Commons instigated an inquiry which was completed in 1818. It was set up under the auspices of the same Lord Brougham who founded *The Edinburgh Review*. This committee studied and severely criticised the 'Great Schools'. The Great Schools, also known as 'The Nine', were Eton, Winchester, Westminster, Charterhouse, St Paul's, Merchant Taylors', Harrow, Rugby and Shrewsbury.[49] All the schools were charities, endowed by statute in perpetuity to provide education to certain stated groups, and as such they came under the Charity Commissioners.[50]

During this period Britain's wealth and power was increasing as a result of Empire. There was a burgeoning middle class and this meant that more people aspired to public school education.[51] Moreover, the expansion of the British Empire meant that many people travelled abroad to serve the needs of government, Church and commerce. The public schools were increasingly called upon to house, as well as educate, the children of absent parents. These children, frequently very young, were often sent 'home' in order to go to school. These were vast journeys from distant lands, as vividly conveyed in Brendon's account *Children of the Raj*.[52] The 'home' to which they were sent was Britain, the home of their parents – but it was not home to children raised in the exotic climates of India or Africa. This merely added to their sense of dislocation, as Kipling vividly described.[53]

With the Victorian era came certain expectations and controls. The intemperate license and wild escapades which had characterised public school life began to become an anachronism in a world of increasing orderliness and standardised public propriety.[54] Moreover, the scandalous reputation of the schools and the headmasters, notorious for their brutality, ran counter to the spread of evangelical religion. Whilst many of these headmasters resisted change, there were certain headmasters who were influential in creating their own reforms. In 1844, the Long Chamber at Eton was demolished at the instigation of two schoolmasters who, as boys, had suffered there. It was converted into cubicles for fifteen boys; others were given bed-sitting rooms in what became known as the 'New Buildings', opened in 1846.[55] At the same time the class sizes were reduced.

In 1861, the Clarendon Commission, a Royal Commission, was convened to 'inquire into the administration, finances, studies, methods, subjects and extent of instruction at 'the Nine'.[56] The inquiry extended to some of the more recently founded public schools, including Marlborough, Cheltenham and Wellington.[57] Witness accounts given to the Commission exposed a previously closed world, the details of which both puzzled and shocked the members of the Commission.[58] People were scandalised when the headmasters were found to be taking illegal amounts of money out of the system, with the only defence that it had been a tradition that had been going on for centuries.[59] 'The uninitiated heard with incredulity that a fag's duties included rising at 3.00 a.m. and working for his master until he [the master] called them at 4 a.m. and thereafter at increasingly frequent intervals.'[60] At Westminster the brutal treatment of younger boys, which included kicking by older ones, was exposed. It became evident that the 'masters had no control over the monitors'; these older boys were in control of the school. They treated the schoolmasters with contempt. Their own hierarchy meant that 'a boy, given permission by a master to leave the room was not free to do so until he had obtained leave from at least three boys in authority: a monitor (sometimes more than one), his immediate senior and the 'lag' (the last person of consequence).'[61]

Despite all this, the Clarendon Commission (which lasted for three years) produced a report which was mainly favourable to the schools. The shock of some of what was revealed was, it seems, ameliorated by men who remembered their experiences positively. It was taken as affirmation that they continued to send their own sons. Thus it was considered, on the evidence of those who had attended them, that these schools provided 'the best possible preparation for the dangers of the imperfect world beyond the school'.[62] This was affirmed in the report:

> It is not easy to estimate the degree to which the English people are indebted to these schools for . . . their capacity to govern others and control themselves, their aptitude for combining freedom with order, their public spirit, their vigour and manliness of character, their strong but not slavish respect for public opinion, their love of healthy sports and exercise. These schools have been the chief nurseries of our statesmen . . . In them . . . men of all the various classes that make up English society, destined for every profession and career, have been brought up on a footing of social equality and have contracted the most enduring friendships and some of the ruling habits of their lives; and they have perhaps the largest share in moulding the character of an English gentleman.[63]

The Commission did recommend reforms in the administration, organisation of governing bodies and the curriculum. However the character of the schools and the system was given 'the firm stamp of . . . approval'.[64] The report brought about 'improved diet and hygiene and better living conditions . . . Fighting, once the criterion of honour, went out of fashion and extreme practices . . . protracted ordeals based on the practices of the prize ring, which had, in the past, led to the death of at least one pupil, ceased to be admired'.[65] The Commission called for more order and discipline whilst acknowledging the importance of the freedom of public school life, considering that it fostered manliness and independence. Chandos points out the long-term effects of these freedoms, in Victorian society, were that they led to 'an authoritarian spirit linked to the morals and manners which were permeating the society'.[66]

The Taunton Commission, a third inquiry which began in 1864, was set up to examine the more numerous new public schools, also endowed grammar schools, that were emerging all over the country. This was a Victorian investigation of incredible scrupulousness, skill and industry. 'Hundreds of inspectors covered the country spending years at their task. They uncovered chaos . . . but came out with a solution.'[67]

The Commission proposed that all the endowments be combined and redistributed on a national scale. This would form the financial basis of a new national system of secondary education. The Taunton Commission drew up detailed plans with the control centralised via Parliament. There was to be a national exam system, regular inspection and a modern curriculum including science. This was to be for everyone, from every class. Those too poor to pay would be educated free, whilst those who could afford to would pay. In this way the merged endowments would be augmented.[68] These proposals were put to Parliament in an 'Endowed Schools Bill', which was passed in 1869. The first grants of public money were voted to this end by Parliament and the Education Commission was set up with powers to introduce the reforms they thought necessary.

The headmasters of the public schools objected to this new scheme. In 1869 they set up their own body, the Headmaster's Conference. The Conference, which is still in existence today, was initially convened in Uppingham in Rutland with only twelve headmasters, but its numbers quickly increased: in 1870 thirty-five headmasters attended, in 1871 fifty. By 1874 Eton and Harrow had joined and the Great Schools dominated the conference.

The reforms and after

Despite these reforms, many of the traditions described continued; fagging, in modified form, persisted as an accepted aspect of most boarding schools until it began to die out in the 1970s. It was abolished in different schools in the years either side of 1977. Current boarders are sceptical about this and inform me that fagging still occurs but, because it is now officially prohibited, it takes place out of the view of the school authorities. It was not just fagging that persisted; as we shall see, many of my patients who attended twentieth-century boarding schools suffered similar indignities to those discussed earlier, but in modified form. Many – but of course not all – endured beatings, bullying, sexual abuse and near-starvation rations.

The lack of structure in the schools prior to the 1860s left the boys without contact with schoolmasters apart from during lessons. Unsupervised, they would invent their own amusements and were often out of control. After the reforms took place this changed: their time became totally regimented. Sports were introduced, along with compulsory cold showers intended to discourage any homosexual activity.[69] The diet in most of the public schools continued to be very poor, and this was partly deliberate. It was thought that a less-generous diet made the boys less sexually stimulated, so evening meals were nutritionally inadequate and took place early. The poor diet combined with extreme exercise sometimes led to deaths, as recorded by one boy at Rugby in 1890. In a letter home to his mother, he tells how a boy fell down on a run and died quickly afterwards.[70]

Gathorne-Hardy concludes that as a result of the various committees and the reforms that followed them, within the period between 1824 and 1900 the public schools had transformed their ethos from 'being anarchic, ill-disciplined, loosely defined societies, uninterested in games, lax about religion, indifferent to sexual license, with huge classes and moderately easy about [social] class'. Now, in the Victorian era, 'they had become highly disciplined, concentrated into very tight, close communities, obsessed with games and every possible ramification of sexual expression, fervently religious, with small classes and snobbish and class conscious.'[71] Writing in the 1970s, he considered that many of their values permeated society in a diluted form because their alumni formed a high proportion of the ruling elite. From my clinical experience with men who have boarded in from the 1970s to the 1990s, I would concur with this.

Royston Lambert[72] and John Wakeford conducted research recording the testimony of boys boarding in public schools in the 1960s. During this period the public schools were class conscious to the extent that they did not accept the children of tradesmen. Wakeford recounts how, in the 1960s, references were sought regarding the parents' social status before the child was considered. He explains how at Harrow the school demanded that the applicant name 'a referee who is an Old Harrovian, or is connected with the school in some other way'.[73] Thus the school perpetuated its traditional ethos of exclusivity.

Although some public school boys have nothing to do with their school once they have left and actively avoid any contact with them, others stay in touch with their schools and their fellow alumni. Loyalty was fostered by school songs, which engendered a sense of belonging and perpetuated an ethos of class exclusivity. Moreover the sibling group in public schools fosters a sense of belonging; many children separated from their parents look instead to the school 'sibling' group for succour and support. Studies of kibbutz life show that children separated from their parents became dependent on each other. Similarly 'public school boys were loyal to their schools, to other public schoolboys and finally to their class.'[74] The late Anthony Storr frequently noticed with his upper-class patients how class love and loyalty, the reassurance this gave, compensated for the way they had been deprived of parental love.[75] The sense of belonging is strengthened by becoming part of the political establishment and can be seen in the old boy's network which in Britain is a well-known means of social advancement, even today. This is evident as many of the members of the current British Government are former public school boys.

Conclusion

In the periods that we have been considering, physical survival was a more pressing issue than the psychological impact of such brutal treatment. However, as psychoanalysis (which was developed in the late nineteenth century) became accepted and childhood became more understood, the general impact of ill treatment of children began to be considered. In spite of the many stories that emerged, such treatment remained unremarked in some boarding schools during the twentieth century. This is because these schools were so much part of the establishment that their ethos was rarely questioned. Orwell's impassioned treatise detailed his experience of starvation and ill treatment in his prep school at the beginning of the twentieth century. He moderated his comments by suggesting that things had changed for the better by the time he was writing.[76] In many schools they had not, as we shall see in the case study which is central to Part 2 of this book. This is written from the viewpoint of a child in a late-twentieth-century boarding school. In this prep school the regime was not dissimilar to those of which we have read in this chapter.

Whilst men were trained to inherit the world, as Empire grew, women – whose role for centuries had been to be subservient to men – continued in this path. The history of girls' schools, which is rather different from that of boys' schools, will be explored in the next chapter.

Notes

1 Gathorne-Hardy, J. (1977) *The Public School Phenomenon, 597–1977*, London, Hodder & Stoughton, 1977, p. 22.
2 Ibid., p. 25.
3 Ibid., p. 22.
4 Ibid., pp. 25–26.
5 *A Renaissance Education: The Schooling of Thomas More's Daughter* (2012) Presented by Dr Helen Castor (TV programme). Broadcast on BBC 4, 5 January.
6 Gathorne-Hardy (1977), op. cit., p. 26.
7 Ibid., p. 27.
8 Ibid., p. 35.
9 Ibid., p.32, footnote.
10 Ibid., p. 31.
11 Brendon, V. (2005/2006) *Children of the Raj*, Phoenix: Orion.
12 Brendon, V. (2009) *Prep School Children: A Class Apart Over Two Centuries*, London: Continuum, p. 23.
13 Gathorne-Hardy (1977), op. cit., p. 29.
14 Ibid., p. 33.
15 John Betjeman, quoted in Gathorne-Hardy, op. cit., p. 34.
16 May, T. (2009) *The Victorian Public School*, Oxford: The Shire Library, p. 30.
17 Chandos, J. (1984) *Boys Together: English Public Schools 1800–1864*, London: Yale University Press.
18 Gathorne-Hardy (1977), op. cit., p. 60.
19 Dickens, C. (1838–1839/1995) *Nicholas Nickleby*, Hertfordshire: Wordsworth Editions Ltd, p. 38.
20 Tomalin, C. (2011) *Charles Dickens: A Life*, London: Viking.
21 Gathorne-Hardy (1977), op. cit., p. 62.
22 Chandos (1984), op. cit., p. 87.
23 Ibid., p. 90.
24 Gathorne-Hardy (1977), op. cit., pp. 62–63.
25 Ibid., p. 60.
26 Ibid., p. 63.
27 Southey, quoted in Gathorne-Hardy (1977), op. cit., p. 60.
28 Chandos (1984), op. cit.
29 Gathorne-Hardy (1977), op. cit.
30 Chandos (1984), op. cit., p. 142.
31 Gathorne-Hardy (1977), op. cit., p. 60.

32 Chandos (1984), op. cit., p. 86.
33 Ibid., p. 86
34 Ibid., p. 88.
35 Ibid., p. 91
36 Ibid., p. 93.
37 Ibid., p. 94.
38 Ibid., p. 99.
39 Ibid., p. 12, quoting the headmaster of Winchester in 1984.
40 Gathorne-Hardy (1977), op. cit., p. 68.
41 Chandos (1984), op. cit., p. 103.
42 Gathorne-Hardy (1977), op. cit., p. 120.
43 Ibid., p. 58.
44 Ibid., pp. 102–103.
45 Ibid., p. 103.
46 Chandos (1984), op. cit., p. 37.
47 Ibid., p. 229.
48 Ibid., p. 322, quoting Reeve in *The Edinburgh Review*, 1861.
49 Gathorne-Hardy (1977), op. cit., p. 97.
50 Ibid., p. 69.
51 Ibid., p. 69.
52 Brendon (2005/2006), op. cit.
53 Kipling, R. (1888/1995) *Baa Baa Black Sheep*, London: Penguin.
54 Chandos (1984), op. cit., p. 320.
55 Gathorne-Hardy (1977), op. cit., p. 96.
56 Ibid., p. 97.
57 Ibid.
58 Chandos (1984), op. cit., p. 324.
59 Gathorne-Hardy (1977), op. cit., p. 97.
60 Chandos (1984), op. cit., p. 325.
61 Ibid., p. 326.
62 Ibid., p. 327.
63 Chandos (1984), op. cit., p. 328, quoting *The Clarendon Commission Report* 20, p. 56.
64 Ibid., p. 328.
65 Ibid., p. 329.
66 Ibid., p. 330.
67 Gathorne-Hardy (1977), op. cit., p. 98.
68 Ibid., p. 98.
69 Hickson, A. (1996) *The Poisoned Bowl: Sex and the Public School*, London: Gerald Duckworth.
70 Ibid., p. 41.
71 Gathorne-Hardy (1977), op. cit., p. 228.
72 Lambert, R. with Millham, S. (1968) *The Hothouse Society*, London: Weidenfeld & Nicholson.
73 Wakeford, J. (1969) *The Cloistered Elite: A Sociological Analysis of the English Public School*, London: Macmillan, p. 45.
74 Gathorne-Hardy (1977), op. cit., p. 131.
75 Ibid.
76 Orwell, G. (1947/2003) *Such, Such Were the Joys*, London: Penguin.

Chapter 3

All girls together
A brief history of boarding schools

> Children cannot articulate their experience in the language of adults. Only after childhood can it be thus expressed. When young we found the school world the reality, the norm, the only rationality. That was its power.
>
> Judith Okely[1]

Schools reflect the ethos of the society that they serve and this is apparent in the history of girls' boarding schools. They were adapted from the long-established tradition of boys' boarding schools and therefore were based on masculine principles. The attitude to girls and their education that will be discussed in this chapter is not exclusive to boarding schools, but it is more extreme than in the day schools because of their residential nature.

Entitlement and disenfranchisement

Henrietta was the only daughter in a wealthy, landowning family with a large estate in the North of England. Following the family tradition like her mother, father and brother, she had been sent to boarding school at 7, in the late twentieth century. She could not recall going to school nor anything about it. Later we will see this is a common form of amnesia, related to the bereavement of being sent to boarding school at a very young age. Henrietta did remember that on her return her beloved nanny was gone; the most significant emotional attachment figure of her early years had been dismissed as no longer needed. Even in adulthood Henrietta's memories of her nanny remained her strongest memories of feeling unconditionally loved, so this clearly was a profound loss.

In this family, wealth and land had been passed through the generations. The men were members of the ruling class. After leaving boarding school, Henrietta, along with others of her class, attended finishing school. Then Henrietta was 'given away in marriage' into another family. Following tradition, she became a full-time wife and mother. Her brother was given his own house and land on the family estate, which he managed alongside his father; he was groomed for a life as a landowner.

Later, as her marriage to this apparently suitable man had failed to provide the income she might have expected, her father gave her an allowance, with her brother's agreement. Thus her father remained a powerful, 'benevolent' but controlling, presence in her life.

Henrietta's story highlights many of the historical differences between male and female social position in the landowning classes. The estate could not be broken up, so inheritance in this, as in other landowning families, went to the eldest son; the younger sons and their sisters did not inherit land. This illustrates the influence of patrimony and so highlights the ethos of disenfranchisement that permeated much of girls' education.

A brief history of women's education

Investigating the traditions of girls' boarding schools reveals many differences between the social position of boys and girls. Education, and boarding schools in particular, were designed for boys and only later adapted to accommodate girls. From their inception, the treatment, attitudes to the person and the taboos in girls' schools were very different from those which we read in the last chapter. Despite the brutality to which they were subjected, boys were 'entitled', whereas girls had no such entitlement. This was literally the case in that inherited titles, as well as the land of the elite classes, were handed down through the male line. In boarding schools this was symbolised by the use of names with boys known by their surname and girls by their first names. For boys of 8 this emphasises the loss of their previous identity as children in a family, but at the same time it bestows on them status, linking them to their fathers and brothers. If two brothers attended the same school they would be known respectively as Smith-major or Smith-minor to identify them, rather than by their first names. Girls were called by their first name, which might imply more kindly care – but Okely points out that it was merely symbolic of patrimony. Girls' surnames were temporary until changed in marriage.[2]

The history of girls' boarding schools is inextricably linked to the social roles of women. Prior to the nineteenth century girls were rarely educated. Working-class girls were put to work as soon as they were able, and often they laboured in factories or in service from an early age. They were expected to conduct manual and physical work; therefore, presumably these women were considered strong. The daughters of the upper classes remained at home waiting for marriage. They were considered to be constitutionally weak and in need of protection – so their education took place in the home, where they were taught either by a governess or by their mothers.[3] There were exceptions, a few daughters of the aristocracy whose education was comparable to that of boys. In the sixteenth century Margaret More, the daughter of Sir Thomas More, was given a wide-ranging education. Along with her two sisters, she studied astronomy, mathematics and languages.[4] Queen Elizabeth I also had an extensive education, which was similar to that of her brother.[5] Unusually, she remained single and was known as a highly educated, independent woman. These were exceptional women. Most of their sex had to wait for girls' education to be taken seriously. This was not until the first Ladies' Academies, or seminaries, were established in the late eighteenth century.

Eventually, due to the tenacity, radical attitude and courage of female thinkers, the prevailing view that women were mentally and constitutionally inferior to men began to change. Generations of women had argued for women's education, including Elizabeth Montague, who in 1750 had formed the Blue Stocking Society, and Catharine Macaulay, author of the eight-volume *History of England* (1763–1783). In her *Letters on Education* (1790), Macauley argued that the apparent intellectual weakness of women was not inherent but due to their lack of education.[6][7] Mary Wollstonecraft developed similar arguments in *The Vindication of the Rights of Woman*.[8] Thus, women began to gradually assert their right to education as well as suffrage.

In the late eighteenth century the first Ladies' Academies were opened. These were small private schools with places for between twenty to fifty boarders. They served the wealthier classes as finishing schools and were often 'run by poor widows or spinsters from the genteel classes. They had few academic pretensions and many social ones'.[9] They were ideologically 'committed to the moral, intellectual and physical training of girls'.[10] The popularity of these academies quickly increased, so that by the nineteenth century their numbers had multiplied. It was not uncommon for them to have as many as 200 students, 'with some growing as large as 900'.[11]

Their success led to the establishment of public schools for girls, amongst the first of which were Cheltenham Ladies College, founded in 1854, and Roedean in 1889.[12] These were formed around the same time that the major reforms in boys' schools were taking place. Based on many of the same principles as the boys' public schools, they were at first chaotic. In many, the girls were out of control, the food was poor and conditions were often cramped and dirty, with children sleeping two or three to a bed.[13] Differences in the care and education of girls and boys were soon to emerge. Whilst traditional schools had left boys to fend for themselves among a horde of other boys, girls were kept in a more dependent state.[14] They were subject to much tighter supervision and control than the boys. This was in keeping with the social order of the time: girls from the wealthier classes were protected, learning the skills they would need as wives and mothers.

The curriculum – accomplishments

In the Ladies' Academies, and in the first girls' public schools, the aim of education was to prepare girls for marriage and motherhood. The stated aim and parental expectation of boys' boarding schools was usually a good academic education alongside the creation of an English gentleman – even though they often fell short of that ambition.[15] In boys' schools the main subjects taught were the Classics, Greek and Latin – but these were not considered fit subjects for women to study. Girls were taught 'the accomplishments', considered to be more befitting their future status as wives and mothers. The accomplishments included sewing, flower and landscape painting, dancing, deportment and etiquette. The girls learned to play musical instruments, perform plays and to recite verse; in some schools a more varied education was provided including languages, mathematics and geography. This 'was intended to turn a young girl into a young lady and enhance her prospects on the marriage market. That was what wealthy fathers paid for'.[16] Women, apart from the working classes, were not expected to earn their own living; they were supported by their families or married to someone else who would support them. It was widely viewed that an educated woman was not marriageable.[17] This view was still around in the 1970s, when Gathorne-Hardy reports a conversation with the headmaster of Roedean who told him of a father 'who claimed he did not mind his daughter taking one "A" level as long as she did not look clever'.[18]

Teachers and their training

There were few alternatives to marriage for women, but teaching was an acceptable option for women who had to earn their own living. Women teachers were also protected; as governesses, for example, they lived in the homes of their pupils. Governesses were often poorly educated, badly paid and treated with condescension.[19] It was often a humiliating role: the governess was not one of the servants but not really an equal to her employers.[20] Women who became schoolteachers in boarding schools also lived in a sheltered environment. This was often an independent community of women. In some cases it was an idealistic and supportive environment in which the teachers could live fulfilling lives in service to the school and the girls in their charge.[21] As teachers, women had the opportunity for an accepted form of employment.

The establishment of training colleges for women teachers was a significant development. In 1848 and 1849, respectively, Queens College for Women and Bedford College were founded. The original remit of training governesses was soon extended to include teachers in general. These colleges significantly influenced women's education and, with their wide curriculum, they produced some notable headmistresses of public schools. Amongst the most famous were Mary Buss who started North London Collegiate for Ladies and Dorothea Beale, the pioneering headmistress of Cheltenham Ladies College. The success of these training colleges inspired a number of others, so that by the 1850s and 1860s girls' education began to change radically.[22] [23]

Due to the tireless campaigning of Emily Davies, who founded Girton College Cambridge, the Endowed Schools Commission of 1864 included girls' schools in their investigation. This was a great triumph because the acceptance 'was a tacit admission that girls had the same right to education as boys'.[24] Then, also due to Davies' campaigning, examinations for girls were established. In 1865 Cambridge allowed girls to sit 'special' examinations for women, followed in 1869 by London University and in 1870 Oxford, Edinburgh and Durham. Davies, however, did not accept that women should sit 'special' examinations and she continued to argue for parity. Eventually in 1878 girls took the same examinations as boys.[25]

Further education

The disparity in the treatment of women and men continued into the universities. It is only relatively recently, 1998, that women who graduated from Cambridge University in the early years of the twentieth century were awarded their degrees. The first women students were examined in 1882 taking, and passing, the same examinations as men – but they were not permitted to graduate. Women were awarded diplomas rather than the full Bachelor of Arts degree. This was another literal case of lack of entitlement. Had they graduated, women would have been admitted to full membership of the university and this was unacceptable to men.

It was 1948 when finally women were permitted to become full members of Cambridge University. The mother of one of my respondents attended Cambridge University after leaving her day school. A medical doctor, now retired, she took her degree in 1942–1944. Because World War II intervened, this was two years instead of three, but in 1947 she qualified as a doctor. Women were not officially accepted into the university until the following year, so although she practised as a doctor, she was not awarded her degree. In 1998 women who had gained degrees prior to 1948 were formally accepted into the university. This belated degree ceremony culminated in a parade, in graduation gowns, through Cambridge on 4 July 1998, in which this doctor took part: it was fifty-one years after her actual graduation.

Another case in point is the pioneer social scientist, reformer and policy activist, Barbara Wootton. As her biographer Ann Oakley explains, Barbara Wootton made history as the first woman elected to the peerage: she was admitted to the House of Lords in 1958. Baroness Wootton graduated in 1919 from Girton College, Cambridge and, like her mother a generation earlier she was unable 'to put the letters "B.A." after her name'.[26] 'The Sex Disqualification [Removal] Act of 1919 theoretically enabled women to exercise most public functions, judicial offices and professions, and to serve as jurors.'[27] However, this took many years to implement. Wootton, whose life spanned nearly a century, commented, 'in 1982, at the age of 85, . . . that young women would be staggered to realise how recent were the gains on which a new feminist movement could build.'[28]

Although neither of these women attended boarding schools, this demonstrates some of the ways in which women during this period had to struggle against their educational disenfranchisement. The lack of status given to women's education in the Ladies' Academies and girls' public schools grew out of a context where women's education was socially marginalised. The eventual parity in the education of women was indeed hard won.

Headmistresses

There were many idealistic headmistresses, often highly committed to their schools and to the education of girls. One of the most influential was Dorothea Beale, whom we have seen was the headmistress of Cheltenham Ladies College from 1858 to 1904. During the early years of reform, roughly 1860–1890, she was a leading spokeswoman for academic standards. She was the founder of St Hilda's College, Oxford for teachers' training. In the Victorian era the schools played an important social role and, in keeping with this ethos, Beale ensured that emphasis was placed on moral-intellectual reform.[29] She was also active in maintaining exclusivity and to this end would not accept girls whose parents were in trade.[30] This was common in major boys' public schools, where (as we have seen) parents were often interviewed before the child was put on the waiting list.[31]

The dedication of progressive female educationalists had mixed impact on the experiences of the girls in boarding schools. Their devotion could be benign, but it could also be intrusively controlling. It is reported that Beale referred to the school as her 'husband', with the presumable implication that the pupils were her 'children'. Mary Buss, headmistress of London Collegiate, who was another significant pioneer of women's education, took sweets with her whenever she visited her juniors. Others would indulge the children, sitting them in a circle and reading to them. It seems this 'maternal' approach would have made the environment a kinder place to be than the violent excesses which characterised the boys' schools. However, in some cases, girls experienced this as 'despotism tempered with sentimentality'.[32] This despotism had a good deal to do with the constraints under which the girls lived. Whilst the teachers may have found this a fulfilling life, there were girls who experienced their boarding schools as little better than imprisonment.

Discipline and control – the Victorian era

That the ethos of girls' schools was more benign than that of boys' schools was, in part, due to the public school reforms of the nineteenth century, which brought about an awareness of the duty of care for the safety of children. The concern about the safety of girls in particular was perhaps because their virtue was to be closely guarded. In some of the first boarding schools, care had been lax and some girls had run away and become pregnant. Probably as a result, during the Victorian era the rules in girls' schools became increasingly rigid. Beatings, which characterised the boys' public schools, were uncommon and, whilst in boys' schools the headmaster's autonomy was often challenged, this was rare in the girls' schools.[33] It is likely that the beatings and abuses in boys' schools may have fostered aggression and exacerbated problems with discipline. Prefects in girls' boarding schools, as in the boys' schools, were often called upon to maintain discipline and perpetuate the moral values of the school. Some headmistresses thought more highly of their prefects than their staff:

> One retired teacher, after a lifetime in boarding schools, concluded that schools were run either for the teachers or the pupil. When they were run for the pupil, the teachers were overworked, underpaid, and without adequate authority.[34]

Prefects could undermine the teachers' authority, a familiar story which, as we saw in Chapter 2, was at times taken to extremes in boys' schools. However the moral imperatives of the Victorian era meant that in girls' schools the discipline was especially rigid.

The 'dictator headmistress' was a product of this period. Such headmistresses were very powerful, overseeing that rules were instilled for all activities. There were prescribed times for everything and the girls' lives were controlled by bells. They were expected to pray, wash, read, walk and sleep in prescribed manners. The girls were always chaperoned, wore uniforms and walked in a crocodile.[35] No mirrors were permitted; little talking was allowed; and hairstyles and even the position in which girls slept were dictated.[36] The girls' lives were regimented by such controls.

Discipline and control – the twentieth century

This type of system continued well into the twentieth century. Judith Okely describes how these rules were enforced in her boarding school in the 1950s by matrons who, in addition to overseeing that the 'no talking after lights out' rule was obeyed, monitored the posture in which the girls slept: 'girls were not to lie on their backs with their knees bent; so sexual shame was instilled.'[37] All activities were controlled by rules and the rooms allocated accordingly; the dormitory, dining room and common room were out of bounds except when time-tabled for their specific purpose. There was no unstructured time even at weekends.[38] This experience was very common. One of my respondents, who had been a boarder in the 1970s, two decades later, reported very similar experiences. In her school too, many places were out of bounds; for example, she could never just choose to go to her bedroom during the day or luxuriate in a bath.

Rather than the beatings that took place in boys' schools, shame was commonly used to control girls. In Okely's school, punishment was withering disapproval from the teachers, backed up by public humiliation. If a girl broke the rules she would be given penalty points and compelled to admit to her misdemeanour in front of the whole school. The girl was expected to show contrition by 'humility, apologetic stance, downcast eyes – possibly tears of defeat'.[39] The more a girl complied with this, the more the self became invisible. From my interviews I find that this treatment was common in girls' boarding schools. The lasting psychological effects of such training may continue to influence the girl in adult life. The true self becomes encapsulated, as the lively, possibly rebellious and non-compliant girl is chastened and then remains hidden. This contributes to an aspect of the creation of Boarding School Syndrome which is different from that manifested by boys. The impulse to hide because they are shamed is a social imperative directed at girls. Girls were intentionally taught to be modest and self-effacing. This was, I submit, no accident: it was the counterpart to the hard exterior presentation expected of boys. It was similar in girls' day schools of the time, but the strictures affected so many more aspects of the life of the child in boarding school. Thus, although girls' boarding schools may have appeared more homely than those of boys, they too were oppressive. In no aspect of life was the girl free to think or respond to her own impulses. This is most notable in relation to the body.

Deportment and girl's bodies

The history of girls' boarding schools is threaded through with subtle forms of social misogyny. An unconscious fear of the power of female sexuality seems to have permeated residential girls' schools. This was evident in the treatment of their bodies. Boarding schools were based on masculine principles and the 'softer' feminine values were eschewed. Girls' developing bodies challenged this masculine ideal with their inconvenient demands for attention. It is hard to ignore the beginning of sexuality when breasts develop and periods start. In preparation for taming this unruly power, it was considered desirable for the young woman to carry herself 'correctly' and so deportment was a significant part of the curriculum.

In the eighteenth and nineteenth centuries the girls were subjected to an assortment of aids to train them to be upright. The corsetry worn by adult women distorted their bodies into preordained shapes, pinching their waists and affecting their breathing. Girls too were subject to wearing such undergarments, but it was not merely corsets that were used in schools. 'Wire structures were devised, to hold the girls' bodies in positions deemed lady-like.'[40] This is recorded by a Mrs Somerville, who, in 1790 at the age of 10, was sent to a boarding school where she was

> Clamped in stiff stays with a steel busk in front, 'while above my frock, bands drew my shoulders back till the shoulder blades met. Then a steel rod, with a semi-circle which went under the chin, was clamped to the steel busk in my stays'.[41]

The female form was thus tortured into submission. It seems that, by their very existence, girls challenged the authorities and, even before their sexuality developed, attempts were made to tame it. Everything to do with their bodies was taboo. In some schools menstruation was never mentioned and at some convents 'they bathed in threes . . . in sort of bell tents, and were never allowed to see their own bodies.'[42] Whilst these taboos were most common in convents they were prevalent in other girls' boarding schools. Although contraptions for enforcing deportment were left behind with the bustles and corsets of earlier centuries, many of the restrictions on the body pervaded schools well into the twentieth century. Okely describes how

> Even when outside the classroom or off the games field, we were to sit, stand and walk erect, chin up, back straight, shoulders well back. At table when not eating, our hands were to rest in our laps. . . . If you were consistently upright you won a red felt badge, embroidered with the word 'Deportment.' This sewn on your tunic was both achievement and defeat.[43]

So, whilst the devices that constrained Mrs Somerville in the eighteenth century were no longer in use, girls in the schools of the mid-twentieth century endured similar strictures. This continued as part of the curriculum of many schools. In the 1970s and 1980s girls were still awarded badges for good deportment.

School uniforms minimised female sexuality. In most private girls' schools in the twentieth century, the gymslip was the favoured form of dress. This flattens the female form. Wearing two pairs of knickers compounded this: Okely records how big navy-blue long-legged ones were worn over smaller ones.[44] This offered double protection from being seen as in any way sexual. Other elements of the school uniform mimicked the clothing worn by boys and men: girls wore 'school ties, lace-up shoes, blazers and striped shirts'.[45] Uniform subjugates the personality by encouraging conformity, for boys as well as girls.

One area where the girl could be free was in sport. However, for a long time sport was considered unhealthy for girls, because of their supposed weak constitution.[46] The pioneering Beale challenged this and introduced sport into Cheltenham Ladies College in the 1850s. Then, later, Netball was invented, a game specifically for girls. At first games were played in corsets and only later were sports clothes for women introduced.[47] Therefore although it was liberating there were considerable restrictions on the way the girls dressed.[48] Games were an escape from the strictures for many girls, but later the compulsion to take part made it another torment for those who were not good at sport.

Comparison between day and boarding schools

None of this was confined to boarding schools, but the difference is that children in day schools have the freedom to be themselves when not at school. In the girls' day schools in the 1950s in the UK, similar regulations applied to those described by Okely; the uniform was almost identical and the constraints on behaviour were comparable, if not quite as draconian. This was part of the social climate in which women were educated at the time. However, there is a significant distinction between the life of the daygirl and that of the boarder. As one of those who attended a private day school, I clearly remember the contrast between school and home. On returning home every evening we were liberated; we could fling off the school uniform and with it the school rules. The daygirl could form friendships, with girls and even boys, outside of school hours – the boarder could not. There was time for unstructured play, pets and reverie.

This is not to idealise day schools or homes; bullying and abuse take place in day schools and also in some homes. The point is that the childhood of day-school pupils differs significantly from that of boarders. Children attending daily are in school for seven or eight hours a day, five, or five and a half, days a week; boarders live in school twenty-four hours a day for several months at a time. For the daygirl home may offer space for psychological restoration, reverie and unstructured play. Boarders do not have this sense of daily liberation; as Okely puts it: 'We were bound in spiders' webs of fine rules and constraints until spontaneity seemed to be a crime.'[49] Several of my informants remember similar situations. One, who boarded in the 1970s, described 'free time' in her school. In the evenings and weekends, the uniform could be taken off (apart from when going to chapel on Sundays). She emphasised that this free time was not relaxing. She recalled the atmosphere of sitting with other girls, 'all cooped up together' in the sitting room in the schoolhouse while overseen by members of staff.

Intimacy

However sympathetic the ethos of the school, children in boarding school are deprived of love and appropriate physical contact. This is still the case in the kinder environment of the twenty-first century boarding school. Some seek solace within the student group, turning to each other for comfort. In some schools the taboo on physical contact was fiercely policed. Young girls together often chatter, invent games and discuss boys, and they are usually physically spontaneous with each other. Some girls' boarding schools in the twentieth century were designed to minimise all such natural acts of friendship. The unstated and probably unconsciously perceived threat was sex.

Wober's interviews in the 1960s reveal the thoughts and aspirations of girls in boarding schools at a time when sex education was limited. In some schools, formal dances were arranged with boys' schools, and in some cases shared lessons took place. The latter was usually when facilities were lacking in the science labs, for example.[50] However, such contact was mostly treated with suspicion. The mixed schools of the present day offer a more natural environment than the single-sex schools of the past. However, some schools remain single-sex, especially for girls.[51]

One significant factor in the psychological development of the child growing up in a boarding school is the lack of intimacy. Young children entering boarding school will long for their mother, father, siblings, nannies and pets – all the natural attachments of a life. There is here a difference between girls and boys. For the boy, if he is not to be burdened with the epithet 'cissy', he must feign independence from the moment of his first arrival in the institution. Thus, he becomes apparently independent but simultaneously does violence to the self. Boys quickly acquire a veneer of masculinity, a kind of bravado to disguise the vulnerable child self. With girls it seems to be a little less violent, perhaps because of the all-female institution.

In the absence of their mothers some of the younger girls form attachments to older girls. One of my respondents, who went to school as a 9 year old, remembered having what was called in her school a 'keen-on'. This was an older girl who became the focus of her attachment. She would wait for this girl to come and tuck her up at night. This was not uncommon and there were a number of other names given to this relationship in different schools, including 'crush', 'pash', 'rave' or 'fad'. The act of naming this association seems to have been tacit acceptance, and it was common for girls to lie awake at night hoping their crush would look in and say goodnight.[52] It was usually the very young girls who attached in this way, which suggests that there was a maternal element. For the child who misses that intimate contact with her mother or nanny, the older girl becomes a part real and part imaginary substitute for this yearned-for loving care. The older girls often enjoyed the special association with the younger one. Boys were permitted no such lapse in their constructed image of masculinity.

As girls developed, such attachments may have acquired an element of sexual attraction, especially at puberty. The younger teachers were also sometimes the focus of crushes. At times they were viewed as role models. The age gap was often not very great, and in some cases lasting friendships developed between senior girls and their teachers. Such friendships happen in day schools too, but they may lack some of the intensity because of the multiple loving and physical relationships to which day-school children are exposed.

These benign relationships were accepted in some schools where love was not rigidly policed. In other boarding schools, personal access to adults and friendships across the age divide were monitored. There were schools where any intimacy was taboo and friendships between girls in different forms were not permitted.[53] This prohibition renders passion totally impossible. Hickson describes similar taboos in some boys' schools.[54] It is, however impossible to legislate against love; in Chapter 15 we will explore this in greater depth.

The lasting effects of lack of intimacy – marriage

The ban on intimacy may have a lasting impact. Some girls rebelled and, on being released from their boarding schools, experimented with sexuality. For others who were more conformist, this led to early marriage, which was in some cases totally lacking in intimacy. Henrietta, with whose story this chapter began, had made a 'suitable marriage' – but she did not really know her husband. He was just the first suitable mate that came along. Like her, he had recently left boarding school and seemed of the right class. He was handsome and from a good family, but in retrospect she realised that they both did what was expected of them: they married but the relationship was devoid of intimacy. They led civil but separate lives with their two children and, while he worked to support the family, she stayed at home. This was an unspoken contract entered into because it was what was expected.

When Henrietta engaged in psychotherapy it was because she was devastated. She had just become aware of her husband's secret homosexual life. Throughout their marriage he had been involved in clandestine meetings with men. Gradually she realised that her boarding school training had primed her for this marriage. On the surface all was well, but she and her husband did not know each other. Neither of them understood how to be emotionally intimate; they made no demands on each other. Boarding school combined with a traditional family may lead to a marriage where the partners remain unknown to each other even after a lifetime of being together. The issue of patrimony and the disenfranchisement of women is threaded through the experience of women like Henrietta.

This was not in the nineteenth but the twenty-first century. Whilst many women in the twenty-first century are not troubled about their social role, and they take their independence and right to work for granted, there is a section of society where these traditional attitudes still prevail. In landowning families, women and the younger sons are not entitled to inherit land. The importance of the integrity of family estates means that only the eldest son inherits land. Therefore boarding school is merely a complement to this traditional upbringing in a patriarchal society. Intimacy and family feeling are less important than history and land. In some traditional upper-class British families this feudal law still stands.

Conclusion

In discussing the respective histories of boys' and girls' boarding schools we have understood a little of the context from which present-day boarding schools have emerged. We have also seen how the experiences of women and men have traditionally been different. For men there is a sense of belonging to an elite. The boys' boarding schools might be understood in terms of subjecting the boy to a lengthy initiation ceremony from which he emerges a man with a strong sense of entitlement. The false masculinity learned in the early days in prep school becomes useful to the man. The old boy's network, which is a well-known means of social advancement in Britain, is an unspoken recognition of the brotherhood of those who have together endured and survived. These boys become men equipped to become part of the British establishment, to run companies and to enter government and, in the past, run the Empire. It was not so for women.

Women were not educated with a sense of entitlement but of service. The boarding schools taught girls to be part of the establishment but in a role of subservience, not to their country but to their men. The punishment by shaming, rather than beating, was one way in which women were trained to keep themselves hidden. Another was inducing shame with regard to their bodies – thus a false modesty, a false femininity, was inculcated in the girl. This is the counterpart to the false masculinity of the men. Thus each learned the social roles they were to play.

In the rest of this book I will turn to the matter of how current psychotherapy patients are psychologically affected by their early boarding school experiences. Sometimes these experiences are prefigured by homes where nannies were the child's first carers or where boarding school is a tradition. Others are the first generation in their family to board, sometimes fulfilling their parents' aspirations. Yet another group board because their parents are posted abroad. These home situations will influence the child's preparation for school.

Notes

1 Okely, J. (1996) *Own and Other Culture*, London: Routledge, p. 149.
2 Ibid., p. 158.

3 Gathorne-Hardy, J. (1977) *The Public School Phenomenon, 597–1977*, London: Hodder & Stoughton, p. 230.
4 *A Renaissance Education: The Schooling of Thomas More's Daughter* (2012) Presented by Dr Helen Castor (TV programme). Broadcast on BBC 4, 5 January.
5 Gathorne-Hardy (1977), op. cit., p. 230.
6 Macaulay, C. (1763–1783) *The History of England from the Accession of James 1 to That of the Brunswick Line* http://plato.stanford.edu/entries/catharine-macaulay/. Macaulay, C. (1790) *Letters on Education* http://en.wikipedia.org/wiki/Catharine_Macaulay.
7 Gathorne-Hardy (1977), op. cit., p. 234.
8 Wollstonecraft, M. (1792) *The Vindication of the Rights of Women*, Kindle edition, in the public domain.
9 Vicinus, M. (1985) *Independent Women: Work and Community for Single Women 1850–1920*, London: Virago, p. 165.
10 Ibid., p. 169.
11 Ibid.
12 Gathorne-Hardy (1977), op. cit., p. 239.
13 Ibid., pp. 231–232.
14 Vicinus (1985), op. cit., p. 166.
15 Brendon, V. (2005/2006) *Children of the Raj*, Phoenix: Orion, p. 35.
16 Watson, N. (1994) *In Hortis Reginae: A History of Queenswood School 1894–1994*, London: James & James, p. 11.
17 Ibid.
18 Gathorne-Hardy (1977), op. cit., p. 234.
19 Ibid., p. 235.
20 Watson (1994), op. cit.
21 Vicinus (1985), op. cit., p. 170.
22 Gathorne-Hardy (1977), op. cit., p. 236.
23 Watson (1994), op. cit., p. 12.
24 Gathorne-Hardy (1977), op. cit., p. 238.
25 Ibid., p. 237.
26 Oakley, A. (2011) *A Critical Woman*, London: Bloomsbury Academic, p. 71.
27 Ibid., p. 68.
28 Ibid., p. 68.
29 Vicinus (1985), op. cit., p. 169.
30 Ibid., p. 167.
31 Wakeford, J. (1969) *The Cloistered Elite: A Sociological Analysis of the English Public School*, London: Macmillan, p. 45.
32 Gathorne-Hardy (1977), op. cit., p. 254.
33 Ibid., p. 249.
34 Vicinus (1985), op. cit., p. 182.
35 Gathorne-Hardy (1977), op. cit., p. 255.
36 Ibid., p. 247.
37 Okely (1996), op.cit., p. 141.
38 Ibid., p. 159.
39 Ibid., p. 161.
40 Gathorne-Hardy (1977), op. cit., p. 232.
41 Ibid.
42 Ibid., pp. 257–258.
43 Okely (1996), op cit., p. 164.
44 Ibid., p. 165.
45 Ibid., p. 144.

46 Watson (1994), op. cit.
47 *Sport and the British* (2012) Presented by Clair Balding. Broadcast on BBC Radio 4; 8 February episode in a thirty-part series looking at the impact of sport on British life.
48 Vicinus (1985), op. cit., p. 183.
49 Okely (1996), op. cit., p. 162.
50 Wober, M. (1971) *English Girls' Boarding Schools*, London: Allen Lane the Penguin Press, p. 65.
51 Lockhart, R. E., Gilpin, A., & Jasiocha, E. (2013) *ISC Census*, London: Independent Schools Council www.isc.co.uk/Resources/Independent%20Schools%20Council/Research%20Archive/Annual%20Census/2013_annualcensus_isc.pdf.
52 Gathorne-Hardy (1997), op. cit., p. 259.
53 Okely (1996), op. cit.
54 Hickson, A. (1996) *The Poisoned Bowl: Sex and the Public School*, London: Gerald Duckworth & Co Ltd.

Part II
Exile and healing

Part II

Chapter 4

Developmental trauma (case study part 1)

> The conflict between the will to deny horrible events and the will to proclaim them aloud is the central dialectic of psychological trauma.
>
> Judith Herman.[1]

In Chapter 2, on the history of boys' boarding schools, we saw that extreme brutality was informally licensed in the eighteenth and nineteenth centuries. The justification was that it toughened the boy up in order to create a man suitable to run the British Empire. Nowhere would he meet hardships worse than those he had already encountered. The experiences, which will be discussed in this chapter, took place in the twentieth century but the legacy of this brutal history is discernable. Due to the reforms described earlier, the conditions in the boarding schools of the mid-twentieth century were less extreme than those described by Chandos[2] and Gathorne-Hardy.[3] However, some continued to treat the boys in their care to the neglect, cruelty and sadistic practices of which we have read. Well-meaning parents left their (often very young) children in the hands of apparently benign adults, but they had little idea of what took place in their absence. This apparent trust is strange considering some of them may themselves have suffered abuses in boarding schools.

In this chapter and the next three I will give close attention to what happens after the parents leave and to the enduring psychological impact of such treatment. The experiences of the person at the centre of this study are far from unique. In tracing the analytic journey of one man who, as a child, was subject to such cruelty in the late twentieth century we are also aware that others suffered similar terrors. The case study is illustrated with pictures made in the course of this analysis. I hope that telling this story will alert practitioners to working with the kind of suffering that may be concealed in the casual comment that a client attended a boarding school. Moreover, this story might warn parents to notice and listen to how their children are on visits or exeats. (The term *exeat* is used in boarding schools to denote a brief leave of absence, such as when parents take their child out of the school for a weekend.)

Those whose experience of boarding school was traumatic may not take their own stories seriously; even as adults they may disregard their own suffering. As children there were no words to articulate the abuses they suffered and they were unable to tell their parents. There was no adult witness to confirm that the treatment they received was wrong. Therefore, in psychotherapy they may tell their story but leave out key elements as irrelevant, or they may gloss over their suffering with a lightness of language or a joke. A child usually assumes his or her experience to be the norm, especially when it was shared with others who took their suffering with apparent stoicism and without complaint. Therefore it is often difficult for the adult in psychotherapy to recognise that the treatment they received was wrong. This may also explain why parents, themselves ex-boarders, may not have 'known' what their children were enduring.

Whilst some children enjoy their school, for those who are mistreated or abused boarding school can be experienced as a form of captivity. In her work on trauma, Herman describes common experiences of trauma in which the person is held against his or her will and subjected to the will of the other. Herman writes that 'whether this is the result of war or of domestic violence the effect on the victim is similar.'[4] The child who is trapped in a boarding school with a ruthless regime is similarly captive. Held against his will and subject to the will of others, the child is powerless.

In view of this, some who experienced living in the worst boarding schools suffered profound developmental trauma. The combination of brutality and captivity resulted for some in a form of post-traumatic stress disorder (PTSD). This is defined as 'an anxiety disorder arising as a delayed and protracted response after experiencing or witnessing a traumatic event involving actual or threatened death or serious injury to self or others'.[5] Children living in boarding school may not be able to articulate it, but they may feel that their own life is threatened. Witnessing ill treatment of others may compound the terror. Too painful to bear, such traumatic memories may be repressed and so remain unconscious into adult life. They find expression in unpredictable behaviours or emotional outbursts, often in reaction to simple triggers. These remain incomprehensible until attention is paid to the events in which they originated. This was the case with Theo.

The first meeting

Theo was aware of my interest in boarding school trauma and had been referred by a colleague, who knew of my work in this field. Theo was typical of those afflicted by Boarding School Syndrome; he was successful in his career and socially able. In his forties, he was married, with three teenage children and some good friends – mostly men. Despite this, the psychological impact of the early hardships he had endured had caused him to experience periods of major psychological distress. His intimate relationships were blighted by his periodic black moods, which his wife described as 'poisonous'. During these he was cut off from others and he became silent for days at a time. The trigger was usually his wife either going away from home or becoming angry. Now, after more than twenty years of marriage, he was driven to seek help because communication between them had broken down and his marriage was in serious difficulty.

Theo had attended a Catholic prep school during the 1970s from the age of 8 until he was 13. Later he attended a major public school until he was 17. His father had been in the military and his schooling was therefore a 'benefit' of his father's work rather than family tradition or wealth. This was not his first experience of psychotherapy. Ten years previously he had seen a psychotherapist for approximately two years. She had helped him to recognise that boarding school had had a damaging impact on him and, most significantly, she had dispelled a recurring dream. Since he was 8 Theo had repeatedly dreamed that he had murdered someone. This was most extreme when he was in his twenties. At that time he was already married and in a job he enjoyed, but this was marred when he experienced a period of three days when he was convinced that the dream was true – that he had actually murdered someone. It was so real that he continually worried about how he would dispose of the body. The intensity of this subsided, but he had still periodically had this dream. It was many years later, when he recounted this in psychotherapy, that the therapist suggested that it was a part of himself that he had murdered. He was immensely relieved by this insight and the dream ceased.

More recently there had been other experiences of short-term counselling. In total he had seen four therapists but, as he put it, none had got to the problem with his mother. He now thought that perhaps some of his anger with his wife was connected to anger with his mother. These accumulated attempts at psychotherapy had left him with the conviction that he was a difficult person to help. He was well defended, intelligent and, apart from the first, he was dismissive of each of the other therapists. This seemed to be a challenge to me – would I be up to it or would I be added to the list? There was an underlying anxiety that no one would be able to tackle his considerable distress.

In the first session he recounted two occasions when his mother had apparently abandoned him. The first was when, aged 8, he was sent to boarding school. The second was when he was 16 and she left his father, leaving Theo with him but taking his youngest sibling with her. The dual aspects of this story seemed to be his mother's apparent lack of care combined with his own extreme anxiety. He felt somehow responsible and so he was concerned about how dangerous he could be. In the initial session practicalities were discussed and arrangements made for further meetings. This completed, Theo turned to me and casually said; 'I guess all the usual things apply – if I am going to murder someone you will inform the police without telling me?' This surprised me, so I said nothing for a while. Reflecting on it, I responded seriously, 'So it seems that you fear you will murder someone?' He said little in response.

With this statement the theme of murder, which had been implicit throughout this first meeting, was made explicit. In his recurring dream he had murdered someone and now this comment. It seemed that Theo considered himself to be a threat – perhaps to me. I think unconsciously he wanted assurance that the analytic frame would be safe and that I would be strong enough to look after us both. He also feared that I would abandon him when I got to know him – 'informing the police'.

This was the first time I had met him, so I was wary; I felt alerted to some unspecific danger. However, I did not feel overly concerned for his or my actual safety. He did not appear threatening. Also, there was a sense that he could understand metaphor and so the symbolic nature of the work. Theo did not appear to think concretely, so this was more likely to be an expression of a psychological state – his fear – rather than a real and present threat. This theme was to recur as analysis progressed, but its origins, complexity and depth would take many months to emerge. It would be much longer before its implications could be integrated and Theo no longer felt like a pariah.

Second session – boarding school – arrival

In the second session Theo reported being very anxious. Now he felt a sense of dread, which he described as 'like having to face a pool full of corpses'. He said that he had been impressed when I picked up on his fear about murder. The topic then turned to his first day at boarding school. Theo conveyed the sense of having been a happy child living in a rural part of Scotland with his parents. The eldest of four children, he loved nature and was a free and curious child. He spent many hours with his friends travelling the area on their bikes and exploring the natural world, investigating the toads and insects that lived in the fields near their home. He remembered being told he was going to boarding school but it meant little to him until the day arrived.

Theo was taken on a long drive with his parents, and then he recalled walking into a dark place. There was a wide entrance hall and here they were greeted by the headmaster, a ghoulish figure wearing tweeds; behind him was a dark corridor that receded into gloom. A terrible sense of foreboding descended upon Theo. His parents disappeared: he was totally alone and helpless. He said, 'The world fell apart; the floor, the walls and the sky all fell in.'

The emotion, as he described it, was very present. This is moment that every prep school child recalls.[6][7] Many older children similarly recall this threshold moment,[8] but at 12 or 13 some are better emotionally equipped to understand it than the very young child. Many writers, including Roald Dahl[9] and Andrew Motion,[10] describe the total bewilderment of the child in this moment of traumatic loss. In this instant the child loses everything and so is bereaved. In each case the facts are a little different, but the emotion is similar – the sense of incredulity and, for many, betrayal begins in that moment. The child is alone in a strange world.

That night in the dormitory Theo knew he was completely alone. Witnessing one boy express what all the little boys were feeling compounded his desolation. The boy stood in the middle of the room and cried for his mummy; he lost control of his bodily functions and messed himself. No one came to help or reassure him. The only reaction was a disembodied voice from a schoolmaster watching from a room above, who called out, 'someone shut that boy up.' Although Theo could not have put it into words, it was then that he realised he was abandoned and dependent on adults who did not care about him; he was alone and in an unsafe place. These children were all 7 or 8 years old.

In reading my account for the purposes of this book Theo tells me that this incident happened when he was 9, nearly two years later. However, he told it in this early session and I heard it as related to the first night. As with other misunderstandings in therapy it is useful to consider their meaning. My retrospective thoughts are that in telling it at this time, Theo was indeed describing how the first night felt to him. Even though it actually occurred two years later, the horror in witnessing the distress of another little boy of his own age affected him deeply. He was a compassionate child and his empathy for a child in such a state was clear.

Terror – the dormitory

The terror of this realisation was very soon followed by horrors. If boys left their beds during the night they were beaten, so they were terrified to move after lights out or to talk to each other. Theo then recounted an incident which had always haunted him. The facts of it were a little unclear, but what seemed to have happened was that a fight had broken out in the courtyard outside the window and someone was badly injured. The children heard shouting, then silence and someone calling for help. Later he was to learn that it was a member of the kitchen staff who had been seriously injured in a fight. The boys heard all this but were too terrified of being beaten to leave their beds to see what had happened or to get help. For most of the night they could hear the calls for help but no one came. The boys were helpless, listening to the cries. The distress and shame as Theo reported this story was intense; he could have done something but, like the other boys, he could not move.

Children have an ethical sensibility from an early age and this is violated if they are forced to act against it. This is a recognised aspect of trauma: Judith Herman describes how in cases of captivity the violation of the person's ethical sensibility – their sense of right and wrong – is compromised.[11] This incident had haunted Theo; he knew it was wrong and he had never been able to speak of it. Even now as he recounted it there was much that could not be spoken. Wordlessly he was able to convey to me that somehow the child had felt to blame, even complicit. His wound had been hidden even from himself until now.

This was indeed traumatic: 'At the moment of trauma the victim is rendered helpless by overwhelming force . . . traumatic events overwhelm the ordinary systems of care that give people a sense of control, connection and meaning.'[12] Donald Kalsched describes his use of the word *trauma* 'to mean any experience that causes the child unbearable psychic pain or anxiety. For an experience to be unbearable means that it overwhelms the usual defensive measures, which Freud[13] described as 'a protective shield against stimuli'.[14]

The little boy knew that care was required but, in his captivity in the dormitory bed, he was helpless and unable to summon adult help. Theo was totally alone and he was at the mercy of forces that were worse than uncaring; they were life threatening. For a child in such a situation the realisation that there are no limits, anything can happen, is terrifying. He is not in control of his life and he is totally, wordlessly overwhelmed. One can imagine that many boys in the early public schools of which we read in Chapter 2 suffered similar trauma: captive and at the mercy of inhuman treatment, little boys have little option but to switch off their emotions.

When Theo returned home after the first term, he was changed: he felt separate from his friends at home and their innocence. He had experienced horrors of which they knew nothing. He watched, as if through a screen, as his siblings and friends did all the things they had done together before – but he was no longer part of them. It did not occur to Theo to talk to his parents about the school. He did not have language to speak of it and his parents did not pick up on his changed state. The horror was wordless; the guilt was always with him, silently haunting him, until the next term when he had to return. This is so often the case: children are unable to articulate what has happened. Moreover, they assume this is normal; his parents sent him to the school, so they apparently know what it is like. If the school is all right, then he must be bad.[15] As an adult the person still cannot speak of such an event because words cannot convey the power of the emotion. Thus the silent suffering of Boarding School Syndrome becomes established.

Transference

Transference is a central element in analysis. It was initially recognised by Freud as repetition of past patterns of relating which are replayed in analysis.[16] Elements of behaviour, the origins of which have been previously unconscious, are brought to light. The emotion unconsciously associated with events of the past may become live in the present analytic relationship. This may temporarily distort perceptions of the relationship with the analyst, but it brings the potential for conscious understanding and so change.

Therefore, as the history is reported aspects of it may replay within the therapeutic relationship. This was the case with Theo. He became anxious before each session. On the doorstep, he greeted me with, 'Hello, how are you?' It would have been reasonable to answer but it is often a good idea to wait to see what such a question means. Theo sat down and we discussed the greeting. It became evident that he was scared of me. After he had told me a little of the horrors he had endured, I had come to personify the terror. The question about my well-being was an attempt to appease, but also to check if I had survived. For many months Theo expected me to reject him. He anticipated that I would find his stories, and so him, unacceptable, and would send him away. We explored this and he said that I seemed cold when I opened the door. It was as if, in his mind, I had become the feared boarding school/abandoning mother. I decided to put this into words, so

I suggested that perhaps he was scared that he would crash in here and I wouldn't be there for him. I was using my understanding of this as transference to make an interpretation.

He seemed relieved and confessed that he had already opened up more here than anywhere before. He said that the worst thing about the school was murdering a part of himself. Then, as a sort of afterthought, he added: 'We all did it – we had to. This was worse than the constant hunger and worse than the fact that all the boys got ill at the same time.' These were both themes that would be returned to. Several times as the psychotherapy progressed he asked me direct questions: 'Can I ever be healed up? Can it ever be connected?' On this occasion, in response, I acknowledged the previous session and how dreadful was the incident with the kitchen staff that he had described. He appeared shocked that I remembered it and reacted physically. It was as if I had physically hit him with something terrifying. Perhaps this was because he had already reverted to the way he had survived in the past by repressing and so forgetting the traumatic experiences. He said quietly and with much emotion: 'They made us cut ourselves in half! Can it ever be put back together? It feels like a chasm; to get to the other side seems immense.'

It would have been misleading to attempt to answer these very serious questions directly. I could not offer reassurance because I could not know how psychotherapy would progress. However, Theo needed to have a sense that there was meaning in the chaos of his feelings. Frequently he struggled with tears that were very near the surface, so I suggested to him that these tears were important. They indicated that he was feeling compassion for the boy he had been and that the grief, although very painful, was ultimately healing. Thus, I was offering hope and showing that – although neither of us knew what would happen – I did have confidence that the suffering in analysis had a purpose. Jung writes of how analysis is about finding symbolic meaning in our dreams. This is the same with communications from the patient. Often these have a purpose of which we are only dimly aware at the beginning of an analysis.[17] Therefore when a patient is remembering or re-experiencing trauma some reassurance is called for. Theo needed to be able to trust, when he felt lost, that I had some sort of mental map of the territory.

Confronting women

Theo increased his sessions to twice a week and began to explore how arguments with his wife terrified him. Theo feared that she might abandon him, but just as significant was his fear of his own destructiveness: he felt he might explode 'like an atom bomb'. Fearing the damage his anger could do to those he loved, he cut off his feelings and retreated into the dark silence he had described. This reaction was a reflex; he did not think about it. It just happened – it was immediate and unconscious. As we discussed this, he began to realise that the rows reduced him to the abandoned 8 year old that he had been when he was first left at school. Simultaneously he was vengeful and was convinced that this was evident to others. He was sure that he was seen as formidable, hugely aggressive and terrifying – especially to women. It was the same with his experience of me in the transference; he feared that he would terrify me with his violent rage and I would abandon him. This was belied by his solicitous demeanour. Eventually, when he repeated this I told him that I experienced him as gentle. He was amazed; he felt so dangerous that he expected all women to be afraid of him. Feedback was needed as his self-image was distorted by his vengeful feelings.

One month into the analysis the first summer break occurred. Already many of the main themes that were to characterise this analysis had been opened up; these included loss, abandonment, revenge and physical as well as psychological poisoning. They were returned to in the autumn when many of the stories were retold. As is often the case in analysis, repetition of the same disturbing events gradually deepens understanding and so lessens their psychological hold.

The first break

Breaks in analysis are often particularly difficult for ex-boarders. I have written in some detail about that elsewhere.[18] This does not often emerge as a problem in the early stages of analysis as the ex-boarder is very used to breaks in relationships. So it was with Theo; at first the breaks apparently did not trouble him. Even so, after the first break, Theo returned wearing shorts displaying newly scarred knees, and he had a badly injured shoulder. He had had a mountain climbing accident, which was unusual as he was a very experienced climber. He thought there was a psychological component to this accident. He had been taken to hospital and then to his brother's house where his family were assembled. Everyone, including his mother, was very kind to him. He became aware that this surprised him; he did not expect to receive kindness. For some months after this, he was in excruciating physical pain from the shoulder injury; he could not sleep at night and, at times, he was reduced to tears. He recognised that this corresponded with the emotional pain he was experiencing in psychotherapy: the physical injury gave him a reason to cry. This accident brought him closer to his mother. Later she sent him oil for his scars, which deeply touched him. He appreciated her care and its symbolic significance; it helped to repair the pain of the past abandonments.

Returning to school

The summer break over, Theo now returned to talking about the school. It was as if the first month had been an introduction and now, trusting me a bit more, he began to recount some of the incidents that had haunted him throughout his life. Significantly this was September, the beginning of the school year, and perhaps the darkening evenings and the autumn atmosphere generated some of the disturbing memories of that time. The first was the story of the PE teacher.

Theo, still only 8, had not been good at cricket. This was the favourite subject of the PE teacher, who therefore took a dislike to him. One day, for no apparent reason, Theo was called out to the front of the class by this teacher, who made him kneel down with his nose on a desk. To the child's disbelief, he held a cricket bat horizontally, in both hands, and then hit him in the face with it; not just once, but repeatedly. The pain, combined with shock at the injustice of this cruel treatment, was then compounded by the teacher's immediate change of face. At that moment the headmaster came into the classroom with some parents who were looking round the school. The teacher said, 'Get up, get up!' There was pretence that all was well. No one except other helpless little boys witnessed this abuse. Recounting this, Theo was overwhelmed by the shame and shock of this incident, but he was also full of rage at the injustice of it.

Theo first told of this incident early in analysis. Then, a few months later, he retold it, this time with more depth of feeling. It was as if he was at first incredulous but then, as I took it seriously, he began to believe himself and to take seriously how abusive this had been. As Theo recounted it for the second time the feelings associated with the event became live in the session. Theo went white; he felt sick; he had trouble breathing and physically regressed. This is the flashback to trauma of which Herman writes so vividly: 'long after the danger is past, traumatised people relive the event as though it were . . . recurring in the present.'[19] The emotional impact of this was fully present in the room. Theo was overwhelmed and speechless.

When a person is re-experiencing trauma, the onus for negotiating the end of the session is with the therapist. The client is in a timeless state and, if possible, the therapist tries to make the ending bearable by gradually bringing the person back into the present. The therapist might therefore need to be more active than usual. I was very aware of the end of this session drawing near and concerned that Theo should recover before leaving. Rothschild writes of the need to help the client to find a safe place in their mind as a place to return to at these times.[20] She does this before regression happens; but, in my experience, regression to trauma is unpredictable and usually occurs without warning. It is helpful to talk simply and clearly, as if to the very young child, at the same time as to the adult. Therefore I calmly talked to Theo, explaining that this was cruel and should not have happened. Gradually Theo returned to the present and his demeanour changed. The colour returned to his face and he was able to speak. He described how he had felt: 'It was like being awake and dreaming; I was actually back there. I am glad I could tell you – I didn't think I could.'

This is what happens with traumatic events: 'the victim is rendered helpless by overwhelming force . . . traumatic events overwhelm the ordinary systems of care that give people a sense of control, connection and meaning.'[21] Moreover, flashbacks are a bit like time travel. As the person relives, in the present, the trauma of the past, it is emotionally live in the room. Theo felt powerless; he was in the grip of overwhelming emotion as he relived this cruelty. This is a characteristic of trauma. As Herman writes, 'psychological trauma is an affliction of the powerless.'[22] At the time, the child had been totally powerless in the face of this abuse.

Before the session ended, as Theo was recovering, he expressed his concern for me. He said, 'It must be difficult being a therapist.' He feared contaminating me with the horror which was so vivid for him. I realised that his fear was that if the horrors were too awful for me to bear, I would send him away. When I suggested this to him, Theo was able to relax a little. The same trauma is often revisited. This one was returned to a few months later.

In this period Theo had already conveyed a sense of significantly traumatic events that had taken place in his first months at prep school. Witnessing the neglect of the other boys and the episode with the kitchen staff was followed by the injury he had suffered being hit in the face with a cricket bat. These events had lastingly affected his relationship to himself, as well as his trust of others. As a child Theo knew that these events were not right but he was helpless. He knew that he was in danger but there was no one to whom to turn.

This child had suddenly to cope alone in the world. Developmentally a child of 8 has only just learned to manage his bodily functions and his relation to food, and now he was plunged into a terrifying and incomprehensible world. The loss of all attachment figures at the same time is a significant bereavement. This experience, as well as captivity, are ubiquitous; Theo's experiences, although particular, are far from unique. The point about telling his tale is to illustrate in depth the traumatic impact of this everyday experience. Most children sent to school at an early age suffer the traumatic separation of the threshold moment and the rupture in their attachments. For Theo it was that initial separation that left him exposed to the further traumas that occurred.

Now his attention turned to the bizarre characters that populated his memories of the school. He was able to introduce me to them through his drawings.

Notes

1. Herman, J. (1992/1997) *Trauma and Recovery: The Aftermath of Violence From Domestic Abuse to Political Terror*, New York: Basic Books, p. 1.
2. Chandos, J. (2001) *Boys Together: English Public Schools 1800–1864*, London: Yale University Press.
3. Gathorne-Hardy, J. (1977) *The Public School Phenomenon*, London, Sydney, Auckland, Toronto: Hodder & Stoughton.
4. Herman (1992/1997), op. cit., pp. 74–75.
5. Colman, A. M. (2001) *The Oxford Dictionary of Psychology*, Oxford: Oxford University Press, p. 572.
6. Schaverien, J. (2004) 'Boarding school: The trauma of the "privileged" child', *Journal of Analytical Psychology* 49 (5), pp. 683–705.
7. Schaverien, J. (2011a) 'Boarding School Syndrome: Broken attachments a hidden trauma', *British Journal of Psychotherapy* 17 (2), pp. 138–155.
8. Partridge, S. (2007) 'Trauma at the threshold: An eight-year-old goes to boarding school', *Attachment* 1 (3), pp. 310–313.
9. Dahl, R. (1984) *Boy: Tales of Childhood*, London: Puffin Books, p. 79.
10. Motion, A. (2006) *In the Blood: A Memoir of My Childhood*, London: Faber & Faber, pp. 99–100.
11. Herman (1992/1997), op. cit.
12. Ibid., p. 33.
13. Freud, S. (1920) *Beyond the Pleasure Principle*, Standard Edition XVIII, London: Hogarth Press, p. 27.

14 Kalsched, D. (1996) *The Inner World of Trauma*, London: Routledge, p. 1.
15 Duffell, N. (2000) *The Making of Them*: London, Lone Arrow Press, p. 140.
16 Freud, S. (1912) *The Dynamics of the Transference*, Standard Edition XII, London: Hogarth.
17 Jung, C. G. (1956/1976) *Symbols of Transformation*, CW 5, Princeton: Bollingen, p. 7.
18 Schaverien, J. (2002) *The Dying Patient in Psychotherapy: Desire, Dreams and Individuation*, New York: Palgrave Macmillan.
19 Herman (1992/1997), op. cit., p. 37.
20 Rothschild, B. (2000) *The Body Remembers: The Psychophysiology of Trauma and Trauma Treatment*, London: W.W. Norton & Co.
21 Herman (1992/1997), op. cit., p. 33.
22 Ibid.

Chapter 5

Mapping the psyche (case study part 2)

> It is curious the degree . . . of squalor and neglect that was taken for granted in the upper-class schools of that period . . . it seemed natural that a little boy of eight or ten should be a miserable, snotty-nosed creature, his face almost permanently dirty, his hands chapped, his nails bitten, his handkerchief a sodden horror, his bottom frequently blue with bruises.
>
> George Orwell[1]

This was written by George Orwell of his prep boarding school, which he attended from 1911, when he was 8, until he left there to go to Eton in 1917. In 1946, when he wrote this, he considered that schools were not as bad as this any more. Sadly, this is far from the truth. The schools continued in the same vein for many decades after he left. Theo attended his prep school in the 1970s but many of Orwell's observations were almost identical to the stories Theo recounted.

We return now to Theo for a close-up account of the experience of living in a cruel preparatory boarding school during the 1970s. Many of Theo's boarding school experiences found a means of externalisation in pictures. Two of the early pictures he made were maps of the school which charted the location of memories. These would be visited and revisited repeatedly. As with many ex-boarders these memories revolved around the dormitory and the dining table, as well as the chapel.

At prep school Theo's experiences had been, literally, unspeakable. Now, as an adult, he was haunted by an inchoate sense that something was amiss, but there were no words to express it. However, when he began to draw, these sense impressions began to form into shapes and then into images. So it was that art began to provide a way of revealing what Theo had never before been able to articulate. Sometimes, as he drew, he described a situation; at other times he would draw and only later find words to describe what it depicted. At first the pictures were rudimentary diagrams which needed words to embellish their meaning. These diagrammatic images[2] were like maps of the psyche, bringing long-repressed memories to consciousness. As Theo became more familiar with the medium, the pictures changed and they began to embody powerful affect. Gradually they began to offer a means of symbolisation.

This is how art mediates in an analysis: it offers a way of revealing imagery which has previously had no other form of representation. It shows what cannot be spoken and mediates between conscious and unconscious, facilitating the beginning of symbolisation.[3] This is why, in working with trauma, art can help articulate otherwise unspeakable experiences.

In my consulting room, art is just one option; as well as a couch and two comfortable chairs, there is a drawing pad and felt tip pens. Other art materials are available, and these I will introduce to a client who seems interested in using paint or larger sheets of paper. Work in progress is stored in a plans chest, in individual folders.[4] Storing pictures is a way of holding imagery that for a while cannot be integrated. During the course of an analysis, the analyst remembers the dreams and stories a client tells; these are held in mind. This is a way of symbolically storing the material of the sessions. With pictures it is similar – but, in them, memories and images are held in a material object and so a concrete solution is required. Stored in the room, they are held within the analytic frame until the material can be integrated.

Themes in analysis often recur repeatedly until they are no longer infused with the charge of unconscious affect. In this chapter I will trace this pattern over a two-month period. It was Freud who first observed that repressed memories would re-present in psychotherapy until they broke through to consciousness.[5] Therefore in analysis a story may be told and then retold, gradually deepening, until eventually it becomes familiar. Jung too observed this pattern and described it as a spiral: the same story may be told from a slightly different place on the spiral as consciousness deepens.[6]

So it was with Theo. Many of the stories were repeated, but with increasing depth of emotion. His pictures give privileged access to this process. The pictures in this chapter are organised by theme and so not always shown in the sequence in which they were made. This analysis reveals how Boarding School Syndrome is created as a necessary defence against unbearable experiences. The dismantling of such defences is not a process lightly undertaken. It took immense courage for Theo to engage with his traumatic history.

This analysis also engaged the analyst in what at times felt like a risky journey. The countertransference is the analyst's emotional response to the client and the material he brings. It is the counterpart of the client's transference and an important guide to understanding the unspoken and often unconscious communications from the client. With Theo this was constantly under review, as is inevitable when working with the return of traumatic memories.

Mapping the territory

Theo became understandably ambivalent following the huge wave of emotion that had engulfed him during the session when he had described the incident with the PE teacher and the cricket bat (Chapter 4). He feared again being overwhelmed by such powerful sense impressions but he also felt better for telling it. He knew there was much more he needed to confront. In the following session he described feeling stuck 'in a dark formless sludge', and he asked me, directly: 'How do I get it out?' I indicated the art materials and suggested that it might help to draw. Theo immediately reached for the pad of paper beside the chair and began drawing a diagram (see Figure 5.1).

Using a felt tip pen on the drawing pad, Theo drew a simple map. As he drew, he explained that this was the entrance hall to the school. Off it was a dark corridor, which always greeted him with a sense of foreboding. The open door on the left led to the dining room. At the top right were the stairs up to the dormitories. In this way Theo showed me the image of this building which was imprinted in his psyche.

Psychologically the left in pictures is often viewed as the unconscious side.[7] Therefore we might understand the open door on the left as the portal which was to lead deeper into analysis. It was opening to permit unconscious memories to surface. Theo was beginning to recall events that had been too unbearable to think about and so they had been repressed. As Theo drew the map, the feeling in the room was live. Then, warming to the task, he drew a second picture, this time of the headmaster (shown in Figure 5.2).

As he drew, Theo described his memories of this man: he was blotchy; his suit was green and orange tweed; and he smelled of ravioli. The colours and the smell were significant because 'it was like it had been buried in the ground for

Figure 5.1 Map 1, 18 November, Year 1.

Figure 5.2 The Headmaster, 18 November, Year 1.

years.' The scratchy black background indicated the blackness of the feelings around him.

Both drawings, the map and the portrait, were resonant with feeling and the atmosphere was intense. Theo was clearly relieved; these images had haunted him since he was a young child. Unable to speak of them, he had locked them in a part of his psyche of which he had little conscious awareness. In this sense, it *had* indeed 'been buried in the ground for years'.

In the following sessions, emboldened by the liberation he felt at bringing these images into the light, he portrayed other teachers. Theo drew a variety of preposterous and often frightening characters (these drawings are not shown due to limits of space).

There had been very few women in the school apart from the matron and the headmaster's wife. The headmaster's wife, as Theo described her, was cruel and took on the proportions of an archetypal witch (Figure 5.3) who moved around the school on crutches. On one occasion Theo was ill and confined to the sanatorium. This was her domain. He remembered that, instead of cough mixture, she gave him Dettol disinfectant to take. This picture, together with that of the headmaster, depicted the bizarre couple in loco parentis; the welfare of the child depended on them.

There was a notable change in Theo's demeanour as he sat back and viewed the drawings; they gave credence to his story. He began to believe himself and he

Figure 5.3 The Headmaster's Wife, November, Year 1.

was overwhelmed. The atmosphere of the school was live in the room and with it the long-buried emotions. Theo was overcome by the emotional impact of his drawings. He found them horrific. Soon I became aware that he was worried about imposing them on me. He feared they would contaminate or upset me. When I realised this and put it into words he seemed relieved.

The intensity of Theo's engagement certainly affected me. I was transported, with him, back in time. I believed and was totally engaged with his story. Countertransference is a useful way of understanding the profound emotional impact on the analyst of such material. However, it is not a theory for the analyst to hide behind. It means being emotionally present but also maintaining the ability to think. Thus although profoundly affected by Theo and his stories, I was also able to preserve my professional equilibrium.

Mapping horror

Theo found art increasingly helpful and, although we did not realise it at the time, the future path of analysis was mapped out in these early pictures. Memories of traumatic incidents now poured onto the paper. The following week Theo came in and immediately picked up the pens and pad, then drew three pictures in quick succession. The first was a second map of the school, the second, evening prayers and the third about food.

This, the second actual map, was a ground plan of the school (Figure 5.4). It was deeper and more complex than the first map. Although the picture is shown here in black and white, the use of red was significant. The locations of memories of bewildering and frightening incidents are detailed. Some had already been described, but other incidents of bullying and abuse were introduced. In each scene Theo is pictured as a red stick figure. In one scene he portrays, also in red, the member of the kitchen staff lying on the ground. He drew the games room where he had escaped a paedophile teacher by being agile, and the room where the PE teacher hit him with a cricket bat. There were the times he was so cold on the sports field that he thought he would die; this is depicted in a shivering figure at the top left of the picture. As he drew the entrance to the school, on the lower left of the picture, he recalled the associated unpleasant smell. There are cowsheds at the top left of the picture, and, in the foreground to the right, a fishing pond. These were peaceful places where he found refuge.

The teachers are arrayed on the right side of the picture, often considered the conscious side. On the left, depicted as an area of shaded map in crayon, are places which it later emerged were associated with more deeply buried traumatic memories. At the lower right, a teacher jumps up and down; Theo explained that he was unpredictable and could be jovial but then suddenly turn. On one occasion, outside the art room, this teacher quite unexpectedly hit Theo so violently that he was lifted off his feet and saw stars. The headmaster is depicted, he would silently creep up to the dormitories, so that his approach was muffled. Then, if he heard

66 Exile and healing

Figure 5.4 Map 2, 23 November, Year 1.

talking, he would pounce and hit the offending boy with a slipper. Theo observed that in the daytime the boys were hit with a leather truncheon but at night it was the slipper.

It was now forty years since these incidents took place. Theo was relieved to have a witness to whom he could show, as well as tell, each of these incidents. Until now, like so many who suffered as children, he had only half-believed these things took place. Being believed began to validate his account. In retrospect I realise that unconsciously Theo was mapping his future analytic journey. These places would be revisited.

Religion

The second picture he made that day was associated with religion (Figure 5.5). Ten years previously Theo had first become aware that there was something wrong when he was attending a christening. During the church service he was suddenly overcome; he felt sick and could not breathe. With his wife's help he had been able to leave the church and sit outside to recover. From that time he could not go into a church without being emotionally overwhelmed. This had made no sense until now. He realised that the physical reaction was similar to the flashbacks he was now experiencing. With the next picture this understanding deepened. Theo never consciously knew what he was going to draw, but as the marks began to form a picture the stories unfolded. The next was the second picture drawn with some urgency on the same November day as the map.

This was a Catholic school and each Sunday evening a teacher would conduct prayers, attended by about fifty of the 150 boys in the school. Theo remembered those evenings as always dark. There was an overwhelming sense of sadness and gloom, with all these little boys far from home. The charcoal that Theo used for this picture conveys the darkness of the room, with the heads of anonymous boys facing a door. Words are written on the picture: 'When the shadows lengthen and the evening comes'. This a quote from the evensong prayer, but it did not offer comfort. Rather the misery of the profound loneliness and homesickness of these dark winter evenings was conveyed. When Theo sat back he was shocked by how realistic this picture seemed to him. The impact of this image on him was immense. We might understand the focus of this drawing to have zoomed in, from the overview of the map, to an emotional close-up. As he drew, the sadness in the room was tangible.

I now explore how Theo revisited themes in his drawings, revealing deeper layers of meaning in each picture. Theo drew his next picture on religion three months later, in February of the first year of analysis. After the second break in analysis there were many times when Theo did not draw. When he did, the process slowed. By February, rather than two or three pictures in a session, he

Figure 5.5 Shadows, 23 November, Year 1.

would often make only one. Theo still dreaded each session. It took a great deal of courage to confront the unpredictable emergence of the horrors that he had endured. They returned with such emotional charge that he was often unexpectedly catapulted into flashbacks to traumatic events. Figure 5.6 was drawn over two sessions: started on a Monday, it was completed the following Wednesday. Drawn in oil pastels on a large sheet of paper, it began with apparently random marks. As the picture took shape, the memories of the Sunday evening spiritual readings returned, accompanied by strong emotions.

Gloom and homesickness continued to affect the boys but it now emerged that the subject matter of the spiritual readings was terrifying. The topic was the lives and deaths of the saints. The fates of individual saints were spelled out: one was flayed alive, while another was sawn in half. Each method of torture was lingered over in forensic detail. The words that Theo scrawled boldly across the page – 'BE SAWN IN HALF' – emphasise the horror. The Stations of the Cross were terrifying. He said 'it was all about torture.' The children were obliged to hear detailed accounts of the effects on the body of crucifixion, how the nails were driven through the wrists and not the centre of the hands. This was compounded because the teaching was that Christ died for their sins, therefore inducing guilt. The child, not understanding, felt he was bad.

Figure 5.6 The Ammonite Priests, 22–24 February, Year 2.

These horror stories were terrifying to a little boy far from the safety of home. He knew he was in the care of adults who did not love or protect him. He had already witnessed life-threatening events in the school and so he knew he was exposed to harm. If the tortures described could befall important adults, like saints, then they could also happen to little boys. The threat was implicit. Theo could not express it in this way but I discerned this from his presentation in the room.

As he recounted this, Theo began to feel ill; his face went white and he had difficulty breathing. He tried to speak but could not form the words; his mouth moved but no sound came. He mouthed one word with his eyes shut, in great pain. He stroked his chest in a gesture of soothing. It became clear that he was in the grip of the terror he had experienced as a child. The adult was gone and in his place there was a speechless, terrified child. It was not difficult to imagine how a child so alone and at the mercy of those teachers would fear for his life. Theo could not formulate the words but it was evident he felt totally vulnerable. He was exposed to adults who could do anything to him.

I kept talking to him and eventually he returned to the present. He was able to tell me the word he was trying to form was 'darkness'. This had indeed been a significant trauma and he had experienced a flashback typical of PTSD. Theo was still regressed and after a while I realised that I needed to intervene in a practical way. It was vital with such regression to attempt to bring him back to safety before the end of the session. When trauma is so live in the room the therapist needs to speak. Ten minutes before the end of the session I suggested that he wrap himself up in the blanket from the couch and then sit in the chair to recover. To break the spell it is sometimes helpful to acknowledge that this should not have happened. This I did with Theo. I explained that he had been powerless; that these people seemed to me to have been sadistic. He had known they did not love him and so, as a child, he had felt unsafe.

Theo then was able to speak a little and realise that this was how he had felt at the christening. He had been overcome in church in the same way he was now. At that time he had not made the link to school and could not understand why being in the church made him feel so ill. Later, he came to realise that the focus of the christening is a baby and this had taken him back to himself as a young child. He seemed a little relieved by this realisation.

The physical impact of these re-presenting memories on Theo was very great. I was concerned. Each time he returned to this or other similarly traumatic memories, the reaction was the same. I was worried about whether his body could survive the impact that he experienced each time a memory came back with such force. I discussed this in supervision and decided that Theo seemed to be strong enough to continue with the work. There was little other option but to continue with the work that had begun. However, it took immense courage for him to come each time, knowing that he could be overwhelmed with horror at any moment.

Food

The third picture, made on the same day as the map and evening prayers, raised another significant topic: food. Like the Sunday evening readings, Theo returned to this subject in a February session; both pictures are shown here (see Figure 5.7 and Figure 5.8). In the analysis of Boarding School Syndrome the relationship of the ex-boarder to food is usually significant. (This will be addressed in more general terms in Chapter 12.) The younger a child is exposed to boarding school, the more likely is disruption to their emotional development and so their appetites. Latency is the developmental time from about 5 or 6 years of age and before puberty. In the normal course of latency, the child learns to accept certain foods and to reject others. The child who is forced to eat food that he or she finds nauseating will dread mealtimes. In institutions there is little subtlety and so this part of individuation is often overridden by inflexible rules. This is compounded when children are always hungry and obliged to compete at meal times, as is often the case in boarding schools.

The third picture made on 23 November conveyed some of the noise and chaos of meal times at school (Figure 5.7). Theo explained that there was never enough to eat, so the boys were always hungry. Mostly the food was horrible but occasionally it was nice – and then 'you ate it very quickly'. If there was stale bread left, it

Figure 5.7 Food 1. 23 November, Year 1.

had to be eaten before the palatable, fresh bread would be served. The meat they were given was condemned as unfit for human consumption and it was always full of veins and tubes. Once Theo found a worm on his plate; this is the moment that he depicted.

The boy in the foreground is horrified at finding the worm. Whilst most of the picture is drawn in black, the worm pictured on the plate is yellow. There is a red outline around the lower part of the boy's face, starting at the ears and outlining the jaw line, emphasising his revulsion. This is echoed in the red tie around his neck. This may indicate the impossibility of swallowing this food. The boy is separated from the rows of featureless black figures in the background, indicating his isolation. At this point Theo remembered how the food was so bad that the boys were always getting ill. Often they all had food poisoning simultaneously. It was bad enough being ill, but because so many were ill at the same time, the basins and the lavatories were all overflowing. This meant it was difficult to approach them even if you were very ill. It seemed that unconsciously this had stayed with Theo as a sense of contamination. He could hardly bring himself to tell me because he said that it was as if he was showing me filth. He feared that in just recounting this he would contaminate me. He felt ashamed and humiliated. Speaking of it felt like breaking a taboo; the words made it real. Gradually we began to understand that Theo felt both poisoned and also poisonous.

The origins of some of the silent rage that his wife described as 'poisonous' began to make sense. Theo felt contaminated and this had to be kept separate from those he loved at all costs. Nor could he permit himself to be angry because of the danger that his poisonous rage could not be contained. Like the basins, it would overflow. Before his fury could come to the fore, in analysis, his sense of having been contaminated by the poisonous experiences at school needed attention. Theo made a picture of the overflowing basins and lavatories (not shown because it is too faintly drawn to reproduce).

The theme of food deepened. Three months later, again in a February session, Theo thought he might make a drawing but (as he often did) he wanted to connect up with his previous pictures first. When he got the pictures out of his folder and looked at them he was visibly shocked; he had forgotten their content. The pictures were concrete evidence of the traumas he had revisited, and the associated feelings returned violently. Between sessions he was able to split off so successfully from the painful memories that they were forgotten. He would leave the pictures and, with them, the associated emotions behind. He knew he had made drawings but he forgot the content, and each time he opened his folder, they shocked him. The pictures were evidence of his traumatic childhood and of the analytic journey so far.

He looked for a while at the one he had made about school food two months previously (Figure 5.7). Then he drew another picture of the contaminated meat (Figure 5.8). Like the second picture of religion, this image went deeper. It was a single picture that took up a whole session. Here in more detail, is a close-up of the tainted meat: it was all tubes and bits. This picture is vividly drawn in coloured

Figure 5.8 Food 2, 10 February, Year 2.

oil pastels. The knees of the boy are in the foreground with the plate before him. The viewpoint is relevant. In Figure 5.7, the viewer is separate, looking at the alienated and horrified boy. Here, the viewer shares the boy's viewpoint and so experiences the tainted food close up.

For Theo, who was hungry all the time at school, food was linked to the repeated trauma of being taken out of school only to return. At half term Theo's parents would take him out for a day. It was fun. Theo was unable to tell them how awful it was at school. He could not say why he could not speak, but it is often the case that a child who is suffering cannot put it into words. His parents did not seem to notice his distress. It seems they were not emotionally attuned to him and perhaps this discouraged speaking about feelings. When words fail, children may express the disquiet as feeling unwell. It is common for a child who does not want to go to school to have a 'tummy ache'. Parents will often understand this as describing the discomfort of anxiety. Homesickness is similar: its causes are emotional but they are expressed physically. The child feels sick.

While returning to school from these exeats Theo was regularly nauseated, but his parents assumed that he was carsick. He thought little of it because 'we were always vomiting at school because the food was so bad.' Reflecting on this now, he realised that the sickness was his way of informing his parents he was unhappy, but they did not understand. He also realised that his system had become accustomed to the meagre diet provided at school and the rich food he had when his parents took him out was therefore indigestible. Emotionally as well, Theo could not digest the rich fare of being with his own family. He briefly had the care and attention of his parents only to lose it again. Theo was incredulous that, after these outings, they would take him back. Each time he was returned to the school his disbelief turned to despair and ultimately to a dreadful resignation. In the process he lost touch with himself.

Thus the three pictures, drawn on a single day in November – the map, the evening prayers and the contaminated food – revealed images that were seared into Theo's psyche. They mapped out events that would be returned to in words and pictures, many times.

Soul murder

Theo still dreaded each session because he could not predict what memories would emerge. As awareness of the psychological impact of the school deepened, each session brought new insights. The next two pictures were made on the same day in December. A story that has already been told in analysis is often retold, as if it is pressing to the fore and requiring conscious attention. So it was that the PE teacher was unexpectedly revisited.

Theo was feeling very sad and stuck; the pain was seated in his chest like a physical block. Crying was almost impossible, so Theo took the felt tip pens and began to draw, without knowing what he was drawing. He drew the picture shown in Figure 5.9.

He was unhappy with the drawing, so he laid it aside and began another one. I usually encourage people to keep rejected pictures, as they may become meaningful later. Theo changed to a different medium. Using black crayon and pastels, he now drew intently the picture shown in Figure 5.10. When he had finished, he looked at it and said quietly: 'It is darkness – it is my soul.' He had drawn a dark cell with a lone figure seated at a desk. He said: 'This is the moment when I killed a part of myself.' Then he drew a sword going through the body and added red for the blood, which falls making a shape on the ground behind the figure. This red is the only colour in the picture. Then, on the floor to the right and behind the seated figure, he drew a black shadow which is reminiscent of a corpse.

We regarded the drawing shown in Figure 5.10 quietly as the full import of his words and the image took hold. After a while, Theo said: 'This is when it happened – within thirty seconds of entering that place.' Then he added: 'I am sure that others who went to boarding school would recognise it.' Theo was right. Many who attended boarding school at an early age would recognise this image: it is a picture of the creation of Boarding School Syndrome. This is what Freud's patient so long ago called 'soul murder'.[8][9][10] Silently we contemplated the magnitude of his words as well as the picture. This had, until this moment, been a very private wound. The picture reveals the secret sorrow and unspoken guilt that, in order to

74 Exile and healing

Figure 5.9 The Cricket Bat, 2 December, Year 1

survive in an alien environment, there was little choice but to do violence to the tender self, to kill off the feeling state, in order to comply with the institution.

This was a very upsetting image. Theo asked me directly: 'How can I get better?' The emotional switch seemed to be a distraction from the enormity of what was before us, but it was also a genuine plea. Theo had shown me his private tragedy and he was worried that his situation was hopeless. He needed reassurance but he knew that this was not the sort of question I could answer directly. The intense feeling in the silence was laden with unshed tears.

Now as we regarded the two pictures, my eye was drawn back to the first one (Figure 5.9); it seemed odd. It had been put aside because the proportions were wrong. Then I realised that it appeared to be someone kneeling beside a desk and I was reminded of the incident with the cricket bat. I kept this observation to

Figure 5.10 Soul Murder, 2 December, Year 1

myself but, in the following session, Theo was musing on how difficult it had been to tell me about that incident. Then I gently suggested that I thought he had drawn it. Theo took the picture out of his folder and, with an almost physical shock, he realised that this was indeed what he had unconsciously drawn. He was swiftly in touch with the emotional impact all over again. Now we understood that the picture had been discarded because it was neither what he had intended to draw, nor what he wanted to see. Unconsciously, the image had re-presented itself, this time visually, demanding his attention.

Here we have seen pair of pictures, drawn on the same day, which brought different aspects of the boarding school trauma into the light and so consciousness.

A moment of kindness

In the following week Theo made another two pictures on the same day. The first was a gentle memory, but another very distressing one quickly followed. In the first picture Theo recalled a young matron who stayed for only one term; he had always remembered her kindness.

In all weathers, even in the coldest winter, the youngest boys used to be out on the sports field wearing short trousers. It was freezing cold, so their hands and knees were sore and often cracked. They used to queue up for this young

Figure 5.11 A Moment of Kindness, 14 December, Year 1.

matron to put cream on their split hands (Figure 5.11). If boys had a cold, she gave them eucalyptus. Theo was emotional, describing this kindness in a life devoid of warmth. In the picture four little boys are shown, patiently waiting for this moment of kindness. Their backs are turned to the viewer, but they stand beside four basins, each of which appears to have a smiling face. Thus the shower room, the scene of many bad experiences, was temporarily transformed into a loving place. This was a reparative memory. This was also reminiscent of his mother recently sending him oil for his scars after his mountaineering accident. Perhaps too analysis was putting some balm on the pain of the emerging memories. He was able to feel relief that comes from a sense of at last being understood. This respite was brief because, in the same session, the dormitory emerged as the location of other traumas.

The dormitory and despair

Two pictures are shown on the same theme, this time the dormitory. The first picture shown was from December (Figure 5.12) and the second was from February the following year (Figure 5.13).

As Theo began to draw his second picture on this December day he told the story of one night when the boy in the next bed to him had an asthma attack.

The boy was breathing with great difficulty and then he began to really struggle for breath. As before, the boys were too terrified of the consequences if they left their beds to summon adult help. They did not even dare to consult with each other. So they stayed in their own beds while this boy was wheezing and gasping for breath. The boys were petrified, turned to stone. Once again their natural compassion for each other was violated and they were too terrified to leave their beds after lights out. The boy survived, but Theo was overwhelmed remembering the pain and shame of the situation. These little boys cared about each other but were ill-equipped to challenge such a callous system. Therefore they did violence to their selves: they cut off emotionally. In this picture there are again four boys drawn in detail; the others are shadowy presences, just suggested by beds.

Once again the trauma was present in the room. Theo was shocked, white and struggling for breath. The words came with difficulty. Perhaps the boy depicted as struggling to breathe was also a part of himself. In the session *he* was indeed speechless and gasping for breath.

A similar regression to trauma occurred in February with another memory of the dormitory. Theo's parents came and took him out for a day. As already discussed, he was unable to tell them how bad it was at the school because he did not have the words. Theo had a very nice day, but on the return journey he was sick. With the understanding that he was merely carsick, his parents returned him to school. Theo now realised that this must have been the first half-term exeat

Figure 5.12 Asthma Agony, 14 December, Year 1.

78 Exile and healing

Figure 5.13 Oh God Help Me, 16 February, Year 2.

because he was shocked – he had half expected that they would rescue him. Although he could not formulate it, he was incredulous. He could not believe that they would take him back and leave him. He could not articulate this sense of things being very wrong. This was made worse because he arrived back at school before the other boys had returned. Theo wandered around aimlessly and the building felt empty. His parents were gone and he was completely alone. Theo was 8 years old and helpless; there was nothing else to do, so he got into bed and cried. No one came and there was no one to witness his distress.

Theo drew this picture in oil pastels as he was talking (Figure 5.13). The bed was black, the boy in blue with a purple cover. He then added these words drawn strongly in red pastels:

'OH GOD HELP ME!'
And then, in smaller red writing, 'aged 8.'

We were both silent in the face of this tragic desertion. The feeling in the room was unbearably sad and we were both close to tears. The plight of this lonely child and his silent cry was profound. Theo said quietly: 'How do you ask for something when there is no one there?' Deeply moved, I said, 'You were traumatised.'

Theo was devastated by the impact of what he had drawn. He was in touch with the complete aloneness of this experience of the small child he had once been. The dormitory is supposed to be a safe place where children can rest and sleep. Both of the pictures made it clear that it had offered no such refuge, but this one was a picture of despair and resignation to his fate: he was completely alone in what looks like a prison cell. At this point the fruitlessness of resisting his fate overwhelmed him.

Later, when he was reviewing his pictures, he was to confess that he felt ashamed of this picture. He felt that he should not have inflicted it on me. He also told me later that when I said 'you were traumatised,' he was deeply touched and near to tears. He was shocked to realise that this was true. This was not just some ordinary set of events; it really was traumatic. So it was that Theo began to take seriously his own reality. Theo, as a child, had not only been bereaved by the initial loss of his home and parents but he had also been captive in an alien environment with no hope of rescue.

In this chapter we have seen that pictures can map the analytic journey and expose to view material that has no other form of symbolisation. The representation of memories in pictures may be the first stage of unveiling the trauma. However, this is no accident and demands understanding. In the next chapter we will see how this facilitates the ability to speak of traumatic events and confront them further.

Notes

1 Orwell, G. (1947/2003) *Such, Such Were the Joys*, London: Penguin, p. 23.
2 Schaverien, J. (1992) *The Revealing Image*, London: Routledge. This edition London: Jessica Kingsley Publishers (1999), p. 86
3 See Schaverien (1992), op. cit., for a full exposition of this process.
4 A plans chest is a large chest of drawers for flat storage of works on paper such as art, engineering or architectural drawings.
5 Freud, S. (1964) *New Introductory Lectures on Psycho-analysis*, Standard Edition XXIV, London: Hogarth Press, p. 106.
6 Jung, C.G. (1969) *Archetypes and the Collective Unconscious*, Collected Works 9, Princeton: Bollingen, p. 362.
7 In the Jungian lexicon the left side is often viewed as the unconscious side; whilst I am sceptical about taking such claims literally, sometimes it is useful to consider as a possibility.
8 Freud, S. (1911/1968) 'Notes on an autobiographical account of a case of paranoia', Standard Edition XII. London: Hogarth Press.
9 Shengold, L. (1989) *Soul Murder: The Effects of Childhood Abuse and Deprivation*, New York: Fawcett Columbine.
10 Schatzman, M. (1973) *Soul Murder: Persecution in the Family*, New York: Random House.

Chapter 6

The distortion of a boy (case study part 3)

> Repeated trauma in adult life erodes the structure of the personality already formed, but repeated trauma in childhood forms and deforms the personality.
> Judith Herman[1]

In the first six months of analysis, from July to February, Theo had relived many of the traumas suffered during his early boarding school experience. Now he began to be better able to remember these events, without immediate regression, and to address their effect on his present life. Spontaneously he moved into a phase of integration. This was reflected in the material of the sessions between April and July and in the pictures that he made during this period.

Relationships

Theo's close relationships began to change as he became better able to understand the origins of some of his behaviour. During the time when the traumatic memories were emerging in analysis, Theo would often return home after his twice-weekly sessions and talk to his wife until late into the evening. Consequently they both began to understand the connection between his early trauma and Theo's retreats from emotional engagement. As a result, their relationship began to improve.

In analysis, Theo, always sensitive to the danger he might pose for those close to him, scrutinised my reactions. Constantly vigilant, he was hypersensitive to any potential rejection. This came to the fore when he thought that I had seemed upset when he recounted one of his traumatic memories. Theo's perceptions were not always accurate, but it was possible that this one was, as much of the material was deeply moving. However, for Theo, any such reaction – real or assumed – confirmed that he was dangerous and that if I were not strong enough to witness his pain, I would reject him. He could not conceive that another person might be sad on his behalf whilst remaining steadfast. So, thinking he might have upset me, rather than check with me, he told his wife. Her response was quite straightforward: she said that if I had been upset, it was probably an appropriate reaction. Reassured, Theo reported it to me. Thus it was that his relationship with his wife, which had been strengthening throughout the work, helped him to return to analysis and discuss his impression.

Packing

This fear of rejection emerged in relation to his wife when they were to go on a family holiday. There had been an argument about packing. Theo couldn't bear it when his wife began packing. It seemed to him that she became serious at this time, and he said, 'When she stops smiling it is as if the sun goes in.' It is common for people who have been 'packed off' to board to have trouble with packing, so I asked about the packing for school. (Here the analyst is more active than usual. This is an intervention informed by my knowledge that this might be a key event in an ex-boarder's story. He would have been unlikely to make this association himself and this is one of the ways in which such key events can be missed in psychotherapy.)

This evoked a vivid childhood memory. In the holidays Theo would be carefree, playing with his local friends – and then, as his mother started packing for him, an awful feeling of doom would descend. Recounting this, he used the same words: 'It was as if the sun went in.' Thus he unconsciously linked his annoyance at his wife to the memory of his mother packing for him to go away to school. When his attention was drawn to the use of the same words he became aware that it was indeed a familiar sense of loss. When his mother packed for him to go away to school it was as if she stopped smiling at him; it was like a withdrawal of love.

His parents seemed not to notice how unhappy he was, but Theo recalled a neighbour who spoke kindly to him as he was leaving to go away to school; he knew she understood. In reporting this it seemed he was aware that his suffering was now recognised. Theo said this therapy was different from the others; it seemed that what was different was that it was both revealing but also staying with the *extent* of the trauma. It is common for those who have suffered trauma to disbelieve the extent of their own suffering and so it may be difficult for the analyst to believe it. Moreover, the client may feel culpable and so responsible for the abuse. Theo seemed to recognise my compassion for his suffering and gradually some compassion for his own anguish emerged. His wife, as well as his analyst, believed him. So, validated, he began to blame himself less. He gradually came to accept that these really were abuses and they should never have happened. He was released from the silence which he had felt compelled to keep most of his life.

Boarding School Syndrome – locked away

The person suffering from Boarding School Syndrome, as with other trauma, may feel distant from his or her own life. Theo described feeling locked away and constantly alert to danger; he could trust no one. Worse was the persistent sound of a drill in his head; he wished it would stop, but there was no way he could control it. This he linked to his state of perpetual vigilance. Even when he was with people,

82 Exile and healing

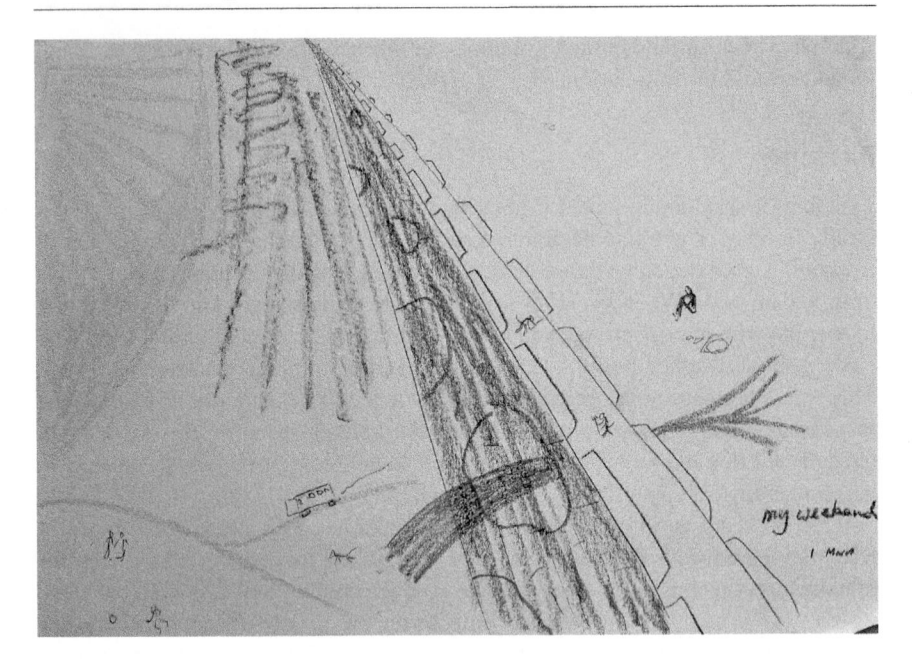

Figure 6.1 The Wall, 1 March, Year 1.

he felt isolated. After a weekend with his family he drew this isolation between him and others as a turreted wall patrolled by demons (Figure 6.1).

On the right side a figure sits alone on the ground, whilst on the left are fields with people playing; this was his family enjoying themselves. At such times he felt completely separate from their ordinary enjoyment. On the top left is a yellow semicircle which seems like a large sun (shown here as the shaded area). Perhaps this was like packing when it felt as if the sun went in. He is cut off from the sun and the other people; he, the boy packed off to boarding school, is alone on the bleak right side of the picture. Regarding the wall, he said, 'I built it; but I can't get over it and it is too huge to knock it down.' There is a thread of green going from one side of the wall to the other, which shows that there is some access. On the right side this has fragile roots whilst on the left it has a strong flow.

Looking at his pictures

As mentioned before, Theo was often visibly shocked when he took his pictures out of his folder to review them. It was as if someone else had made them. Although he remembered making them, he had forgotten the subject matter. The pictures had been split off, just as the original incidents they portrayed had been forgotten. Slightly awed by them, he commented on how powerful they were; he said, 'They bring it all to the fore.' He looked at one and said, 'You could not say that! It conveys so much more.' Acknowledging their significance, I suggested that the pictures were like bricks in that wall; perhaps he was gradually dismantling it, picture by picture.

Talking to his parents

At the beginning of analysis Theo had been vengeful and very angry with his parents. He had wanted to punish them by telling them all about school. He realised that they were now old and he could not tell them the details, but he needed some acknowledgement from them. He began to realise that the worst thing about boarding school was that his parents should have known and did not. Analysis had permitted him to realise the extent of his anger and it now became more possible to consider talking to them. Theo met with his father and told him some of what he now knew about school. They discussed it at some length and his father was genuinely sorry that he had not realised. Theo now began to think about how he might approach his mother and decided to visit her. They had had a really good talk, and when he told her about school, she asked, 'why didn't you tell me?' It is very common for parents to ask this question and it is not easy one to answer. Children just take what happens to them as normal and often do not question it until they are adult. Okely writes of this: 'My mother has often said since, "But why did you not tell me?" We, my sister and I, could not discriminate that which now sounds bizarre. Whenever I inwardly questioned aspects of this education, I thought myself mad.'[2] For many, this continues into adult life: the children, now adults, are unable to say why they did not tell their parents at the time.

Theo was relieved; he felt seen and heard by his parents. The past could not be undone, but such acknowledgement repairs some of the sense of abandonment. Part of the problem for a child who has suffered in the absence of parents is that, as they did not rescue him, it seemed they condoned the ill treatment. Theo now moved into a more positive phase; his relationships began to improve and the wall gradually began to come down. The relief was evidenced by a spontaneous change in the subject matter and drawing style of his pictures.

The tortoise

Theo kept tortoises and they were coming back to life after the winter. He explained how they hibernated in winter and then returned in the summer; now he could have them in the open. The metaphor for his situation was evident: the boy went to boarding school in the dark winter months and then returned home in the summer. His story was now known and so he too was in the open; the winter of the earlier analytic sessions had turned to spring. The tortoise was symbolic of the vulnerable child self, hidden away in a protective carapace, like Theo when he had arrived.

Theo took great pleasure in drawing his tortoise (Figure 6.2). There is little black in this picture; it is drawn in orange and brown pastels on a green grass-like

Figure 6.2 The Tortoise, 31 March, Year 1.

background. He relaxed and, for the first time, there was a lighter feel to the atmosphere in the room. The picture is drawn in a noticeably different style. It seemed as if it was the child who drew the pictures of the past horrors of school. The adult now drew this friendly creature who had a place in his present life. As Theo placed this picture in his folder with the others, he said, 'Perhaps it will counteract them a little.' Thus he was aware that he had moved into a better place.

The garden in spring

This heralded a positive phase where Theo drew the things he most loved. He spent one whole session drawing the garden he and his wife had created (Figure 6.3).

As he drew, Theo explained where the tortoises lived, and he described each tree and the different sections he had created. This seemed like relief, renewal and a psychological spring. Theo had left the dark and oppressive psychological state associated with school, so this was like a map celebrating his present life. This picture, like the one of the tortoise, has an aesthetic quality; it fills the paper and is drawn with skill and colour. Since it is shown in black and white, it is hard to imagine the fresh spring-like quality of this picture. The green, which we saw as the thread coming through the wall in Figure 6.1, is evenly distributed throughout the picture. The tree in the centre of the picture is dark but balanced with bright greens and oranges.

Figure 6.3 Our Garden in Spring, 21 April, Year 1.

Meeting the boy

When Theo metaphorically returned to school, it was from a different position. He had found some photos of himself as a schoolboy. He described his appearance, then he decided to draw it.

In pencil he drew a very serious little boy (Figure 6.4), wearing glasses and a school uniform. He realised that he enjoyed drawing this because he could think more kindly of this boy now. He was beginning to forgive that boy and realise that none of it had been his fault. He began to be released from the prison of self-blame. The picture is sensitively drawn in pencil. Here the boy is seen from the perspective of the adult. Thus from the phase of *identification* of the earlier pictures there is an *acknowledgement* and thus a separation of two aspects of the self.[3] The adult can see the child portrayed, as if from a distance, embodied and held in the picture. Thus he is a little separate from his traumatic experiences.

Rage

Having established safe ground, Theo began to confront his anger. At prep school he had not been subject to bullying by boys. It seemed that they had stuck together; it was the staff who had inflicted inappropriate punishments. When he left the prep school he went to a well-known public school where, in comparison

Figure 6.4 The Boy, 5 May, Year 1.

with the prep school, the treatment was easy. He was confronted by bullying in the student group briefly at first, but it was nothing compared with the torments of his prep school. Moreover, at about this time he had a revelation: he saw himself in a mirror and became aware that he had become muscular and very strong. He knew then that he could never again be bullied. As well as his physicality, he was psychologically stronger than anyone else. He knew he could be meaner, and this became evident to him when a boy unfairly kicked him during a rugby match. The next time there was a scrum, he took the opportunity to hit that boy. This is depicted in the picture shown in Figure 6.5. He was shocked by his own violence and deeply ashamed in telling this story. This brought to light another aspect of the rage of which he was so scared. Theo's extreme self-control was mustered to keep this aspect of himself at bay. He was worried about how vengeful he had been on this occasion.

Theo made another picture (not shown because it is faintly drawn) of when he was about 7, before he was sent to school. The place he lived with his parents was 'crawling with wildlife'. In the picture the boy is looking under stones for little insects and amphibians. Theo was free and happily engaged in this activity with his friends. He compared this picture with the pencil drawing of the schoolboy (Figure 6.4) and the one of the older boy fighting (Figure 6.5). As he regarded the three together he reflected on what his life would have been like, as he put it, 'without the middle bit'. (That is, without going to boarding school.) Then, referring to his life in prep school, he said, 'I wasn't there'. The tragedy here is that

Figure 6.5 The Fight, 12 May, Year 1.

he was describing five years of his childhood when he was not really present, not fully alive.

In trauma, very often the only way to survive is to disassociate. This is what Theo was describing: for a considerable chunk of his childhood, he was not emotionally present. This is very common; one man described it as locking his feelings in a box and just getting on with it. Theo looked from the pencil drawing of the schoolboy to the rugby field picture and said sadly, 'That one made the other . . . the distortion of a boy.'

As already noted with the quote with which this chapter began, repeated trauma in childhood deforms the personality. This seems to be what Theo was describing: he had had to fight hard to keep some integrity in this school, but the boy he had been was distorted by the experience. In psychotherapy we were trying to retrieve the boy and liberate him from the prison of self-blame and fear.

Taking care of the boy

It was sometime later, in July the same year, that Theo began to realise that the little boy needed protection. This happened in a surprising way. Theo was talking about his fear of his own violence. We were thinking about this quite calmly when I suggested that the violent impulse came from his need to protect the child we had seen in the drawing. Theo was completely overcome; this was a shattering revelation and he reacted physically. It was only later that he was able to tell me why he had been so shocked. It had never occurred to him that the boy *could* be

88 Exile and healing

protected or that he might have had a *right* to be protected. He said he would try to draw this, then he drew two pictures.

In the centre of the first picture (Figure 6.6) is a man, the adult Theo. Within his body, seated near his heart, he drew a smaller seated figure. Looking at the picture we see the words: 'You are Safe with Me.'

The words were drawn in the following order: 1, 'Safe'; 2, 'You are'; 3, 'with me'. I think this slightly alters the meaning. 'Safe', drawn first, refers to the small figure; the 'You are' may also refer to this small figure. 'You are Safe' is reassuring. 'With Me', added later, seems to indicate repair and refer to the larger containing figure. So here is an inner representation of a protective parental self-image. The small part of himself is being taken care of by a kindly adult aspect of himself. This acknowledged what had been missing. Theo was now beginning to find it in analysis and with his family, but most of all within himself.

The realisation that he should have been protected brought his rage to the surface. He imagined returning to the prep school as a grown man. He would show them: 'I could kill them, beat them all up.' More quietly, he reflected: 'But I can't do that – I can't change it – this is how it was.' This is significant, marking the beginning of separating out how it was from how it should have been. It was the beginning of acceptance. Theo then drew a second picture (Figure 6.7).

Figure 6.6 You Are Safe With Me, 14 July, Year 2.

Figure 6.7 Lonely, 14 July, Year 2.

This simple picture of a child in a bed is drawn in coloured pastels on an otherwise blank sheet of paper. It is so expressive that we just regarded it together. It did not need to be embellished – there was just one word that passed between us: 'lonely'.

Mother – betrayal – the journey

Now with a stronger sense of the present, and also the very little boy he had been, Theo started to confront the deepest sadness. This was the immense grief of the loss of his mother when he was 8. This first surfaced with this picture of a lonely little boy in bed. It was summer and one year since Theo first came into analysis. He was going away alone on a long journey. This led to memories of the journey to and from school.

The first time his parents took him to the school, but after that he alone travelled by train from Scotland to the South of England. He described each stage of the journey and how it took him 'deeper and deeper down to hell'. Theo had to change trains at a huge station where he was met with other boys and teachers. The dread increased until he arrived at the school – and then the bed: 'A bed is supposed to be a safe and cosy place but it was not like that; it was just a place you did not want to be, where you slept.'

I suggested that perhaps, as a boy, the only sense he had been able to make of being sent away was that he was bad. He thought this was probably true and the feeling deepened. Theo described the separation from his mother, the moment of parting and his incredulity as he watched her leave the station platform. He could not believe that she was just getting on with her life. He knew the routine: she would go for a coffee with the neighbour and then carry on washing clothes, cleaning the house, doing all the normal things. Theo said: 'If you are going to be shot I don't think you believe it. There are these people with guns but people *don't do that to other people!*' (This was how it had felt – mothers don't just abandon their children.) 'I had to stop thinking because if I thought about it, it was impossible; *it ripped your mind apart*. I could not think of her at home – gradually my home self faded and the school self took over. I was going back to that place and she was just getting on with everyday things.'

He realised how often this was repeated, and each time it was a shock. Every term he went through this: his mother putting him on the train and then leaving him. At this point there was little needed from me, but sometimes a word can help and so I offered one. I said, 'I think you are describing a sense of *betrayal* as well as loss.' This was the beginning of a long phase where the relationship with his mother was explored consciously, and unconsciously replayed, through the transference.

Regression – January to March, Year 2

It was January and the evenings were dark. This may have contributed to the negative transference which emerged a year and half into the analysis. Theo had had some experience working in groups, and he started to complain that my approach was too laid back and too slow. He started to become sure that I knew techniques that would help him more quickly but that I was holding back. These complaints were related to the awfulness he was experiencing. Often he would regress to the trauma of the school, feeling the intense horror of it. He was much less defended and so it would sometimes take him by surprise. It was less the memories of actual events than the general overwhelming horror of being there and unable to escape, the sense of imprisonment.

During this time Theo did not make pictures, but he lived the emotional impact. He blamed me for not rescuing him from the pain, and he blamed me for not preventing him from feeling it during the time between sessions. This was very serious because there were times when he sat in the chair writhing in anguish, unable to speak. I did question myself and wondered if I could do anything to make it easier for him. Supervision is important in order to check out one's judgement in such situations. At this point, I discussed this in supervision.

I realised I was witnessing how it had been at night-time in school when there was nothing to distract Theo from the pain. When he was in these states it was difficult for him to return to the present. Sometimes he would punch his fist in the air quite violently, explaining that this was his tried and tested way of bringing himself back to the present – through violence. Other times, he would speak of his children and come back into the present that way. Recognising that he did not have the words to speak of what was happening to him when he was in this state I would check out with him what was helpful. He wanted to keep going although he desperately needed to cry but could not. I suggested that this was like doing surgery without an anaesthetic and he agreed, adding 'on yourself'. This was 'time travel' – he was journeying back into the past and thus realising just how horrific it had been.

Betrayal – letter to mother

In April of the following year (Year 2) a friend of Theo's who had done a counselling course suggested he write a letter to his mother that he may not post. He did so and brought it to several sessions with the intention of reading it aloud. However, he became aware that he could only do so if he read it quickly without emotional engagement. When he engaged with what he had written, he was overcome and unable to speak. Eventually he was able to read it in broken sentences that were barely audible: 'How could she leave me in that place? It was pure terror... don't speak... silence... don't cry... don't move.' As he spoke, his voice was choked up and the words were barely audible. There was a very present sense of the terrified child who needed to take up no space at all because of the punishments that the dormitory held after dark.

I commented that he had been able to cry on other occasions, but he said that it was easy: it was about the school, this was worse because it was about his mother. He persisted with it over the next few sessions, but the emotion was so huge that he really struggled. Eventually he read very slowly and with great difficulty: 'Why didn't you, my mother, notice that your own son was in a place where children were beaten, starved, abused, frightened, shouted at humiliated, neglected.' So here he acknowledged to himself the facts of the situation. He had been treated intolerably and he should have been rescued.

Then, in June of Year 2, having spent a month or more addressing his rage, Theo made a decision to visit his mother. He enjoyed spending time with her and – although he did not talk to her about the letter, nor did he show it to her – he felt liberated. He had been able to let go of the blame. Then he asked me a direct question: 'I know you don't usually answer. But I would like to ask you something.' I encouraged him to ask the question without guaranteeing an answer. Eventually he said that the question was, 'Are you alright?' In my usual exploratory way I noted that he always feared that he was too much for me. Perhaps that is what he was asking. We explored this from different angles for a while, and then I said: 'How would it be for you if I said I was alright?' He said that would be good, because it would mean he had not contaminated me. However, I realised that this discussion was not relieving the tension, so after contemplating it for a while, I answered: 'I am alright.' Theo visibly relaxed. Part of his struggle had been feeling he could not share the horror to which he had been subjected without

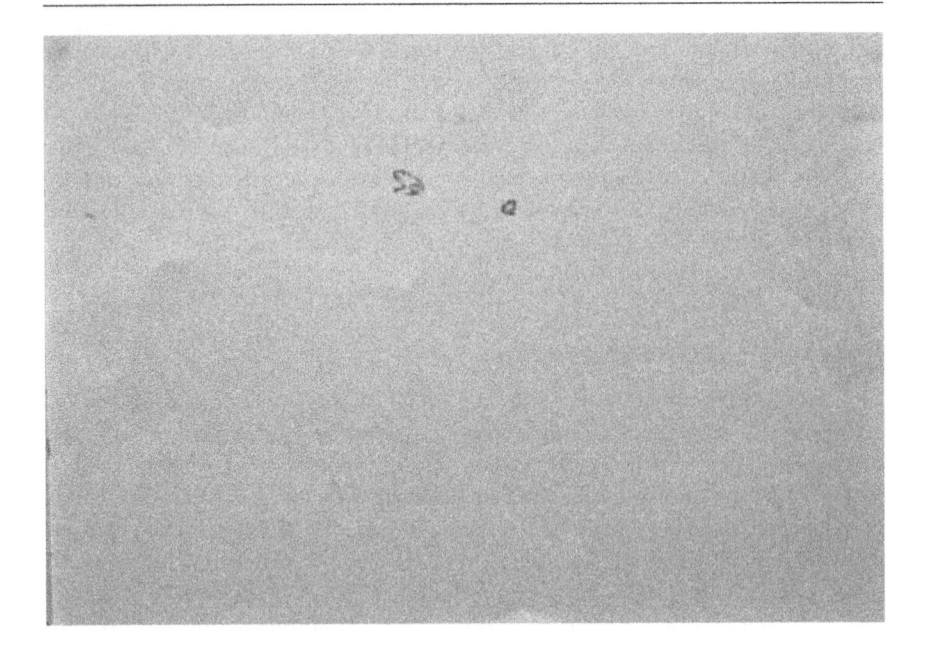

Figure 6.8 Toads, 15 June, Year 2.

contaminating the other person. So when I admitted that I was all right, he could trust that I had not been damaged. The relief after this series of sessions, as well as the visit to his mother, was reflected in his next picture.

Theo was in a playful mood; he had been on a walk and seen a tiny, baby toad. It was in an unsuitable place on open ground so, very carefully, he had lifted it and moved it to more moist ground where it had a better chance of survival. He drew it in the picture shown in Figure 6.8.

The first toad he drew was not small enough, so he drew another one on the same paper. However, regarded as a single picture, this shows two toads in close proximity but with their backs to each other. There was some discussion about toads and then I pointed out that a toad is a bit like a tortoise without a shell. I also noticed that the toads look like mother and child: a small one and a larger one. I asked: 'What do toad mothers do?' Theo replied: 'Oh, they are off doing their own thing – they aren't maternal at all'.

His words revealed the unconscious implication of his drawing and he was evidently moved: it was acceptance of his mother after the recent contact he had with her. She was his mother and there was an affectionate bond, but she was off doing her own thing, as she had been when he was at boarding school. He could now accept her as she actually was – flawed, but still his mother. He no longer needed her to look after him. This positive phase was two years into the analysis. In the next chapter I will consider the final phase of Theo's analysis.

Notes

1 Herman, J. (1992/1997) *Trauma and Recovery: The Aftermath of Violence From Domestic Abuse to Political Terror*, New York: Basic Books, p. 96.
2 Okely, J. (1996) *Own and Other Culture*, London: Routledge, p. 149.
3 Schaverien, J. (1992) *The Revealing Image*, London: Routledge. This edition London: Jessica Kingsley Publishers (1999), p. 106.

Chapter 7

The return
Trauma and the developing brain (case study part 4)

It was July, two years after Theo began his analysis. Some of the intensity of the emotional damage was gradually receding into the past, but then another series of distressing episodes occurred. The trigger was an event which will be described in detail. It illustrates how trauma can have an impact on the developing brain and how it may be worked with in analysis. Although painfully live for a period of time, the trauma may eventually be consigned to history.

A new wood floor had been laid in my consulting room a few months previously. It had been laid on damp concrete and, as a result, it had buckled, creating a large domed shape in the middle of the room. Although it was covered with a rug, a considerable bulge was evident. Theo began by reporting his week, then he paused and commented on the floor. I explained what had happened. He said he was relieved to realise it was the wood, because when he came in, he had wondered to himself what I had got under the rug. I asked what he had imagined. At this he was immediately plunged into a flashback. His demeanour changed and he looked terrified: his face turned white, his breathing came in gasps. He tried to speak; although his mouth moved, no words were formed. He was clearly overwhelmed and in the grip of some horror. Eventually, haltingly, and in a barely audible whisper, he said, 'I can't say it.'

As we have already seen, in working with extreme trauma, it is important for the client to be returned to the present before leaving. On this occasion, however, this was not fully achieved. More than once-weekly frequency can be significant in this regard. Theo returned two days later and was then able to begin to discuss what had happened. This had been the worst flashback yet and Theo was anxious when talking about it in case it recurred.

When Theo read this chapter in order to give consent for his story to be published, he reminded me of the significance of what he had imagined and been unable to put into words. Theo writes: 'The episode when your rug hid a bump in the floor. You may remember I came to believe that you might have hidden a corpse under it. That's what I meant when I said, "I can't say it." It's obviously a ridiculous notion, but at that time, and in that mental and emotional place, I believed it. It shows the waking terror, which the analysis sometimes induced – for a short period (which may actually have been weeks, on and off). I really could not tell the difference between what was in my head and what was real. It also suggests how my unconscious was prepared to seize on almost any object to try to heal itself.'

So it was this trigger in the outer world that had returned him to the psychological state induced by his recurring dream that he had murdered someone. There had been a period of three days when he was in his twenties when he had walked around awake, but sure he had killed someone. He had been terrified, wondering how he had disposed of the body. This dream had ceased after his first psychotherapist told him that it was part of himself he had killed. (The incident is described in Chapter 4). It probably stopped because the interpretation had transformed the concrete belief. It gave it symbolic meaning and this created a space for imagination – a space between the thought and the deed. This concrete state had recurred and again he believed there was a corpse, this time hidden under my floor. He reflects further on its symbolic significance with hindsight: 'I think the corpse had the significance of an accuser or mute witness to a crime, and I was literally terrified of it coming to light.' Such is the power of this kind of regression: it brings the psychological past into the present with vivid and sometimes overwhelming imagery. This further came to light through more pictures. Theo was still anxious but, to further explore his terror, he began to draw the cellar at the prep school (Figure 7.1). He explained that this was where the showers and sinks were.

The cellar had a domed roof and was below ground level. It was approached through a long dark tunnel. There was no natural light in this basement. As he

Figure 7.1 The Cellar 1, 6 July, Year 2.

talked Theo hovered on the brink of terror. This theme continued in the next session. During the intervening week he had been trying to work out what the bump in the floor represented. Theo felt sure that he had tackled all the school demons and so he had been surprised by his reaction. However he realised that this violent reaction to my question about the floor suggested that there was something. For several sessions he continued to wonder about why the bulge in the floor had so upset him. Then one day, as he discussed it, he was abruptly catapulted into a similar violent regression. Now he began to tell what had happened, in a barely audible whisper. Disjointed words emerged, separated by what felt like minutes, but listening intently, I gradually discerned:

> A boy was beaten. . . . [Then when he came out there were other little boys there to look after him.] We were very little . . . the sinks. . . . [He remembered the sinks. It was all very disjointed and spoken in a tiny voice, muffled, as if the little boy he had been at the time was speaking from a long way away.]. . . . The boys thought you could make it better if you had hot and cold water . . . his hands were clasped around him. Then we went with him into the cellar . . . past the snooker table . . . through the tunnel to the sinks . . . hands in the sinks . . . it didn't work . . . screams . . . terror.

If the readers find this hard to comprehend, then they are in the same state of unknowing that I was at the time. After what seemed like a long time, shaken, Theo began to return to the present and asked if I had heard what he had said. I acknowledged that indeed I had heard (although with great difficulty). He explained that it was alarming because he could now actually hear the terrified screams of the boy. This past event was live in the room. By the end of this session Theo was able to distance a little from the experience by talking about it and so he returned to the present. This is an important theoretical distinction: when he was in the terrifying memory he was *talking from that actual place*, he was *reporting the events*. Then, as a little distance occurred he began to talk *about it*.

This is how psychotherapy works: at first the trauma is live in the room and understood through a combination of actions and words that convey the essence of traumatic experience. This is the flashback, when the incident is relived in the present. Then, as the person speaks *about* the ordeal, they are separated a little from it. This is why finding words is essential in mediating trauma. The analyst adapts during this process. At first, during the flashback, the analyst is a present and alert witness, but may have to accept that she does not fully understand. Then, eventually, the client begins the second phase, of talking *about* the incident and remembering from the perspective of the present. Here the analyst may begin to understand more and attempt to help in separating past from present. The process of gradual separation may continue for a number of weeks or even months as the incident is discussed and revisited.

The split

Over time it became clear that this had been a key moment. Theo had felt the utter helplessness and despair of his captivity. It was a moment of pure terror and ultimate betrayal. It was the realisation that his parents had left him and there really was no adult to whom to appeal for comfort. The headmaster had beaten the boy's hands with a leather-covered truncheon. Theo's innate sense was that this was very wrong, but these were adults. They were all-powerful and could inflict cruel punishment at will. Theo knew he was powerless and so the horror and his vulnerability had been locked up in his psyche. Truly repressed and so forgotten until now, this was the moment when the psychological split was complete. The meaning of a picture made the previous year now became clear (Figure 7.2). He got it out and we regarded it together.

This was a picture of an incident that took place when Theo had been at school for about a year. The place is outside and the toilets in the background frame a little boy. Standing alone on the left of the picture in front of the toilet block is the boy who messed himself and cried for his mummy. As already described in Chapter 4, I had at first understood this to be in the dormitory on the first night. However, Theo explained that this incident took place a year later. It was a deeply traumatic event. With such an event, time sometimes becomes telescoped in the

Figure 7.2 The Split, 24 November, Year 1.

telling or in the listening. If we approach this picture as interpreting a dream, we might consider all the elements in the picture to be aspects of the artist. Therefore the boy would then be both the child in the story and also an aspect of Theo, framed by the toilet block entrance. The materials used in this picture, and the way it is drawn, are significant.

The child and the school building, viewed from outside, are depicted in pencil. The dominant aspect of the picture is the back of a head in the foreground. This Theo said is the back his head; it is divided by a jagged line, giving a sense of the terror of that moment. The right side of the head is drawn in red pastels and forms a bright red claw, clenching half of the head. (In this black and white reproduction the red is the darker side of the head.) In contrast, the left half is lightly drawn in the same pencil as the rest of the picture. He said this is 'when the split occurred between the home self and the school self'. He says it felt like a ripping apart of two parts of himself. This seems to show the moment when, cleaved from the gentle child who lived at home, Theo shut down emotionally. In order to cope with extreme cruelty, the child ceases feeling emotional reactions. This is common – and necessary for survival – but unconsciously it causes a rift between two aspects of the self: the feeling self and the thinking self. The continuity of the child's sense of being is at this point ruptured.

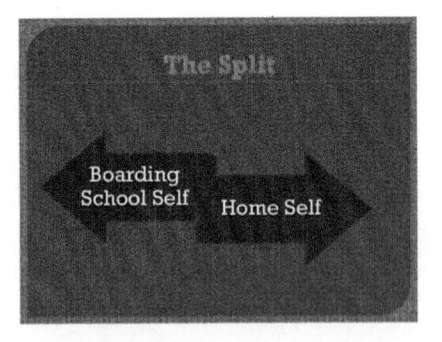

The boarding school self and the home self are from that moment separated. The child who has lost all that is familiar has to appear to conform in order to survive. Secretly he or she may be resisting, so that whilst appearing to play the game the way the bullies, the staff or other representatives of the system require, a fragment of the former self remains intact. This is the moment of the creation of Boarding School Syndrome: vulnerability is hidden from then on. The initial traumatic event varies but the effect is the same. In Jungian terms this is a division between Eros and Logos. It is an *encapsulation of the self that takes place in a moment and may last a lifetime*.

There is increasing evidence of the psychological effects of trauma on the development of the brain. Alan Schore's seminal work on the emotional development of infants is highly significant,[1] as is the exploration by Sue Gerhardt.[2] It is clear that traumatic events can profoundly affect the brain of older children as well as infants, as studies by Lanius and colleagues into sexual abuse and the impact of trauma on health and disease have demonstrated.[3] [4] The brain of the child is sensitive to impingement and therefore repeated traumatic events may well influence developmental pathways. It seems that this is what Theo had unconsciously portrayed.

McGilchrist has shown how the two hemispheres of the brain develop separately and have distinct but linked functions.[5] The left hemisphere develops later than the right and is the language centre, the part that manages emotions. The right is the part responsible for more intuitive and creative aspects of the personality. In the light of this, Theo's picture might be understood to depict the distortion of the brain in the moment of trauma. The sides of the head are depicted in two halves; the viewpoint is that of the artist, so the right hemisphere is portrayed in red. This is the emotional centre, as McGilchrist puts it: 'The right hemisphere as birds and animals show us, is "on the look out" . . . This requires a mode of attention that is broader and more flexible than that of the left hemisphere.'[6] It is responsible for every type of attention except focussed attention.[7] The left hemisphere is 'better able to integrate perceptual processes, particularly bringing together different kinds of information for different senses'.[8]

Wilkinson discusses this in relation to psychotherapy, suggesting that the right hemisphere 'influences the . . . strategies of affect regulation for coping and survival'.[9] It is responsible for internal models of attachment and is more mature at birth than the left hemisphere. The left hemisphere matures later, as the child acquires linguistic and analytic ability. Thus it 'enables a new experience of agency, of relating and of separateness'.[10] This is significant for the young child in a boarding school because if the left side of the brain is not yet sufficiently developed to manage the emotional impact of broken attachments, something will have to happen. I think this is what we see portrayed in Theo's picture.

As we saw, Theo said: 'This was when the split occurred between the home self and the school self. . . . It felt like a ripping apart of two parts of myself.' We might understand this in the light of brain function. The left hemisphere, depicted in pencil, is the language centre that deals with cognitive understanding and manages complex emotions. This was not yet fully mature. It is ripped apart from the right hemisphere, depicted in red, the emotional and so self-side. Theo at 8 years of age was ill-equipped to make sense of the magnitude of the cruelty he witnessed. Therefore, terrified by the repeated traumas, his emotions were frozen. In the absence of a caring adult there was no witness and no one to help him process the experience by giving it words.

Wilkinson makes the point that, in analysis, it is important for the therapist to be in contact with the emotional or non-verbal aspects of the person. Only then can it become possible 'for the left-brain to fully process traumatic experience'.[11] This is the difference between being overwhelmed by a flashback and having the capacity to reflect on the situation and process it. As a small child, Theo was not developed enough to cope. The executive functioning of the left hemisphere did not have the capacity to process all that had happened to the child. This is where

100 Exile and healing

an adult is needed to help the immature child process experience. In the absence of an adult, Theo had to develop a premature control. It is as if the right side, the emotional and attachment centre, seized up. The repair in analysis is to begin to separate past from present by talking and making simple distinctions between then and now. In working with trauma, part of the work 'will involve naming the self-states through which in normal development the person moves seamlessly'.[12] This is what parents and carers do for young children; they explain events to the child and this has the effect of developing left-brain functioning.

During analysis Theo began to understand that he had been a very little boy in these early days at school and so he did not have the language to make sense of what happened. He began to identify different parts of himself and to understand their functioning. This was vividly conveyed in another picture made four months later (Figure 7.3). This too shows these two aspects of the self: the prematurely

Figure 7.3 The Controller, 30 March, Year 2.

developed executive functioning aspect and the vulnerable child self. Theo was again talking about how difficult it was for him to cry. He described an internal battle between the vulnerable part that felt moved to cry and the part of him that had learned to hold that firmly in check. His compassion for the boy was tempered by a strong internal injunction that it was not safe to express his grief, this he named 'the Controller'. He personified it in a drawing.

The Controller was the inner protector who held the boy in a tight grip. This picture is reminiscent of the picture we saw in the last chapter; 'You Are Safe With Me' (Figure 6.6). However, the Controller is a less benevolent and fiercer personification of that aspect of the self. The Controller prevents the child from seeing, crying, speaking or even moving. Later, as we returned to consider the vivid screams of the boy in the cellar, Theo linked it to the drill that he heard in his head and he realised that the drill was an aspect of the Controller. I understood this as a distraction from the horror: if the drill were loud enough, the screams would be drowned out. Perhaps this is an auditory form of repression. As we discussed this, I ventured that he might ask the Controller to stand back. It can be useful to separate aspects of the experience. Responding to this idea, Theo signalled and said, 'Go and stand by the door!' Imaginatively, this freed him to speak from the boy part. In the absence of parental figures Theo was forced to find a way of looking after himself. Ill-equipped, he had evoked a strong and monstrous protector to help him. It had served a useful purpose at the time but now this protector was sabotaging his intimate relationships.

Anger – after the summer break

After the second summer break, Theo was angry. Previously he had been unable to express any negative feelings towards me, but now he had had enough of the pain and wanted to stop psychotherapy. He declared that reliving the memory of that cellar had been too painful. Moreover, when that memory first emerged he had needed to be held. He realised that I do not do that, but he experienced me as too rigid. He was white with anger for most of the session, during which I said little. Then Theo asked me directly how I felt about him working towards ending, and I quietly said that I thought it was too soon to stop. Furious, he said he wouldn't return for his second session that week. I acknowledged that he was free to make this choice. However, I pointed out how angry he was with me and reminded him that we both knew that this was something he had previously feared. If he did not return for a whole week he might lose touch with it – I wondered if that was what he wanted. This seemed to make sense. He agreed to come on Wednesday, but on the proviso that he would drop one of his two sessions in a few weeks. The tirade continued over two more sessions. Theo wanted to stop, but he knew that it was best to work towards ending. He wanted to think about how to do that.

It seemed to me that the transference was very active at this time. Theo's fury with me was partly a response to my absence during the summer break. He may well have felt that I had abandoned him. For those whose childhood was punctuated with comings and goings to and from boarding school it is common to suffer profoundly during the breaks; it replays their abandonment at school. To begin with it is usually unconscious, but once into analysis it can evoke just such an angry reaction.[13] The anger with me was also in part evoked by his fury with his mother. It was she who abandoned him to the cellar and she who should have been there to hold him as a child when he was distressed.

It was important, in analysis, to permit the full expression of his anger and so I did not yet interpret this. It was not easy to sit with such rage but it was important that it was out in the open. It was only later that I pointed out that if I had offered to hold him, it would not have made up for the absence of adults to hold him when these terrible events occurred. I noted that in the past I held him with my words – but perhaps, on that occasion, he had felt too far away to be reached. This was especially hard when the summer break had come so soon after this event.

There were several other elements to his rage. It seemed that he could not imagine how analysis would end other than angrily. But most of all he was scared of falling into the cellar again. The anger deflected him from this. The Controller was angry, and he was taking care of the boy as he had always done. Then one day, when Theo was still angrily thinking about ending, I explained the reason I did not think he was yet ready to leave. Evoking the image of surgery, I said that it was as if we were midway through a procedure and I did not want him to leave with an open wound.

That made sense to Theo; it showed that I cared and he stopped talking about leaving. Almost immediately, as if the anger had been a distraction, he regressed again into the painful memory of the cellar. Again he was terrified because he could hear the screams of the little boy. It was so real it was like a tape recorder in his head. Then he explained, from a rather different place, how he had been one of four little boys all standing around terrified. Then his anger, the well-tested way of dealing with such adversity, came to the fore with the fantasy of what he would do to the headmaster. It is common for men who have been abused by teachers to have fantasies about what they, as men, would now do to the perpetrator. So Theo imagined that first he would kill him violently, and then rescue the boy. At the end of the session, as a way of distancing him from the trauma, I suggested that he try to leave the memory here with me. Imaginatively it seemed to work to have a place to symbolically store it, as in the pictures. I handed him a little glass apple that I keep in my room. Theo held the apple and concentrated hard, looking into it. Then he said with humour, 'It gets more like Harry Potter in here all the time!'

Theo now settled back into analysis twice a week. He said that it had helped when I had said, 'I don't want to let you go with a gaping wound,' because it gave him a reason for staying that made sense. (It is interesting that I remembered it as *open* wound and he heard it as a *gaping* wound.) This provided an image and so meaning to the pain and distress he was experiencing. It may also have given a sense that I thought that the pain would eventually ease. It seemed that the split in his head, shown in the drawing in Figure 7.2 had opened up; this was the wound and he was acutely vulnerable.

Revisiting the school

Theo had often considered visiting the school. Now he made contact, and, after making the appropriate checks, an appointment was made for him and his wife to visit. The current headmaster invited them to an open day, when current students would show them around. This was some months ahead and Theo worked towards it, thinking about how it would be. Then, early in the third year of analysis, he and his wife travelled to the school.

The building remained the same but the school had changed; it was now a co-educational day school. Two students, a girl and a boy, showed them around. The girl was 11 and Theo was struck by how little she was. I pointed out that she was three years older than he had been. It is important to draw attention to the smallness of the child who experienced the trauma, because the adult can rarely imagine just how small they were. This is part of separating out aspects of the self as well as past from present. Theo visited the dormitory, which was now an IT suite. He met teachers and other staff who knew about the previous reputation of the school; several people remembered the old regime, although none of the original staff remained. He was told that the school had been part subsidised by the military for the children of their serving personnel. Therefore, they did not have to make an effort to attract students. The headmaster had been notorious and even in the local pub the landlord knew of the school's reputation.

Then Theo visited the cellar and saw that it had been transformed into a well-lit woodwork room. Theo documented his visit, taking photographs, which he brought to compare with his drawings. He was immensely relieved that the regime to which he had been subject was no longer in existence, but also to have his story objectively corroborated. This was a very important part of his healing.

Soon after this, Theo made contact through email with others who had been at this prep school at the same time. The 'sibling group' at prep school had been important and it seemed the boys had looked after each other rather kindly. However, most of these men seemed not to want to discuss this painful history. Theo had a long phone conversation with one man and some email exhanges with others, but contact soon ceased. Mostly it seemed the memories had been buried and they did not want to return to them. This was very different than his public school experience; there the sibling group had remained strong and transformed into adult friendships.

Betrayal and trust

The process of emotionally returning to the school continued for several more months. There were still times when Theo would regress unexpectedly and violently. However, this was also a period of repair, in which he was kinder when considering the small boy he had been. In some sessions Theo was quite cheerful – but he could still hear a drill, an actual noise in the back of his head, like a warning. This he could not switch off. I suggested that it might be that he couldn't trust being happy, and he agreed it was about trust. It was also about betrayal. It became clear that betrayal by the adults who should have cared for him had been significant. Theo was haunted because he had been forced to betray himself. He did not put it this way but it was clear that as a child he had had ethical values that he had been forced to betray. Witnessing cruelty to others and being unable to intervene when he knew something was wrong meant he had had to suspend his ethical self. It had made him feel complicit.

One day as we were discussing his history at school I said to him, 'You know it was not your fault.' This was just an innocent remark and so I was again taken aback by his huge reaction. Theo was unable to speak. It was not until the next session that he was able to tell me that this comment had turned his reality upside down. It became clear that Theo had blamed himself. When I had said, 'It was not your fault,' he was taken off guard and his vulnerability was exposed. It was a huge relief, but he found it difficult to explain how it felt. I sensed it and offered, 'Perhaps you felt naked?' That seemed right: he was naked without his armour. For a few sessions Theo explored the feeling of guilt. He reflected on how religion instilled guilt and wondered if a child of 8 could feel responsible for being bad. We thought about how very young he was when he heard that child screaming. He was again overcome, but then he found the words and said, 'That is when I was broken.'

Recalling the boy

Theo began to truly realise how small and helpless he had been. More kindly pencil drawings of the boy were made. Once when he had been silently staring into space I inquired about the silence. He said, imagining how little he had been, he had seen an image of a baby mouse. It had no hair and its eyes were not open. This was a revelation. Theo realised how small he had been when that part of him was killed off. Even though his own children had passed through these phases he had not really associated his own childhood experiences with theirs. Remembering the dreams of having committed murder, he realised that he had indeed committed a crime. He said: 'It was as if there were two of us. It was as if I had a little brother and just killed him because he felt too much.'

Aware that his present feelings were related to that part of himself, I suggested that perhaps he had not completely killed him, but rather it was as if he had been hidden away, all shrivelled up. I told him Freud used the term *soul murder*. Theo was evidently relieved at the end of this session. He felt that I had said more than usual. I suggested that perhaps he was ready to permit me to understand. It was a relief for him to think that might be possible. So it was that this vulnerable part of him began to come to life.

Reconciliation between the parts of him that had been split asunder was beginning to take place. It was very moving to witness as he took the picture of the boy and apologised to him. He was forgiving, understanding that he had been unable to do anything. Separation was taking place between the abandoned child and the caretaker part of himself; the Controller was releasing his grip and a kinder, more compassionate adult man was emerging. Usually his pictures were left in my room but he took the picture of the boy home with him. He kept it above his desk; a reminder that he had re-emerged.

The cellar drawing

Trauma is often visited and then revisited until at last it no longer carries the huge emotional charge it once did. The cellar was revisited nearly a year after its significance first came to light. It was now June, nearly three years after analysis began. Periodically the cellar would again come violently to the fore. Theo described it as like hitting a brick wall – it was always shocking and unexpected. He was worried that this regression to trauma would recur intermittently and often unpredictably. I too was concerned. Although I did have a sense that things were gradually changing, it was not yet possible to integrate the experience. It was still becoming familiar to him, and I thought it would change over time if we kept talking about it. Theo had recently read a book by Judith Herman, who described some of the process he had been through. She confirmed some of what I had said to him.[14] He was relieved because he now trusted that there was a map of the territory.

I suggested that another drawing might be a way of externalising the trauma of the cellar. Theo wanted to draw but feared what he might see, so he struggled for a while before he took up the paper and pastels. As he started to draw, the domed shape of the cellar ceiling took form. Then, having drawn the room, he could not bear to put the people in. He described the slope of the roof, the lack of light, and the position of the showers and basins. The drawing conveyed a claustrophobic sense of this underground space (Figure 7.4).

The next time, Theo could not at first bear to look at the picture. It brought that cellar, live, into the room. He marvelled that he had had the courage to draw it. Then he compared the drawing with the photo of the cellar, taken on his recent visit, and was satisfied that the drawing was pretty accurate. He wanted to place the figures in the picture, so he sat on the floor with the drawing in front of him. Then tentatively he drew a figure by the basins. With increased confidence, he drew two more figures. Finally he drew the figure in the centre at the front of the picture. This was himself – the witness.

This time he was able to tell me the story without regressing. He explained that there had been two other boys and the boy who had been beaten. The two other boys seemed to know what to do; it was a school tradition. They poured hot water in one basin and cold in another. Then the injured boy's hands were submerged in one basin, then the other. Theo did not know the routine, so he did not have a role; he just watched helplessly. I pointed out that witnessing it, even though he was not beaten, was traumatising. It was the ultimate betrayal because now he realised that nothing was taboo. Witnessing a child in such distress was frightening. The context, where the stories of the suffering of the saints were so vivid, increased the impact. Now Theo realised that this was where he learned that no one could

106   Exile and healing

Figure 7.4 The Cellar 2, 11 & 13 June, Year 3.

be trusted. He said that this horror had always been with him: it was known and unknown at the same time.

It is notable that the boys are kindly drawn and the one at the centre of the picture is realistic. The position is a similar back view to that of the split head (Figure 7.2) but here the head is not split. The childlike proportions of the figure are realistic rather than distorted. Perhaps this reveals both acceptance of the reality – he was just a little boy – and also separation from the incident, in that he is an observer. Again before he left, hoping to be able to leave the fear behind in my room, Theo took the apple and imaginatively placed the memory in it. It seemed that some healing was taking place and in this way he was symbolically able to separate from the horror.

Respite

The following week Theo was cheerful and reported that he had not felt too bad at the weekend. He was surprised how good he felt after last time. That noise in his head was a little less now. He had been terrified of drawing the cellar again and was surprised that he had not felt more upset whilst doing so. He said with some relief that it was now out. It was evident that seeing the event was better than having it trapped in his head. He then looked at the picture and appeared stricken, but recovered without falling into full flashback. Theo said it was as if a door had been slammed on this event; previously there had been no going there. He had talked about it and drawn it before. It was on the map he made right at the beginning, but the associated feelings had only now come to the fore.

This was a year since the floor had come up, domed like the cellar roof. He knew that this was the key memory. He reflected that he thought he really did get through that school without ever being beaten with the truncheon. He was hit with other things, but never had that beating. I wondered if perhaps he felt guilty about that. He thought he probably did: 'Why should I have got away with it?'

The summer break was approaching, so Theo thought again about ending. He said he was not ready yet because he could still feel troubled. I said that he would know when he was ready to end; one day he would have better things to do than to come here.

Dream

This positive phase was followed by what seemed to be a healing dream: Theo was walking in some barns like ones belonging to his parents' neighbour. (This was the husband of the woman who was kind to him when he was leaving for school.) He went in through a dark tunnel and there were a series of joined-up barns all made of wood. In the centre of one of them there was a tower of firewood. There was a party going on somewhere else and he thought his wife was there. The tower was made of sticks all joined together. They were not tied and he had to walk on it. It was a bit unsafe and he had to jump down about 6 feet but he landed on his feet and was OK.

Theo said that the feeling of the dream was quite nice. There was a sense of familiarity about the place. Shafts of light were coming in from skylights. I suggested to him that this was his barn; it was his reparation of that awful cellar. Like the cellar, it was entered via a tunnel. The difference is that light has been shone into it and it feels quite good. It seemed to me that the pile of wood at the centre was a self-image. It was high but not rigid. He could risk walking on it and then jump down from it and land on his feet.

End of cellar

Following this, Theo was still in good spirits the next time and said that he was worried that it wouldn't last. I pointed out that perhaps the good feeling was evoked by his dream. This dream was his, so he could always return it. He reflected that perhaps it was his own (psychological) house. He thought that there might even have been music going on. He asked me if I thought he would get bad again. Although I did not answer that directly, I tried to help him think about the approaching long summer break. In the following session he brought that up at the beginning. Lying on the couch, he said, 'Well, I guess we need to talk about what happens when you go away.' Remembering the previous summer, he said: 'Mostly it happens before I realise it; I get shut into myself. I feel abandoned.'

I pointed out the difference between the past and present. Although once he had been abandoned to danger, this was not the case now – it was simply that I would be away and he would be at home.

As we reflected on the work so far, I pointed out that it had been important that I had believed his story. Theo said: 'There were times when you were the only person in this room who did believe it.'

During this, the third summer break, Theo was fine. He enjoyed the summer and was pleased to come back to analysis without having felt totally abandoned. During the next months he spent time reviewing his pictures and so working towards ending. Although he felt much in reviewing the pictures, he did not fall into the flashbacks again with any of the incidents depicted. It was as if, in reviewing them, he was consigning them to the past.

At the end of our work together September, four years after he first came, we reviewed how it had been. I told Theo I was writing his story, and he said people would say 'it is not like that now.' Then he made the point that I think is most significant. He said perhaps the cruelty would not be so extreme these days, but the worst thing for him, despite all the cruelty, was when he came to realise the terrible loss of the abandonment by his parents.

The cruelty he experienced had toughened him up, as it was intended to, to make of the boy a hard man who would feel nothing and then send him off to war. He had used his righteous anger to fire himself up; he would take on anyone who might threaten him or his family. What is more, he knew he could do so. Most significant, though, was when he got back further in his memory. The worst was remembering the loss, epitomised by the image of his mother at the station. The aloneness he felt then was the deepest: 'the primary wound'. He asked me, in writing, to be sure that I made that point.

I hope that through Theo's story this point has come through to the reader. He took his pictures away with him to burn them with the help of his wife. They no longer had the power to hurt him, and he could now talk about his experiences without being re-traumatised. The immense courage it took to confront this traumatic childhood needs to be acknowledged along with my gratitude to Theo for permitting me to tell his story.

We now leave Theo and turn to general points raised by his story and the experiences of others who suffered trauma in different ways though their experiences of boarding school.

Notes

1 Schore, A. N. (1994) *Affect Regulation and Origins of the Self*, Hillsdale, New Jersey: Lawrence Erlbaum Associates.
2 Gerhardt, S. (2004) *Why Love Matters*, London: Routledge.
3 Lanius, R. A., Vermetten, E., & Pain, C. (eds) (2010) *The Impact of Early Life Trauma on Health and Disease: The Hidden Epidemic*, Cambridge: Cambridge University Press.

4 Van der Kolk, B. A., & d'Andrea, W. (2010) 'Towards a developmental trauma disorder diagnosis for childhood interpersonal trauma', in Lanius, R. A., Vermetten, E., & Pain C. (eds), *The Impact of Early Life Trauma on Health and Disease: The Hidden Epidemic*, Cambridge: Cambridge University Press, pp. 57–67.
5 McGilchrist, I. (2009) *The Master and His Emissary*, London: Yale University Press.
6 Ibid., p. 38.
7 Ibid., p. 39.
8 Ibid., p. 42.
9 Wilkinson, M. (2006) *Coming Into Mind*, London: Routledge, p. 19.
10 Ibid., p. 20.
11 Ibid., p. 180.
12 Ibid., p. 185.
13 Schaverien, J. (2002) *The Dying Patient in Psychotherapy: Desire, Dreams and Individuation*, New York: Palgrave Macmillan.
14 Herman, J. (1992/1997) *Trauma and Recovery: The Aftermath of Violence From Domestic Abuse to Political Terror*, New York: Basic Books.

Part III
Broken attachments
A hidden trauma

Chapter 8

A hidden trauma
Amnesia

Amnesia is a recognised symptom of traumatic stress. It is the result of a form of psychological splitting whereby, in an overwhelming situation, the psyche closes down. In order to survive, a part of the self is shut off from consciousness. This is a spontaneous effect of what Kalsched has called 'the self-care system'. This, he suggests, is an adaptive response to an unbearable situation.[1] Even when the boarding school is relatively benign, the young child sent away from home to live with strangers may experience unbearable emotional stress. Not all but very many children are affected in this way. Therefore the 'self care system' comes into play, blunting some of the emotional impact. The research on trauma has noted memory loss to be a common symptom of traumatic stress.[2] This loss of recall for certain incidents is a less dramatic expression of post-traumatic stress disorder (PTSD) than the 'vivid intrusions of traumatic images and sensations' more commonly associated with it.[3]

Now in his fifties, at the age of 10 Robert had been sent from the country where his father was a diplomat to boarding school in Britain. After several years in psychotherapy his limited recollection of his childhood had improved and some early memories had returned. Even so he was unable to recall going to the boarding school. He could not remember the very first day or any subsequent occasions when he returned at the beginning of term. He knew, because he was told, that his grandparents had met him from the airplane and they had taken him to school. He could recall none of that. He could, however, remember the end of term when his grandparents would come to the school, take him to the airport and put him on the plane to re-join his parents for the vacation. It seems likely that, for Robert, the start of each term and the associated sense of loss had been too much to bear and so he shut down emotionally, forgetting his arrival at the school.

We are beginning to build a picture of some of the ways in which early boarding causes trauma and to see a pattern in the psychological presentation. In some cases the initial rupture with home is *apparently* recovered from reasonably quickly, as the child adapts. There are some children who genuinely seem to adapt to the new situation and engage in peer group activities with relish. However, many children are damaged by the separation and a minority do not recover, becoming severely mentally ill. Of those children who apparently cope well, some later, as adults, realise that they are suffering without understanding the cause. These are often the ones who seek psychotherapy for generalised depression, relationship difficulties, separation anxiety or a sense of emotional numbness, which may manifest as not feeling as if they are genuinely living their own lives. Much of this can be traced to the unconscious strategy for coping with the 'hidden' trauma of the initial bereavement. For a few, who have been bullied by staff or fellow students, what emerges is previously undiagnosed PTSD.

There may be certain predisposing factors, related to early attachment patterns, which influence how children cope with the early separation. This I have discussed in an earlier publication,[4] and the idea was developed by Power.[5] However, regardless of the nature of the primary attachments, early boarding can be an insult to the personal integrity of the child.

Trauma has become a rather overused term, which is hardly surprising when we consider how common it is. The term originates in the Greek language, where *trauma* means *wound*. The *New Oxford Dictionary* definition is: 'Emotional shock following a stressful event or physical injury'.[6] Bessel Van der Kolk and Alexander McFarlane cite evidence that a large proportion of the population has suffered or witnessed some form of trauma in their early lives, or in adolescence. Moreover, they point out that this is inevitably a part of the human condition, as is evident in art and literature, where tragedy has been the subject matter for generations. They draw attention to differences between those who suffer trauma and are soon able to resume their lives, leaving the memory behind, and others who become fixated on the traumatic event/s.[7] It is this fixation that may develop into more severe reactions, including PTSD. Clearly the details of each case need to be differentiated. In this chapter, the aetiology as well as the clinical picture of trauma and memory loss is explored. It is then proposed that describing the suffering of some ex-boarders as a 'hidden trauma' is not an exaggeration.

Amnesia and dissociation

Amnesia has been central in the treatment of trauma since this category of distress was first recognised. In her critical appraisal, Ruth Leys attributes the first use of the term *trauma* to the British physician John Erichsen, who during the 1860s identified the trauma syndrome in victims suffering from the fright of railway accidents.[8] Later it was called *traumatic neurosis* by the neurologist Paul Oppenheim, working in Berlin. The clinical picture was investigated by Charcot, Janet and Freud, who described it as 'the wounding of the mind brought about by sudden, unexpected emotional shock'.[9] At that time, in the 1890s, the favoured treatment was hypnosis.

When Freud began to apply his psychoanalytic method to the treatment of hysteria, he was at first informed by his early experiences working with Janet and Breuer using hypnosis.[10,11] Freud traced symptoms of psychological distress in his patients back to painful past events. He observed that these re-present in psychoanalysis with an insistent pressure until their origin is acknowledged. The 'return of the repressed' is the lifting of the curtain of amnesia.[12] This is often evoked by abreaction: the sudden, and often violent, return of unconscious memories in the present of the analytic encounter. Freud noticed that many of his 'hysterical' patients recalled childhood incest; however, under social pressure he came to disbelieve his own findings, concluding that the stories he heard were incest fantasy, generated by repressed wishes. Thus a form of cultural, as well as personal, amnesia became associated with this particular trauma. It was nearly a hundred years before Freud's initial observations were validated and the prevalence of sexual abuse in childhood was given credence.

In the early days of the twentieth century the debates between Freud and Jung at first revolved around the splitting in the personality that had been observed in the early treatments by hypnosis. As Kalsched puts it: 'Freud found that behind the hysterical symptoms of his patients lay some painful affect that had remained in a "strangulated" state and that this affect was attached to a memory that was cut off from consciousness.'[13] Kalsched helpfully summarises: 'Instead of a lesion in the brain, Freud proposed that trauma created a lesion in the psyche (a splitting of the ego).'[14] It is this splitting of the ego that causes dissociation, which is central in understanding the psyche of the ex-boarder.

Memory loss gradually became a recognised consequence of trauma. Psychiatrists and neurologists noticed this through attention to the physical symptoms of 'shell shock' suffered by soldiers returning from World War I and later World War II. The prominent British psychiatrist William Sargent was influential in the 1940s. He observed that the debilitating symptoms men suffered after witnessing the horrors of war seemed to be alleviated by reliving the original events. Sargent favoured the use of hypnosis and physical treatments rather than psychoanalysis, which he regarded with scepticism.[15] In the treatment of one particular traumatised survivor of Dunkirk, Sargent 'rediscovered the method of cathartic abreaction that Breuer and Freud had first introduced in the 1890s to treat hysteria'.[16] Sargent administered sodium amytal, initially to alleviate the physical symptoms of the state of terror with which this patient presented. The transformation in the patient was immediate; the physical tremors ceased and the man was then able to recall an event which had been so abhorrent that he had forgotten it. This led Sargent to experiment with clinically administered doses to help sufferers to recall battle traumas. He realised that because the horrors they had experienced were beyond recall they were converted into bodily symptoms. Once they were remembered, the amnesia was overcome, leading to lessening of the symptoms.[17]

The understanding that many of those traumatised by war experienced amnesia influenced treatment. It became evident that those who had been soldiers in World War II, as well as Holocaust survivors, did not speak of what they had witnessed.[18] The memories were split off and life continued without conscious recall.[19] As trauma research developed in the last decades of the twentieth century, 'dissociation' was increasingly recognised as a symptom. There is not space to reference all of this research but certain events were key. Different events produce different lasting effects. The psychological effects of witnessing mass murder and imprisonment during the Holocaust has been well documented by many, including Kerstenberg[20] and Bettelheim.[21] Clearly, different experiences produce different forms of lasting suffering. Some are recalled vividly whilst others are forgotten. Jay Lifton has written movingly about the numbing psychological effect produced by the horror of the bombs dropped on Hiroshima and Nagasaki.[22] These forms of suffering had a cultural as well as personal impact. On a more personal level, dissociation is well known in the presentation of those who have suffered child sexual abuse. This is a very private form of suffering.[23] Working with refugees from more recent conflicts, Papadopoulos proposes that despite the fact that a person is traumatised he or she may gain from the experience.[24,25] This brave observation is substantiated by some of his case material. Therefore it is important not to merely see the traumatised individual as a victim.

During the 1970s Judith Herman, working with women's liberation groups, became aware that women who had suffered sexual assault, domestic abuse, captivity and torture at the hands of abusive partners were also traumatised. This was the catalyst for her seminal work *Trauma and Recovery*.[26] It was in the same decade that Bessel van der Kolk identified the lack of literature on trauma. Research was needed to understand the psychological state of soldiers with whom he was working who returned to the USA from the Vietnam War. Thus he began his influential writings on trauma.[27]

It was the cumulative effect of the research by these and other practitioners that eventually led to the recognition of PTSD as a diagnostic category in the 1980 edition of the *Diagnostic and Statistical Manual of Mental Disorders* (DSM III). The types of trauma recognised included 'victims of rape, torture and motor vehicle accidents',[28] as well as those traumatised by war. Common features were that 'the person has been exposed to a traumatic event which involved actual or threatened death or serious injury, or a threat to the physical integrity of self or others'.[29] This recognition led to extensive scientific studies.[30] Later editions of the DSM have included additional categories, running now to twenty pages in DSM V. With regard to our discussion, it is of note that dissociative amnesia is a recognised outcome of traumatic events.[31] This has a particular impact when the trauma took place during childhood.

Childhood trauma

Approaches to treatment over the last century have been diverse, but there seems to be general agreement that, under extreme forms of emotional stress, survival mechanisms create a split in the personality. As a result, a form of dissociation takes place whereby traumatic events may be completely forgotten for years and recalled only when symptomatic behaviour demands attention. In the case of PTSD this splitting mechanism is severe and the resulting amnesia may make diagnosis difficult. This may be especially the case with childhood trauma.

In analysing Boarding School Syndrome, it is childhood trauma that we are considering. This has a different psychological impact from trauma experienced by adults. In Chapter 6 we have seen that Theo movingly described his experience, depicted in his drawings, as 'the distortion of a boy'. These were his own words for the deformity Herman describes.[32]

In Herman's view, the diagnosis in DSM III did not do justice to 'complex and prolonged trauma' experienced by abused children. This she differentiates from 'more circumscribed traumatic events'. Therefore she proposed an additional diagnostic category: 'complex post-traumatic stress disorder'.[33] Van der Kolk and d'Andrea also found the definitions of PTSD inadequate for understanding 'chronically traumatised children'. They too proposed a separate category: 'Developmental Trauma Disorder (DTD)'.[34] This nomenclature draws attention respectively to (a) the prolonged nature of some childhood trauma and (b) its developmental impact.

These observations are validated by recent research into the effects of adverse early life experiences on brain development. In 1994 Alan Schore published his seminal book, *Affect Regulation and the Development of the Self*. Since then, research in this area has burgeoned. Some of Freud's early findings have been endorsed by evidence from neuroscience. Advances in understanding of the effects of trauma on the developing brain have identified the impact on affect regulation and empathy.[35][36] This work has generated a number of publications linking this research to psychotherapy.[37][38][39][40][41][42]

Witnessing and the narrative function

In the case of childhood trauma, memory impairment is complicated because of developmental factors. A child does not have the mental capacity for creating a coherent narrative out of traumatic events. He or she is unable to tell him- or herself, or anyone else, the story of what has happened and then process it. Therefore *'adults, who were chronically traumatized as children, suffer from generalized impairment of memories for both cultural and autobiographical events.'*[43] [Italics mine.] Children who lose all their primary attachment figures and their home at the same time cannot process what has happened.

It is too much to bear, and there is no way that the child can comprehend the multitude of consequent emotions without adult mediation. In boarding school there was no adult to enable the development of mentalisation. Mentalisation, put simply, is the ability to think about experience. Developmentally it is an outcome of attachment relationships where the parenting adult is empathically attuned to the child.[44][45] Some boarding school children feel that their very survival is threatened and there is rarely a parental figure to compensate for the loss of the actual parents. If there is a sympathetic witness it is possible to speak of the events. It is when the traumatic memory is not spoken of that it may remain unintegrated. In some cases this may lead to dissociation.[46]

Therefore what is lost in boarding school is the narrative function for emotional experience. It is easy enough to see this in play with young children. Those who attend a day school often arrive home eager to recount the story of their day. The ups and downs are processed as they tell their experiences to their parents. In this way those emotional events become part of a personal narrative. Traumatic events are similar – if they can be told they are gradually detoxified, thus eventually accepted as part of the person's personal history. It is then an accessible narrative and no longer unconsciously dominates their life. When there is no such witness the trauma may become embodied, leading to conversion symptoms such as digestive problems, migraines, chronic pain poor energy and a large number of other physiological indicators.[47] This may be because the event that caused it is remembered in an embodied sense, but not recalled cognitively and so it cannot be consigned to the past.[48] There is sometimes an unconscious retracing, a repetition which is an unconscious attempt to try to capture the elusive elements of the feelings.

Traumatised individuals are prone to experience the present with physical sensations associated with their past and to act accordingly. Therefore an approach that attends to bodily symptoms and links the person to their bodily experiences may help. The ex-boarder may need to learn that it is safe to have feelings. For a child in boarding school, such as those described in the history chapters or in the portrait of Theo, the trauma was constant and inescapable. In Theo's pictures the subject matter re-emerged unbidden as he made random marks on the paper. As he was able to take in what he had drawn, the memories first became active in the present, and then gradually they were relegated to the past. Through analysis they became integrated as part of the personal history with a narrative that could be told. Thus, in the creation of narrative, witnessing by the therapist is formative.

Psychotherapy presentation

Adults who suffered trauma as children are often well adjusted; they may hold down jobs and maintain relationships. It is only when under extreme pressure that the trauma may re-present in incongruous behaviours. This is because trauma is not primarily remembered as a story. Rather it is stored in mind and brain as images, sounds, smells, and physical sensations and enactments.[49,50] Thus the person may present in psychotherapy complaining of a feeling of numbness, as if not really living in his or her own life; there may be incomprehensible bodily sensations with no apparent physiological cause. The person may become scared, irrationally angry or aroused by some other emotion which is triggered by an unbidden memory. Thus a form of sensory memory may suddenly overwhelm the sufferer. Angry outbursts may occur, triggered by a current situation but inappropriate in their intensity, as we saw with Theo. The reaction is deeply troubling because its origin is apparently incomprehensible. In many cases this is because there is a blank where memory should be and hyper-arousal occurs. All of these symptoms have been noted with some ex-boarders who present in psychotherapy.

The body remembers

PTSD is like time travel: a person may be safely living in the present and is suddenly, incomprehensibly, catapulted back in time and confronted with terror or unprocessed grief from the past. Thus amnesia and the subsequent unbidden return of the memories, often in embodied form, can cause an apparently incomprehensible reaction that leads the person to seek psychological help. Associated with this may be a violent alarm state that overwhelms the person, catapulting them back into the past. Alarm states erase people's sense of time: 'because the brain areas responsible for executive functioning go off line under threat, frightened people lose touch with the flow of time and get stuck in a terrifying, seemingly, never ending present.'[51] This supports the hypothesis that, in some cases, early boarding traumatises children by separating them from a coherent narrative of their life. The young boarding school child is subject to prolonged stress and, in some cases, repeated trauma. This may go some way to understanding the often successful, intellectual achievements alongside the emotional inarticulacy sometimes observed.

Given that the person was a child and therefore did not have the 'mental capacities for constructing a coherent narrative', it is little wonder that the ex-boarder, now adult, may be suddenly shocked by the return of a split-off memory. This may occur when the unconscious survival strategy breaks down and the veil of amnesia is lifted. This may happen quite unexpectedly, accompanied by sudden violent emotions.

Jackie was 47 when she came to see me for psychotherapy after she had been shocked to find herself crying uncontrollably when her eldest child left home. Jackie and her husband had taken their daughter to another country, leaving her there to study. Jackie was surprised to find that, on the return journey, she became overwhelmed by distress. She cried all the way home in the car and at the airport, and continued when they arrived home. For the whole of the next week she cried uncontrollably. Jackie realised that this reaction was more than an ordinary expression of loss and then, coincidentally, that week she read an article in *The Sunday Times Magazine* about children being sent away to school at 8.[52] This triggered a memory and suddenly she connected her extreme sense of loss with her experience of being taken to boarding school at 6. Jackie knew that it was appropriate that she was sad that her daughter was going away. However, she also realised that her reaction was more extreme than this warranted. She now understood that the weeping was commensurate with the devastating loss experienced by the 6-year-old child that she had once been.

Traumatic events that are split off permit the sufferer to engage in life without conscious remembrance of the distress. Babette Rothschild reminds us that the body has a way of remembering what the mind cannot recall.[53] 'The return of the repressed' in psychoanalysis is the return to consciousness of the split-off, previously unconscious, memory of some unbearable situation.[54,55] This is what happened here. Without consciously remembering, Jackie's body suddenly and violently reacted to the emotions from her long-forgotten childhood trauma. Kalsched writes that 'for an experience to be unbearable means that it overwhelms the usual defensive measures which Freud described as "a protective shield against stimuli"'.[56,57] When Jackie unexpectedly found herself overcome by emotion, it seems that this protective shield had been breached. Like a dam which had burst its banks, the previously repressed distress at her abandonment had returned unbidden, devastating her adult self. This violent return of memory can be helpful in eventually alleviating suffering by admitting its cause to conscious awareness. The relief comes in finding the meaning of such events.

Jackie had been sent to school, as she put it, 'at nearly seven', from another continent where her father was working. She remembered little of the long airplane journeys and nothing at all of arriving at school. Later her mother confessed that she had not wanted to send her children away but she had been obliged to choose between her husband and her children. If she had returned to live in the UK with her children, she would have sacrificed her marriage. Like so many other women, this mother was forced to make the impossible choice between her marriage and her children. Brendon gives many examples of women over the centuries faced with making just such a choice.[58][59] Jackie's mother told her later that she had been heartbroken; she was very close to her daughter and could not bear to be parted from her. The mothers' stories are significant in this. Many have been bereft going along with what was expected of them. This was a tragedy of the dominance of patriarchy. Women who objected were often silenced with the comments that 'this is the tradition,' 'it is best for the child' and 'it will be the making of him or her.' So it was that many women went against their intuitive sense of what was right and gave in to the authority of the man or their parents. So the patriarchal tradition continued to the detriment of children.

The unambiguous admission from the parent in later life, that he or she did not want to let the child go, helps for some in repairing the trauma. It is important for the child to know that she was loved and was not easily given up. It also indicates the emotional atmosphere in which the child was separated from her mother. It is likely that the child too was heartbroken but she could not recall that. The only indication of this was the extreme grief reaction she experienced after leaving her own daughter. It seemed that the emotional impact of this traumatic loss had been 'forgotten' until the curtain of amnesia lifted. It returned in the bodily experience of being overwhelmed with grief and then in identifying its source. This return of the memory is a relief because it creates meaning out of an otherwise incomprehensible reaction.

This hidden trauma had been buried but was latent. A previous analysis, lasting three years, had uncovered the sense of loss but not the extent of the emotional impact of this wound. That was concealed from consciousness. This was a very personal form of amnesia but it had a cultural element. Jackie was not the only child at the school experiencing this loss; like the other girls, she was expected not to make a fuss. No one mediated her distress and she had to 'get on with it'.

Melanie Klein's work on the psychological splitting mechanism has permeated much psychoanalytic thinking. It is highly relevant in understanding the amnesia experienced after trauma. In her seminal paper 'Notes on some schizoid mechanisms', Klein outlines splitting in relation to projection and introjection.[60] This gives a framework for thinking about the psychological impact for a child abandoned in boarding school. The child desperately needs to keep the inner image or memory of the mother, or other primary caretaker, good. These inner images are his or her 'internal objects', and in the absence of a loving adult these are important in sustaining the child. In order to maintain good internal objects the child may project the good parts of the self into them. In Jackie's case this good object was the memory of her mother. However, if the mother is then lost, that part of the self is also lost. The child is then alone and feeling bad. She or he has to manage the bad feelings somehow – and so in order to preserve the good image of the mother, the bad feelings are experienced as a hated part of the self. This establishes a self-punishing psychological splitting mechanism which may continue into adulthood. This is very familiar in the treatment of Boarding School Syndrome.

Now an adult, Jackie understood her mother's predicament, the choice she had been forced to make between her husband and her child. It took rather longer to access her feelings of anger and come to realise that, however her mother had suffered, she could/should have protected her child. Thus there was anger wrapped up in the grief of this too-early bereavement.

The social pressure to forget – cultural amnesia

Herman points out that amnesia occurs on a cultural as well as personal level.[61] As we have seen, Freud came to doubt his own evidence of sexual abuse in his patients. That may well have been due to cultural pressure. In claiming that boarding school induces trauma, there is a similar cultural opposition. It is clear that not all ex-boarders suffer such extreme effects, but the initial entry to the school may be traumatic for many. There is a culture of acceptance and so children may appear to recover quite quickly. However, in some cases – especially where the treatment was cruel and the child feared for her or his life – PTSD occurs. Additional losses are incurred by those sent from abroad (such as Jackie and Robert). I will return to this in Chapter 11. The point is that the children, now adults, lack a coherent narrative account of their own early lives and there is rarely anyone who was present to corroborate it.

The hidden trauma – in conclusion

I return briefly to Robert with whom this chapter began. His lack of recall of the journey to school seemed to be connected to having to leave his home and his family. As a boy he could not make sense of his loss, and there was no adult witness to help him to find words for his bereavement. Robert remembers that the group of boys whose parents lived abroad tried to console each other. They would rationalise their situation by telling each other that they were lucky because, unlike the boys with families in the UK, their parents had little option but to send them to boarding school. They thought the others must feel rejected, as their parents had a choice. Thus they externalised their own sense of rejection, psychologically attributing it to the other boys.

Robert and Jackie both suffered a form of amnesia; the memories of each of them had been affected by their very different early losses. This had not impaired their success as adults and, until late in life, neither of them had apparently been troubled by this lack of memory for one aspect of their childhood. Robert sought psychotherapy because of a sense of unease; he was depressed despite his apparent success. Jackie's situation was more dramatic in that the memory returned violently, triggered by current life events. The common features of this trauma were that at the point of entering school they both lost their primary attachment figures and their homes abroad. Therefore the narrative of their lives was severely ruptured. They were very young: Robert was 10 and Jackie only 6. The lack of continuity in the life stories was profound. There were gaps in memory between the times their parents left them and the times they were picked up. These children both suffered trauma from this culturally accepted event.

To describe the lasting effects of early boarding as a hidden trauma is not an exaggeration. These are not children taken into the care of the local authority because of family breakdown but they are casualties of a system of apparent privilege. The child in boarding school may be exposed to the trauma of prolonged separation, bullying and loss. This has an impact on emotional development. This is the hidden trauma of many of the most successful ex-boarders as well as those who are apparent casualties in society. In the following two chapters we will make a closer examination of two aspects of this trauma. These are bereavement, which is addressed in Chapter 9, and captivity, which will be discussed in Chapter 10.

Notes

1. Kalsched, D. (1996) *The Inner World of Trauma*, London: Routledge, p. 84.
2. Herman, J. (1992/1997) *Trauma and Recovery: The Aftermath of Violence From Domestic Abuse to Political Terror*, New York: Basic Books, pp. 7, 26.
3. Van der Kolk, B. A. (1996) 'Trauma and memory', in *Traumatic Stress*, Van der Kolk, B. A., McFarlane, A. C., & Weisaeth, L. (eds), London: Guilford Press, p. 283.
4. Schaverien, J. (2004) 'Boarding school: The trauma of the "privileged" child', *Journal of Analytical Psychology* 49 (5), pp. 683–705.
5. Power, A. (2013) 'Early boarding: Rich children in care, their adaptation to loss of attachment' *Attachment* 7 (2), pp. 186–201.
6. Pearsall, J., & Hanks, P. (eds) (2001) *The New Oxford Dictionary of English*, Oxford: Oxford University Press, p. 1,972.
7. Van der Kolk, B. A., & McFarlane, A. C. (1996) 'The black hole of trauma' in *Traumatic Stress*, Van der Kolk, B. A., McFarlane, A. C., & Weisaeth, L. (eds), London: Guilford Press, pp. 3-5.
8. Leys, R. (2000) *Trauma: A Genealogy*, Chicago: University of Chicago Press, p. 3.
9. Ibid., p. 4.
10. Jones, E. (1953/1983) *Sigmund Freud Life and Work*, vol. 1, London: Hogarth Press.
11. Kalsched (1996), op. cit., p. 69.
12. Jones (1953/1983), op. cit., p. 304.
13. Kalsched (1996), op. cit., p. 69.
14. Ibid., p. 70.
15. Dr Kenneth Simon, personal communication, 2000.

16 Leys (2000), op. cit., p. 192.
17 Ibid., pp. 191–192.
18 Of course, there were those who remembered vividly after World War II and wrote their memoirs as a way of disseminating their experiences.
19 Herman (1992/1997), op. cit., p. 20.
20 Kerstenberg, J. (1985) 'Child survivors of the Holocaust – 40 years later', *Journal of the American Academy of Child Psychiatry* 24, pp. 408–412.
21 Bettelheim, B. (1960/1986) *The Informed Heart*, London: Peregrine Books.
22 Lifton, R. J. (1967) *Death in Life: Survivors of Hiroshima*, New York: Simon & Schuster.
23 Messler Davies J., & Frawley, M. G. (1994) *Treating the Adult Survivor of Childhood Sexual Abuse*, New York, Basic Books.
24 Papadopoulos, R. (ed) (2002) *Therapeutic Care for Refugees: No Place Like Home*, London: Karnac Books.
25 Papadopoulos, R. (2006) 'Refugees and psychological trauma: Psychosocial perspectives' http://isites.harvard.edu/fs/docs/icb.topic920418.files/arc_1_10refandpsych-1.pdf.
26 Herman (1992/1997), op. cit.
27 At the *Journal of Analytical Psychology* conference in April 2013, in Boston, Van de Kolk described how he went to the library in 1972 asking for all the books they had on trauma, and there were none.
28 Van der Kolk, B. A., & d'Andrea, W. (2010) 'Towards a developmental trauma disorder diagnosis for childhood interpersonal trauma', in Lanius, R. A., Vermetten, E., & Pain C. (eds), *The Impact of Early Life Trauma on Health and Disease: The Hidden Epidemic*, Cambridge: Cambridge University Press, p. 27.
29 American Psychiatric Association (1980). *Diagnostic and Statistical Manual of mental disorders,* third edition. Washington, DC: American Psychiatric Press.
30 Van der Kolk, B. A., & d'Andrea, W. (2010) 'Towards a developmental trauma disorder diagnosis for childhood interpersonal trauma', in Lanius, R. A., Vermetten, E., & Pain C. (eds), *The Impact of Early Life Trauma on Health and Disease: The Hidden Epidemic*, Cambridge: Cambridge University Press, p. 57.
31 American Psychiatric Association (2013). *Diagnostic and Statistical Manual of Mental Disorders*, fifth edition, Washington, DC: American Psychiatric Association, p. 271.
32 Herman (1992/1997), op. cit., p. 96.
33 Ibid., p. 119.
34 Van der Kolk, & d'Andrea (2010), op. cit., p. 57.
35 Baron Cohen, S. (2011) *Zero Degrees of Empathy: A New Theory of Human Cruelty*, London: Allen Lane.
36 McGilchrist, I. (2009) *The Master and His Emissary*, London: Yale University Press.
37 Gerhardt, S. (2004) *Why Love Matters*, London: Routledge.
38 Wilkinson, M. (2006) *Coming Into Mind*, London: Routledge.
39 Wilkinson, M. (2010) *Changing Minds in Psychotherapy*, London: W. W. Norton & Co.
40 Lanius, R. A., Vermetten, E., & Pain, C. (eds) (2010) *The Impact of Early Life Trauma on Health and Disease: The Hidden Epidemic*, Cambridge: Cambridge University Press.
41 Knox, J. (2003) *Archetype, Attachment, Analysis*, New York: Brunner Routledge.
42 Knox, J. (2011) *Self-Agency in Psychotherapy*, London: W. W. Norton & Co.
43 Van der Kolk (1996), op. cit., p. 283.
44 Fonagy, P., & Target, M. (2000) 'Playing with reality: iii. The persistence of dual psychic reality in borderline patients', *The International Journal of Psychoanalysis* 81, pp. 853–873.
45 Bateman, A., & Fonagy, P. (2013) 'Mentalization-based treatment', *Psychoanalytic Inquiry* 33, pp. 595–613.

46 Van der Kolk, & McFarlane (1996), op. cit., p. 7.
47 Van der Kolk, & d'Andrea (2010), op. cit., p. 62.
48 Rothschild, B. (2000) *The Body Remembers: The Psychophysiology of Trauma and Trauma Treatment*, London: W.W. Norton & Co.
49 Van der Kolk, B. A., & Fisler, R. (1995) 'Dissociation and the fragmentary nature of traumatic memories: Background and experimental evidence', *Journal of Traumatic Stress* 8, pp. 505–525.
50 Van der Kolk, & d'Andrea (2010), op. cit., p. 65.
51 Ibid., p. 59.
52 Williams, S. (2013) 'What's it like to go away to school at 8?' *The Sunday Times Magazine* (31 August).
53 Rothschild (2000), op. cit.
54 Freud, S. (1939) *Moses and Monotheism*, Standard Edition XXIII, London, Hogarth Press.
55 Van der Kolk, B. A., & Kaddish, W. (1987) 'Amnesia, dissociation and the return of the repressed,' in Van der Kolk, B. (ed), *Psychological Trauma*, Arlington, Virginia: American Psychiatric Press, pp. 173–190. Quoted in Van der Kolk (1996), op. cit., p. 284.
56 Freud, S. (1920) *Beyond the Pleasure Principle*, Standard Edition XVIII, London, Hogarth Press.
57 Kalsched (1996), op. cit., p. 1.
58 Brendon, V. (2005/2006) *Children of the Raj*, Phoenix: Orion.
59 Brendon, V. (2009) *Prep School Children: A Class Apart Over Two Centuries*, London: Continuum.
60 Klein, M. (1946/1975) 'Notes on some schizoid mechanisms', in *Envy and Gratitude, the Writings of Melanie Klein*, vol. 3, London: Hogarth Press, p. 5.
61 Herman (1992/1997), op. cit., p. 20.

Chapter 9

Broken attachments
The bereaved child

> When a love tie is severed, a reaction, emotional and behavioural, is set in train, which we call grief.
>
> Colin Murray Parkes[1]

In Chapter 2 we saw how extreme brutality was prevalent in boarding schools throughout numerous generations. Clearly there were psychological consequences of such treatment. We saw in Chapter 8 that for some the first day at school is forgotten. For others, as we will see in this chapter, that day is seared into their memory as a life-changing moment. I turn now to the psychological impact not of brutality but of separation on the development of the child. The premise is that the broken attachments of the first days in boarding school amount to a significant, but unrecognised, form of bereavement.

Bereavement is a prolonged grief reaction to the loss of a significant person. It most commonly refers to the death of a partner or parent, but Colin Murray Parkes suggests that understanding bereavement can contribute to appreciation of the effects of other forms of loss.[2] Therefore the losses of the child sent to boarding school at a young age might well be seen in this light. Early boarding breaks intimate bonds and subjects the child to traumatic loss. This initial loss is significantly wounding, even for children living in the best of schools. The autobiographies of well-known writers attest to this and, in this chapter, their words complement the material from psychotherapy.

The young child at boarding school, whilst fed and housed – sometimes quite well – may none the less feel a sense of homelessness. The child may long for his or her parents and all that belonging symbolises. However, as time progresses, this may become an idealised version of the real home; it becomes a place of the imagination. House parents, however good, are no substitute for real ones. The repeated experience of returning home as a stranger and then leaving, just as the child has settled back in, builds a psychological pattern, an expectation of being left which is often unconsciously active in later life. These patterns of disrupted attachments are often replayed within a marriage or long-term partnership.

Charles was successful in his career and had apparently fulfilled the promise of his boarding school education. He was a senior executive in an international telecoms company and he travelled all over the world. Yet, suddenly, he was struck down by extreme psychological distress with symptoms that he could not comprehend. He referred himself for psychotherapy after he found himself amassing pills with the intention of taking them all. Not consciously suicidal, he had been extremely shocked and realised that he needed to seek psychological help.

Two years previously his twenty-year marriage had broken down, culminating in an acrimonious divorce. Now he was in a new relationship and his partner's psychological understanding of him had led him to realise that he had previously lived an emotionally isolated life. Now he began to consider his life and his relationships more deeply. It emerged that he had married at an early age to someone he met as soon as he left school. With little understanding of intimacy, he had chosen someone whom he described as cold and unforgiving. The marriage had worked because they had led traditionally separate lives. Charles was the provider, putting his work before everything else, and his wife had looked after the children and the home. He now deeply regretted missing much of the early lives of his children.

As we pursued his story it became clear that boarding school had set Charles on the path for this way of living. He had been taken to his boarding school at the age of 9. This was a big family event that involved his grandparents as well as his parents. He remembered how they had all accompanied him into the dormitory and helped him to unpack. Then quite suddenly they left. Charles looked around and they were gone.

This is the traumatic, life-changing moment that is either totally forgotten (as we saw in Chapter 8) or else recalled in powerful emotional detail. In that instant he realised with a sense of shock what it meant to be in boarding school. He remembered thinking to himself that he was now alone. He had no one to depend on but himself, so as he put it, 'he had better get on with it!' From this moment on he had been fiercely independent. His parents had returned to their lives abroad, his father to his work and his mother to her social life and caring for his younger sister. In the holidays Charles would stay with his grandparents. He formed a very close relationship with his grandmother, so he was bereft when she suddenly died two years later. This was handled in a way typical of the time. Charles was told of her death, but he received no special attention; he remained at school and was not taken to the funeral. This further compounded his sense of loss, but he had to deal with his feelings alone. He was now doubly bereaved: he had lost his home with his parents and sister when he went to the school, and now he lost his grandmother too. From then on, realising that he was dependent on his own resources, he worked very hard and just got on with the task of growing up, independent of everyone. Thus he appeared to himself, as well as others, to have done very well at school.

His marriage had followed a similar pattern. He did not depend on his wife, but he provided for her and their children. His success was based on an ability to put his work before his family and also before his own psychological welfare. He could be very sensitive and gentle, but he was ruthless in his work. He had learned to live this way early in his life. The philosophy by which he lived was, 'concentrate on work and do not mind that you have been abandoned.' This ruthlessness made him invaluable in his company. There were times when he described making fellow workers redundant. They were not performing adequately and so they must go; he did not consider how they would feel about this. However, it seemed his new relationship had changed him and he now realised what he had missed earlier in his life. His way of living no longer fitted, hence his desperation. His whole system rebelled against the way he was working and he was forced to stop and take stock.

Reframing Charles's early boarding school experience, we might understand that he was traumatised by the sudden loss of his parents, his grandmother, and all that was familiar to him. The term *homesickness* does not do justice to the depth of the losses to which the boarding school child is subjected: Charles, like Theo, was *bereaved*. Moreover, from the moment when his family had left the school he was captive, living in a situation not of his own choosing and which he was helpless to change.

For many it is the simple fact of boarding that constitutes a traumatic bereavement. The rupture in emotional attachment is the first boarding school trauma. The child must learn to live without love. If there is additional abuse and bullying, as with Theo, this is intensified – but even for those who suffer little overt cruelty, it is still traumatic. This is because boarding breaks intimate bonds and causes the child to live for a significant part of his or her childhood subject to an unsympathetic regime, effectively in captivity.

Parents take the school on trust; reassured by the public face of the school, they leave the child with the assumption that he or she will be well cared for. They may be told that the child will soon overcome any homesickness, so they leave, comforted by this understanding, whilst the child is bereft. The parents are often from then onwards unaware of any frightening incidents that befall the child. Generations of well-meaning parents have left their – often very young – children in the hands of apparently benign adults with little idea of what took place in their absence. The trust is based on little or no evidence.

Boarding School Syndrome – breaking emotional bonds

Boarding School Syndrome is created through multi-layered discrepancies between the perception of the child, new to the school, and the behaviour of adults around him or her. The deprivation of liberty and the profound culture shock is tempered with mixed messages. The child raised with ethical sensibilities soon observes that teachers and older children treat as normal strangely incongruous behaviours, such as beatings and regimentation. The child is unhappy but given the message that school is good for him or her. The parents appear to condone its ethos, yet the child may perceive that they too are unhappy at the separation. The contradiction between the parents' words and their emotional reaction causes the child to doubt her or his own perception.

The anomalies accumulate as the child progresses through the system, but acculturation takes place and the child appears to conform. Emotionally, however, the confusion remains, causing a split between the feeling self and the thinking self. This creates a wound; it breaks intimate attachments and damages the continuity of the self.

Attachment

Attachment is a powerful need of the dependent human being. Bowlby's research on this theme was published in his three-volume *Attachment and Loss*.[3] Along with Mary Ainsworth, he conducted research with children in children's homes, observing the profound psychological effects of broken attachments.[4,5] Anna Freud worked with children separated from their parents during World War II,[6,7] and Donald Winnicott's work with young children and their families has influenced approaches to psychological treatment for decades.[8,9] In the 1950s and 1960s research began to give evidence backing up the psychoanalytic understanding of the attachment needs of infants. Harlow's experiments with infant rhesus monkeys demonstrated the effects of maternal deprivation and extrapolated from this the importance of the early bond for human infants.[10] For many years James and Joyce Robertson conducted research in which they filmed very young children left in children's homes or hospitals for relatively short stays. These films give clear evidence of the profound psychological impact of this separation.[11,12]

This work has been amply validated by more recent infant research demonstrating the importance of parental bonds and interactions with small children. Starting with Daniel Stern's work in this field, the literature has been developed especially in the USA.[13] Since the 1990s the expanding literature on the importance of attachment on brain development has further validated these findings, demonstrating that there are physiological changes in the brain if attachment is inadequate, as we saw in Chapter 7.[14,15] The importance of the reciprocity of the infant-mother relationship has been researched in some depth and links made with the therapist-patient dyad.[16,17] This research has been extended to consideration of the type of therapeutic interventions that might be offered.[18,19] Sue Gerhardt's work on why love matters offers a very personal account of the importance of early emotional regulation for the immune system. She considers her own mother's personality, upbringing and early fatal illness.[20] This research provides a strong body of evidence that the human infant and young child develop best in a loving relationship.

Therefore it seems likely that early boarding, which ruptures early emotional attachments and subjects the child to living without love, would have psychological repercussions. The younger a child is exposed to the system, the greater the trauma is likely to be. In my interviews with adults, as well as with my psychotherapy clients, it emerges that this 'threshold moment'[21] is either completely forgotten or else it is vividly recalled. It is often described with wry humour in the autobiographies of successful men such as Stephen Fry,[22] Wilfred Bion[23] and John Peel.[24] Evacuated in 1939 as a consequence of World War II, Oliver Sacks does not use humour but rather conveys some of the horror of living in a particularly cruel prep school.[25] Even when these writers do not explicitly state this in their autobiographies, it is clear that the losses of the primary attachments were significant.

Arrival – autobiographies of boarding school

The stories of Theo and Charles have described the moment of separation. Theo said, 'In that instant the world fell apart; the floor, the walls and the sky all fell in.' Charles declared, 'From that moment I knew I was alone in the world and just had to get on with it.'

In order to convey the impact of the moment of separation, I turn to the published autobiographies of two well-known writers who both describe it vividly: Roald Dahl, the children's author, and Sir Andrew Motion, who was poet laureate of the UK from 1999 to 2009. These two men are from different generations, but each describes, with the hindsight of an adult, the traumatic incomprehension of the child in the moment of loss.

Roald Dahl's is an account of boarding in the early years of the twentieth century.[26] His parents were Norwegian but his father had, as a young man, moved to Wales, where he created a successful business. Dahl senior wanted the best possible education for his only son (he had five daughters) and so planned to send him to a British boarding school. Before Dahl was old enough to go to school his father died, but, when the time came, his mother was true to his father's wishes. So it was that in 1925 the 9-year-old Dahl was taken to a small prep school in Weston Super Mare, as near as his mother could find to their home in Cardiff. His description of the preparation and the journey is one to which generations of ex-boarders could relate:

> On the first day of my first term I set out in a taxi in the afternoon with my mother . . . every piece of clothing I wore was brand new and had my name on it . . . and into the taxi that was taking us went my brand new trunk and my brand new tuck box, and both had R. Dahl painted on them in black.[27]

There was hope and anticipation in this exciting new beginning, but also apprehension: 'I had absolutely no idea of what was in store for me. I had never spent a single night away from our large family before.'[28] They arrived at the school, and here he conveys another ubiquitous aspect of the experience:

> As we got out of the taxi, I saw the whole driveway abustle with small boys and their parents and their trunks and a man I took to be the Headmaster swimming around among them shaking everybody by the hand. . . . I have

already told you that *all* Headmasters are giants and this one was no exception. He advanced upon my mother and shook her by the hand, then he shook me by the hand and as he did so he gave me the kind of flashing grin a shark might give to a small fish just before he gobbles it up. . . . 'Right' he said to me. 'Off you go and report to Matron.' And to my mother he said briskly, 'Goodbye, Mrs Dahl. I shouldn't linger if I were you. We'll look after him.'

My mother got the message. She kissed me on the cheek and said goodbye and climbed right back into the taxi. The Headmaster moved away and I was left standing there beside my brand new trunk and my brand new tuck box. I began to cry.[29]

The simplicity of this tale belies the desolation such a small child feels in this moment. The understatement gives a sense of how the child is helpless and can do nothing to alter the situation. For the first time in his life, he is alone and dependent for survival on his own resources. The image of the giant/shark/headmaster conveys the archetypal power that strange adults in positions of power take on for small children. This story of loss would be unremarkable, but we are attending to the deeper impact of this commonplace bereavement. Dahl wrote to his mother every week for the rest of her life but he never again lived with her.

Another version of the story, this time from a later generation, also conveys the trauma of this threshold moment. Andrew Motion's evocative account of a 1950s childhood is overshadowed by a tragic accident suffered by his mother when he was 16.[30] He creates the sense of freedom of a middle-class childhood, overseen by loving parents. The child played alone or with his younger brother, exploring the garden and locality. He attended the local day school and returned home each evening. The impending sense of dread is conveyed as the idea was introduced that he would soon be going to boarding school a hundred miles away from his home. This was incomprehensible to the child: 'How far *is* a hundred miles?' Prior to this the headmaster, a friend of Motion's paternal grandfather, was invited to his parents' home to meet him. This did nothing to ease the transition.

Motion was nearly 8 when his parents drove him to Maidwell Hall in Northamptonshire. The confusion of arriving, mixed with the obligation he felt not to upset his mother, is conveyed in the words of the child: ' "I'm afraid poor mum is rather upset," dad said softly, as though he was letting me into a secret.'[31] Thus his own emotional turmoil about the impending separation was coloured by consideration of his mother's feelings. This split is one way the first stage of Boarding School Syndrome is created. The boy appears to be a 'little man' but, whilst seeming strong, the vulnerable self begins to retract in favour of a false self-persona. The child's sense of unreality is evoked:

This wasn't my hand opening the car door. It wasn't my voice telling mum she mustn't worry, I was fine. These weren't my new indoor shoes slipping on the gravel because we had forgotten to scratch them to make them grip.

> This wasn't me helping dad cart the trunk towards the glass front door. These weren't mum's steps hurrying after.[32]

This distancing from the emotional self is typical. The impending trauma is so great that the child emotionally absents himself; it is just too painful to be fully alive in the moment. This is the beginning of disassociation, a split that is essential for survival. It enables the child to appear to be coping, even though that is far from the emotional reality.

Motion's first impressions of the school include his observation of the boys:

> We were in a long hall – panelled walls, yellow wood floor. And there were boys everywhere, walking in groups, or running and sliding then strolling again if they thought a grown-up was watching. They looked like little men in their tweed jackets.[33]

Then the farewell: his parents wanted to see where he was going to sleep (which today would be considered a normal request) but the headmaster said, 'No – do that at half term.' The parents were advised to just leave because there was 'lots for him to do this evening'. The boy reflects: 'Why was he talking as if I did not exist?'[34] Thus it was that the parents were advised by the headmaster to leave without 'making a fuss'.

The moment-to-moment distancing from self is described in the approach to the dreaded separation:

> All the way in the car I had broken the journey into miles, and half miles, and quarter miles, and hundreds of yards, and inches. That way, I still had ages with mum and dad, if we took the trunk upstairs to my dormitory together, then came downstairs together and said goodbye. I could make every second feel like an hour. But Beak (the Headmaster) had decided we were at the end. As the thought sank in my neck suddenly went floppy and I stared at the floor.[35]

Desolate, his thoughts are still for his mother, who was crying. Like his dad, he had to be a man and look after her:

> Then mum tapped me on the tip of my nose with her finger and it was brilliant . . . after that she caught hold of dad's sleeve and they moved away. It's done, I thought. I'm on the other side of saying goodbye. But as the glass door closed behind them, mum peeped over her shoulder. She was really crying now, so when she tried to blow a kiss her lips crumpled and wouldn't make the right shape . . . she never stopped walking, not even when she turned round to look at me for the last time, as their footsteps started to crunch over the gravel.[36]

So it was that both these boys were left alone in a strange environment, Dahl crying and Motion staring at the floor. Even when the child cries, there is little comfort because it does not elicit the anticipated adult caring response. Sometimes other boys do their best to offer solace, but the boy who cries soon realises there is no point in doing so. Whilst Dahl's mother apparently did not cry, Motion's mother did so. Portrayed by his father as vulnerable, she had permission to show she was affected, unlike the child who, 'as a man', was expected to be strong. The child cannot imagine that his or her parents are upset at leaving and so, even as an adult, it can be comforting to realise that they were. (In some schools it was accepted that mothers might cry, so they were advised to wear sunglasses so that their children would not see this display of emotion.)[37] This raises the question of how and why these mothers, both clearly very caring and palpably upset, could bear to let their children go. What sanction was it that might cause them to so deny their own intuitive reactions? Is this merely the law of the father, the paternal injunction to turn their little boys into men? This is a question that calls for further research. The term *homesickness* does not do justice to the immensity of the grief suffered by the child in this moment of loss. The profound anguish of this separation is actually bereavement, but it is not treated as such. Therefore the appropriate reaction, which would be acknowledgment and mourning, cannot take place.

Dahl and Motion are both highly successful men, so it could be argued that boarding school did them no harm. However, each has remembered that first day in sufficient detail to write about it in later years. The reasons they were given for being sent away to school are common ones. In both cases British tradition was behind this everyday breaking of attachment bonds. Dahl's father, an immigrant, aspired to the best British education for his son. Motion's father had himself attended public school, therefore it was family tradition. It seems from their stories that both mothers would have preferred not to send their child away but they thought it was for the best. Parents may trust the school to look after their child, often upon the recommendation of some respected adult. A respected colleague of his father recommended Theo's school. The headmaster in Motion's school was a friend of his grandfather.[38] Did the grandfather know that his friend grew canes in the grounds for the express purpose of beating the boys?[39] So it is that the parents' trust in the adults in the schools are often insufficiently researched and ultimately misplaced.

Bereavement

Let us look in a little more detail at how this common story, this moment of loss, could be reframed as bereavement. Colin Murray Parkes created the first research-based study of bereavement in adult life.[40] Significantly, he was a colleague of John Bowlby and his work extends that of Bowlby on attachment. One of his main contributions was to identify the stages of the grief process. Murray Parkes suggests that his understanding of bereavement can help with understanding forms of loss such as divorce, unemployment or physical disability.[41] To this

I am now adding early boarding. Murray Parkes summarises seven features that seem to be major aspects of many bereavements:

1. A process of realization, i.e. the way in which the bereaved moves from denial or avoidance of recognition of the loss towards acceptance.
2. An alarm reaction – anxiety, restlessness, and the physiological accompaniments of fear.
3. An urge to search and find the lost person in some form.
4. Anger and guilt, including outbursts . . .
5. Feelings of internal loss of self or mutilation.
6. Identification phenomena . . .
7. Pathological variants of grief, i.e. the reaction may be excessive and prolonged . . . [42]

Many children left in boarding school are subject to a similar process, but without the recognition of what has been lost. They lose their parents and with them the emotionally dependent state of the childhood they have previously known. They are still totally reliant on adults and have no control over their fate. The lost innocence of the childhood state can never again be regained; even when they return home for vacations they are changed by the experience.

Mourning

The bereaved person is usually permitted a period of mourning. However, for the child in boarding school their losses are minimised and glossed over as insignificant. This contributes to the hidden aspect of the trauma. The child is bereft, alone and feeling the loss of those people who have always loved and cared for him or her. The familiar in every sense is gone: family and place are all lost in one moment. The stages of reaction to bereavement described by Murray Parkes are relevant to the child in boarding school. Below is my list of how these stages may be adapted to the psychological reaction of the child bereaved in boarding school.

1. The first reaction to finding him- or herself in boarding school is shock. The reaction in the moment when the parents leave is acute shock, numbness and disbelief. This is not unlike the reaction to a death.
2. Alarm, terror and the realisation of captivity may be part of this but it cannot be expressed. There are no words for the magnitude of what has occurred.
3. The loss then dawns and the next phase of separation, which in this case is called *homesickness*, causes pain that comes in waves. It is often a yearning for the mother in particular, perhaps searching for her to reappear. The child may hope that this is all a mistake and anticipate that soon she will appear to collect him or her.
4. The reality is nothing like the stories that have been read in preparation.

5. Despair then follows: like the person bereaved, the child is helpless to alter the situation.
6. The child may cry. However, the longed-for comfort is not forthcoming and so acceptance gradually follows.
7. Anger, guilt, restlessness and inability to concentrate may be symptoms. Here the child may be distracted by enjoyment of sport or lessons.
8. The loss of self is important because for a small child the mother, or in some cases the nanny, is closely identified with a sense of self. That self-object is not dead but gone to another remote world – a world to which the child no longer has access. Thus the dependent childhood state is broken.
9. The final phase in bereavement is acceptance, and it is similar with this bereavement too. Children accept their lot and get on with it, no longer expecting to be rescued by loving adults. Cut off from the emotions that cause so much pain, they live without intimacy.

This process was evident in the television documentary *Leaving Home at 8*.[43] The cameras followed an 8-year-old girl going through the first term at school. She was very upset during the first term and she displayed attachment-seeking behaviour, clinging to her mother. On another occasion, when her own mother was not there, she attached to the mother of another child, hopeful for attention. However, by the second term, she is shown enjoying herself and does not seem to be upset. She has apparently adapted and no longer displays her emotions. So it is that, in the film, we witness the creation of Boarding School Syndrome.

Actual bereavement

In addition to this emotional bereavement some children are actually bereaved in that one of their parents or grandparents has died either before they attend the school or, like Charles, during the time they are there. In the past it was often the case that after the death of a parent, especially the father, the child was sent to boarding school. Sometimes, if the father died in war, the school was paid for by his employer, the military or perhaps by a charity concerned about the welfare of the child. The problem with this was that the child was doubly bereaved, losing not one, but two parents. Others suffered the death of a parent when they were away at school and, in some cases, the need for mourning was completely denied. The child was expected to carry on as normal, often not even attending the funeral. This all fits with the attitude to psychological distress that if it is ignored it will go away. This contributes to the creation of an adult who is unable to attend to his or her emotional life.

One woman reported that her father died when she was at school. By chance she was in a dormitory with three other girls who had all lost their fathers. This was not seen as a benefit, as it might be today, in that they could support each other emotionally. Rather they were all treated as pariahs and not permitted to discuss it. Soon they were separated, moved to different dormitories. The rationale seems to be that grief would be emotionally contagious.

So it was with Charles, the man with whom this chapter began. His grandmother died, but he was not taken out of the school or included in the funeral. There is little doubt that he had benefitted from his boarding school training. He knew how to be ruthless in work. However, this ruthlessness had blighted his intimate life. He had not known how to be in a loving relationship. As a consequence he chose for his first wife someone who would not make emotional demands on him. During analysis he took a break from his work and reassessed his life. It took a relatively short period of therapy for him to understand how his early life had formed him. He made changes that enabled him to live an emotionally full life, giving more time and attention to his own needs. His new relationship offered him an opportunity for a kind of intimacy that he had never before experienced. He now saw how his life might have been and needed to mourn his losses in analysis before he was free to go forward with a richer attitude to his life.

Conclusion

In this chapter I have examined in detail the moment of loss for the small child sent to boarding school. This I have reframed as a form of bereavement. Broken attachments and the rupture of intimate bonds occur for many young children sent to boarding school. It seems that some children soon adjust; they appear to cope and adapt happily enough to living in two different places. Some schools are progressive and some children genuinely enjoyed living in them. For others the disruption is unmanageable: they become used to school in term time and then have to leave their friends to return home. There they are rarely any longer simply children who belong in a family. For those unhappy at school, the holidays are blighted by the knowledge that the return to school looms ahead. For them the whole separation takes place again each term. Its repetition is a significant aspect of the process, which for some is a re-traumatisation each time.

In the next chapter I look further at the anatomy of this hidden trauma and address an additional aspect, captivity.

Notes

1 Murray Parkes, C. (1972) *Bereavement: Studies of Grief in Adult Life*, Harmondsworth: Penguin Books, p. 11.
2 Ibid., p. 212.
3 Bowlby, J. (1969) *Attachment*, Attachment and Loss, vol. 1, London: Hogarth Press; (1973) *Separation: Anxiety and Anger*, Attachment and Loss, vol. 2, London: Hogarth Press; (1980) *Loss: Sadness and Depression*, Attachment and Loss, vol. 3, London: Hogarth Press.
4 Ainsworth, M. D., & Bell, S. M (1970) 'Attachment, exploration, and separation: Illustrated by one year olds in a strange situation', *Child Development* 41 (1), pp. 49–67.
5 Ainsworth, M. S. (1989) 'Attachments beyond infancy', *American Psychologist*, 44 (4), pp. 709–716.
6 Freud, A. (1992) *Ego and Mechanisms of Defense*, London: Hogarth Press.
7 Freud, A. (1965) *Normality and Pathology in Childhood*, London: Hogarth Press.
8 Winnicott, D. W. (1971) *Playing and Reality*, Harmondsworth: Penguin.

9 Winnicott, D. W. (1958/1982) *Through Pediatrics to Psychoanalysis*, London: Hogarth Press.
10 Harlow, H. F. (1959) 'Love in infant monkeys', *Scientific American* 200 (6), pp. 64–74.
11 *Young Children in Brief Separation* (1971). Five-film series produced by James and Joyce Robertson.
12 *A Two-Year-Old Goes to Hospital* (1952). Film produced by James and Joyce Robertson www.youtube.com/watch?v=s14Q-_Bxc_U.
13 Stern, D. (1985) *The Interpersonal World of the Infant*, New York: Basic Books.
14 Schore, A. N. (1994) *Affect Regulation and Origins of the Self*, Hillsdale, New Jersey: Lawrence Erlbaum Associates.
15 McGilchrist, I. (2009) *The Master and His Emissary*, London: Yale University Press.
16 Tronick, E. Z. (2003) 'Of course all relationships are unique: How co-creative processes generate unique mother-infant and patient-therapist relationships', *Psychoanalytic Inquiry* 23, pp. 473–491.
17 Beebe, B., & Lachmann, F. M. (2002/2005) *Infant Research and Adult Treatment*, London, Analytic Press.
18 Stern, D. N. et al. (1998) 'Non-interpretive mechanisms in psychoanalytic therapy: The "something more" than interpretation', *The International Journal of Psychoanalysis* 79, pp. 903–921.
19 Trevarthen, C. (2009) 'The intersubjective psychobiology of human meaning: Learning of culture depends on interest for co-operative practical work-and affection for the joyful art of good company', *Psychoanalytic Dialogues* 19, pp. 507–518.
20 Gerhardt, S. (2004) *Why Love Matters*, London: Routledge, p. 93.
21 Partridge, S. (2007) 'Trauma at the threshold: An eight year-old goes to boarding school', *Attachment* 1 (3), pp. 310–313.
22 Fry, S. (2004) *Moab Is My Washpot*, London: Arrow Books.
23 Bion, W. R. (1982) *The Long Weekend 1897–1919, Part of a Life*, London: Karnac Books.
24 Peel, J. & Ravenscroft, S. (2006) *Margrave of the Marshes*, London: Random House.
25 Sacks, O. (2001) *Uncle Tungsten*, London: Picador, p. 20.
26 Dahl, R. (1984) *Boy: Tales of Childhood*, London: Puffin Books.
27 Ibid., pp. 75–76.
28 Ibid., p. 78.
29 Ibid., p. 79.
30 Motion, A. (2006) *In the Blood: A Memoir of My Childhood*, London: Faber & Faber.
31 Ibid., p. 98.
32 Ibid.
33 Ibid.
34 Ibid., p. 99.
35 Ibid., p. 100.
36 Ibid., pp. 100–101.
37 James Foucar of Boarding Concern, personal communication.
38 Motion (2006), op. cit., pp. 90–92.
39 Ibid., p. 113.
40 Murray Parkes (1972), op. cit.
41 Ibid., p. 212.
42 Ibid., p. 213.
43 *Leaving home at 8* (2010) Cutting Edge Programme on Channel 4 www.channel4.com/programmes/leaving-home-at-8/episode-guide/series-1/episode-1.

Chapter 10

The captive child
Abandonment

> Psychological trauma is an affliction of the powerless.
>
> Judith Herman[1]

> Children have fewer capacities for constructing a coherent narrative out of traumatic events.
>
> Bessel Van der Kolk[2]

The anatomy of boarding school trauma

In the last two chapters I have started to build a picture of the lasting psychological legacy of boarding school trauma, addressing elements which may contribute to the creation of Boarding School Syndrome. We have seen that the memory of the threshold moment may be obliterated by a protective amnesia or, alternatively, it may be forever etched in the psyche of the child. Whether or not the memory is conscious, it may unconsciously influence intimate adult relationships. Homesickness following the losses sustained in the first days at school has been reframed as grief and bereavement. I turn now to another aspect of boarding school life that requires reframing: the long-term residential nature of the experience.

Some children seem to adapt, after the initial upset of arrival, and to genuinely enjoy being part of a large 'sibling' group. Some come from homes where their lives are stressful and for them boarding school is a relief. The traditional rules and sporting activities may offer a sense of fair play and consistent care which is lacking in their homes. As one of my patients said, 'At least at school you knew where the punishments were coming from.' In his school there were fagging, bullying and beatings – even so, it was better than his home. Some children do evidently thrive in this setting, as some of my respondents have helped me to see. However, for others their experience of boarding in school is little better than a form of imprisonment. Benign terms may be applied, such as the current vogue for calling it a 'sleepover'.[3][4] This does not alter the fact that for twenty-four hours a day, for months at a time, the child lives – usually against their will – in an institutional setting away from their home.

Imprisonment

It is not uncommon for ex-boarders to flippantly refer to boarding school as 'imprisonment'. John le Carre dryly described his time in boarding school as having 'spent 11 years in the Gulag'.[5] The comparison is usually made with ironic but resigned humour. This technique, of employing humour to acknowledge an unpalatable truth, is acquired in school. Children soon learn to mask their vulnerability with a veneer of wit. However, this jocularity distracts from the underlying distress of living deprived of liberty for a substantial part of childhood.

Stephen Fry was informed by having experience of both the penal and boarding school systems and he makes the comparison explicit. Immediately after leaving school, Fry was arrested for using a credit card that he had stolen from the parents of a friend. The way he describes this, it was likely to have been an expression of his psychological confusion at leaving public school. Having spent ten years in institutional care, he had become accustomed to it. Fry served a short term in prison and considered that he was well prepared to survive because it was just like boarding school:

> I knew how to tease authority enough to be popular with the inmates and tolerated by the screws; I knew how to stay cheerful and think up diversions, scams and pranks. I knew, ironically, given my inability to do so in real boarding schools, how to survive.[6]

Thus he employed strategies learned in boarding school to handle imprisonment. He suggests that others, not trained in boarding school, might have been less prepared.

As we have seen, the regime in most girls' schools is less brutal than that of boys' schools. As we saw in Chapter 3, it is nonetheless rigid. Order and conformity in girls' schools is maintained not by beatings and brutality, but by inducing humiliation and shame.[7] Judith Okely's boarding school was on the Isle of Wight, also the site of a maximum-security prison. The parallels between the two were not lost on Okely, even as a child. She realised that, like the prisoners, she and her schoolmates were captive: they were not free to leave and, because it was an island, there was no point in trying to escape. Moreover, like the prisoners, they had to adhere to a strict regime which controlled every aspect of their being.[8] Whilst the island nature of her school was specific, the point she makes about imprisonment is more generally applicable, particularly to girls' schools. This treatment of girls was in part due to the fear of female sexuality, which was for many years a dominating influence in the treatment of girls.

Similar to the prisoner, the child in a boarding school is powerless to leave and lives a life of institutionalised captivity. Subject to a rigid regime, he or she has to learn obedience to the will of others (senior students and staff). The school, like prison, is often far from home – in some cases in a different country – making the concept of escape remote. The child, like the prisoner, is 'doing time' and waiting for their eventual release. At the end of term the child is released, but on parole, provisionally, to be returned to the school after a brief respite. Most significantly, and also like the prisoner, the child lives deprived of love, intimate touch and physical care. However, unlike the prisoner the child has committed no crime – he or she is young and vulnerable. This is a formative time and therefore a child may feel that his or her own survival, physical and emotional, is under threat.

The distress of children in boarding school is rarely understood to be an appropriate reaction to being detained against their will. This is not the only form of captivity to go unseen in society, and a comparison may be helpful. Herman has pointed out that the suffering of women and children trapped in abusive relationships is a hidden form of captivity.[9] As she puts it, they are 'held against their will and subjected to the will of the other'.[10] The comparison with the child in a boarding school might at first seem unlikely. However, the child too is captive, held against his or her will and subject to the will of others. This is indeed a hidden trauma but it is also a commonplace occurrence. Perhaps this is the reason that society has been blind to the suffering endured by its 'privileged' children over the centuries.

Dissociation and the captive child

The trauma of long-term captivity on the child is rarely acknowledged, but inevitably there are psychological consequences. Dissociation may be one of these; it is initially an unconscious but adaptive reaction to an intolerable situation. Dissociation may manifest as a sense of feeling permanently distant from the world around the sufferer. This is a recognised symptom of post-traumatic stress disorder (PTSD). It is also a symptom of Boarding School Syndrome that may be identified in many of the ex-boarders who present for psychotherapy. Described in the *Diagnostic and Statistical Manual of Mental Disorders* under the heading of 'Post Traumatic Stress Disorder', symptoms of dissociation include:

Depersonalisation: Persistent or recurrent experiences of feeling detached from, and as if one were an outside observer of, one's mental processes or body (e.g. feeling as if one were in a dream; feeling a sense of unreality of self or body or of time moving slowly).
Derealisation: Persistent or recurrent experiences of unreality of surroundings (e.g. the world around the individual is experienced as unreal, dream-like, distant or distorted).[11]

Thus it is that a person may live an apparently normal life, with a job and family, and yet, as a result of the trauma, always feel as if they are not really participating in their own life. This was the case with Rose. The thread of captivity runs through Rose's story and so I will attend to it in some detail.

Rose – Boarding School Syndrome with dissociative symptoms

Rose was 38, and married with three children. She had been working in a part-time job as a receptionist in a hotel for the last ten years. She came to see me because she had felt numb and at a distance from herself all her adult life. Struggling to describe the sense of it, she used a number of metaphors. She said it felt as if she was living with a paper bag over her head, a bit as you do when you have had flu; she felt distant, as if residing in the back of her head, observing, but not really participating in life.

Although unaware of it, Rose was describing the symptoms of dissociation. Rose had first realised something was amiss when she was 17 and due to leave the boarding school she had attended since she was 11. She remembered thinking that she just did not feel right; it was a sense of not living her own life. Since then this feeling had always been with her. Rose was worried that there was something seriously wrong and had consulted numerous doctors. Her symptoms had been fully investigated and no physical cause found. She had had the mercury fillings in her teeth removed because she thought that the cause might be mercury poisoning. She had tried acupuncture and various other approaches, all to no avail.

Rose sought psychotherapy after reading an article in a newspaper about children of 8 who were sent to boarding school.[12] This was the same article that led Jackie, whom we met in Chapter 8, to seek psychotherapy. Rose began to wonder if her problem might be linked to her school experience. She came to see me in despair, thinking that nothing could help. Very quickly she began to recount her story, beginning with the momentous first day. In common with others, she thought she may be making a fuss about nothing and so she told her story casually and in a matter-of-fact way. I took it very seriously.

Rose – trauma one – the first day

The boarding school Rose had attended was a long way from her parents' home. Her mother, an only child, had been to boarding school herself – so when her daughter reached 11, it seemed automatic that she too was sent away. Rose described her dormitory, high up in the attic of the building. From there she had a view of the entrance to the school. She recalled watching, helplessly, from this window as her parents drove away on that first day, leaving her bewildered and bereft. This attic dormitory window was to become a significant metaphor for Rose's psychological state. It remained imprinted in her psyche even today. From here Rose would look wistfully out at the lit sitting rooms of the houses in the town. She would longingly imagine the ordinary lives of the people who lived there. The yearning was intensified because there was a group of daygirls in the school. Rose envied their uncomplicated life, returning each evening to their homes and parents. The attic was therefore a powerful image of being shut out of a life she could see others enjoying.

Grief and mourning

Rose was bereaved, although she would not have expressed it thus. There had been no way of protesting. The term *homesickness* is inadequate for such immense losses (as we saw in Chapter 9). In any other circumstances, for an 11-year-old child to be suddenly wrenched from all that is familiar would be recognised as deeply wounding. To a child, suddenly alone, the world feels very unsafe. For Rose, as for so many others, there were no words to express the emotional pain of her losses. This meant that there was no way of symbolising the experience. She was bereaved and captive in an alien environment. This contributes inarticulate terror to the moment of abandonment; the child is helpless and speechless.

Rose cried for many nights, as she put it, 'until there were no more tears left'. As in other forms of bereavement, a grieving period is appropriate. It is common for the bereaved to seek, yearn and long for the lost loved object/person, before eventually a form of acceptance is attained.[13] The losses incurred by the child sent away to school evoke a similar pattern of behaviour. The primary loss is of the mother, but the grief is also for the dependent state of childhood. It is the premature death of the child-self that is the most significant loss. This can never be regained because when the child returns home she or he is inevitably changed, no longer innocent and trusting but watchful and alert for rejection.

No one says to the child 'you are going to be imprisoned in this institution for the next x number of years', but this realisation gradually dawns. At first disbelieving, the child slowly comes to realise that her parents *really* are not returning. This unspeakable loss causes a psychological freezing: the child is literally 'lost for words'. An encapsulation of the self takes place and a protective shell is formed. This contributes in some cases to dissociation, which may be an aspect of Boarding School Syndrome. From then on the child lives communally but feels no longer known intimately by their parents. An unconscious but deep and permanent lack of trust of loving relationships may ensue.

Rose became vigilant; unconsciously, the anticipation of abandonment was ever present. We have seen that as an adult, the ex-boarder may, against their own desires, prematurely cut off from intimate relationships. It is an unconscious impulse to abandon the love object before she or he abandons you.[14] Even when physically present, the ex-boarder may maintain an unconscious emotional fallback position. She or he keeps an 'I can cope alone' mentality so that, if abandoned again, it is less likely to hurt. This contributes to the dissociative state and to the numbness that Rose described.

One of the definitions of trauma, as we saw earlier, is that the person is 'deeply distressed by a shocking event'. This is what I am describing here and therefore what is commonly given the rather bland name of *homesickness* by adults is a totally inadequate description. It is dismissed as a necessary ill, from which the child will soon recover, while it is actually a symptom of undiagnosed trauma.

The regime and punishment

In this captivity the child, like the prisoner, is subject to an inflexible regime: there are rules governing all aspects of behaviour. The day is timetabled and punctuated with bells or alarms. These denote the time to get up and wash: mealtimes, lessons, homework and prayers all adhere to a strict time. At night, bedtime and even lights out were, and sometimes still are, strictly timetabled. With uniforms, the dress code is strictly controlled. In the past when my patients were children, the food served had to be eaten whether or not the child liked it.

The rules in the schools attended by many of my respondents and patients were confusing for the child new to the school. They were rarely made explicit; rather they were imparted by tradition, passed from one generation of pupils to the next. Therefore it was not until the rules were infringed that they became known. The child might be punished without understanding the rule violated.

Rose – trauma two – breaking the rules

Rose shared the attic dormitory with five other girls. One evening after lights out these girls came out of their room and enjoyed playing in the corridor. However, this spontaneous fun was soon curtailed by senior girls whose role it was to police the corridor. Rose and her friends were punished. Separately they were taken into the senior common room where there were about ten or twelve older girls. Rose's punishment was that she was made to stand up and talk for five minutes on a random topic selected by the older girls. In this case it was the string of a tennis racket. Rose knew nothing of this topic and it was a frightening and totally humiliating experience.

If we consider this misdemeanour, it is evident that the younger girls had been excitedly playing as many 11 year olds would at a sleepover with their friends. But these little girls were not free; they were imprisoned and bound by a strict regime. The type of punishment is typical of that meted out in girls' schools and is based not on physical violence but on psychological control. Conformity is established through shame and humiliation.[15] Humiliated, Rose quickly learned that spontaneity was taboo. It is likely that an accumulation of such episodes led her to begin unconsciously to dissociate. In order to conform to the regime she became separated from her true spontaneous nature.

The rules in schools are passed on through the generations and often enforced by older children. However, when children are permitted to mete out punishments, bullying is tacitly condoned as a privilege of seniority. Sometimes these punishments are fair. However, there are times when older children take advantage of such privileges. For the younger children living in a school, the proximity of the regime and its bullies is never escaped. Captivity brings the victim into prolonged contact with the perpetrator and, as Judith Herman points out, this proximity creates a relationship based on coercive control.[16] The effect is the same whether the victim is taken captive entirely by force, as in the case of prisoners and hostages, or by a combination of force, intimidation and enticement. This latter is the fate of 'religious cult members, battered women and abused children'.[17] It also applies to the child in a boarding school. She or he is *coerced* to stay and *intimidated* by the rules of the system and by the threat of punishment.

However, the most confusing element here is *enticement*. The adults, parents and the staff all maintain that this is in the child's best interest. It is a privilege to attend this school. The child knows that his or her parents pay a lot of money for this 'very special' education and this makes it difficult to complain. The paradox at the heart of this problem is that child who hates or fears the school doubts his or her own perception and thinks that she or he has got it wrong. This is very evident in Colin Luke's film *The Making of Them*, which vividly conveys children trying to come to terms with the gap between their own perception and what their parents have told them.[18]

There is a more sinister element that a minority of children experience which presents itself in the guise of being treated as 'special'. They may be selected by a more powerful child or an adult and favoured, but the affection comes at a price.[19] This may be extreme control enforced by threats of withdrawal of love or some other more sinister peril. As Herman puts it, 'in captivity the psychology of the victim is shaped by the actions and beliefs of the perpetrator.'[20] The child's psychology in these cases is certainly influenced by the actions of the perpetrator. There is added torment and confusion when the perpetrator coerces the child into compliance with sexual abuse. This 'special relationship' may blight the whole time the child spends in the school. Living in such close proximity, it only takes one other child or one predatory adult to make the life of the child a misery. It is worse at night when the smaller children are exposed to these perpetrators.

The trust that parents invest in the school may be abused. Parents mean well and are usually vigilant in defending their children, but in this situation they abdicate parental responsibility in favour of unknown adults. These adults now become the most powerful people in the life of the child. In some cases a good teacher may make the whole experience bearable but in others the child lives a troubled life. Once they leave the school, parents have no real sense of how their children are treated in their absence.

Rose – trauma three – the bid for freedom

The fantasy of escape often accompanies imprisonment. If an opportunity to run away presents itself, it is sometimes taken. Rose made a bid for freedom and this brought her sharply up against the invisible walls of the institution.

The accumulation of distressing situations built up until, one day, when Rose and another girl found the opportunity, they ran away. It was an occasion of sports events between the schoolhouses, so the situation was more relaxed than usual. The school was in the centre of a town and Rose remembered walking out of the school grounds and out of town, along a dark country lane. They were not quite 12 and had no clear plan of where they were going. A police car drew up and its occupants asked where they were going. Her companion replied: 'We are running away.' They were then taken in the car to the police station. There they were shown a cell with a hard wooden bed in it and they were warned that this is where they would end up if they ran away again. The headmistress was called and she fetched them in her car.

When they returned to the school the other girls greeted them with a wall of silence. They had been disappointed because the sports event had been cancelled while the search for Rose and her friend was mounted. Blamed for this, they were 'sent to Coventry' by the other girls in their house. This means they were ostracised by the other girls, who ignored their presence and refused to talk to them. Rose did not remember for how long, but it was several days at least. It was in this way that they learned that it was useless to try to escape.

This bid for freedom led to the terrifying threat of a real police cell. That was the final straw. The innocence of the spontaneous child was crushed and it was substituted with a distorted self-image. Rose began to sense that she must be a very bad person. It is likely the dissociation with which she presented in psychotherapy began as a result of these accumulated events. It may have been at this point that she became psychologically distanced, feeling she was not really participating in her own life.

The headmistress told Rose that she had told her parents, but her parents did not come to the school, nor does she recall them ever discussing it with her. So it seemed to Rose that this big event in her life made no impression on her parents. (It may be that the headmistress told the parents that it had been dealt with and not to come.) However, this event contributed to a sense of resignation and hopelessness. The girl with whom she ran away was taken away from the school a year later, so perhaps her parents responded to her unhappiness. Continuing in the school, Rose now knew that there was no escape; she was there for as long as her parents decreed. Perhaps this failed bid for freedom was the final straw in this realisation for Rose. She had more courage and determination than most, so she had attempted to liberate herself. But this seems to have been the moment when she gave up resisting her fate.

The drawing

As we saw with Theo, there are times when illustrations facilitate the deepening of a narrative, giving weight to experience. Rose told her story lightly; she was distant from it. It took some time for her to begin to own its deeper emotional impact. Thinking about how small her own children were at 11 helped her to begin at last to recognise the gravity of what had happened to her. So did my response. Rose told me that she had been shocked when I took the account of her attempted escape very seriously. During the following week she had continued to think about it in a more deeply affective way, realising that the police cell had been a terrifying threat. I suggested that she might find it helpful to draw it and show me what it was like. This she did and the result is a simple line drawing, a diagram of the memory of a space seen just once (Figure 10.1). However its impact had continued to affect her throughout her life.

Figure 10.1 The Police Cell.

Not unlike the first map that Theo drew, this is a simple drawing with felt tip pen on white paper. On one side of the picture is the hard wooden bed and on the other side an empty room. The drawing may not look powerful but its impact on the artist was evidently very strong. It was drawn in order to show me, but in drawing it, Rose showed herself the bleakness of this warning. Escape meant the threat of a police cell and the risk of an even more lonely bed than the one in the dormitory. She was warned that if she tried to escape again she would find herself in a real prison. This confirmed the deeply unconscious sense that she was imprisoned in school because she was bad.

Looking at the picture after she had drawn it, Rose seemed rather satisfied. It seemed that she saw the previously internal image from a different perspective: it was now external. In this way, she was distanced a little from an image that had unconsciously haunted her all her life. As an adult Rose could still feel the emotions of the child but she could also begin to process them.

Repetition

Part of the trauma of boarding school is its repetition. After the shock and distress of separation there may be weekend visits by parents. However, most schools at this time discouraged parental visits because 'they only upset the child'. Then at the end of the first term the eagerly awaited vacation comes. Most parents arrive on time to fetch their children home. However, some parents were always late. One man remembers that at the end of each term he was always the last to be fetched. He recalled waiting for his parents at the end of the school drive with his bags and his younger brother, long after all the other children had left.

It was similar for Rose; at the end of term she too was always the last to be collected. The pattern was that, at the end of term, the girls whose parents lived in the UK would be collected on a Wednesday evening. Rose's mother was afraid to drive at night, so she would collect Rose on Thursday morning. This was the day when the girls from abroad left for the airport. Everyone, including Rose, awoke very early on these days. The other girls left, and Rose was alone in the school. She wandered the empty corridors, watching from her window for her mother's car to appear. Eventually, but long after all the other girls had left, her mother arrived. She said now, 'If it were my child I would be there on the Wednesday no matter what.' Tellingly, her children attend day schools.

Some children whose parents lived abroad did not return home. They stayed with relatives, or friends of their parents or even, in some cases, spent the vacation in the school. For them abandonment was total. Even for the child who returned to home, the school holidays emphasised their powerlessness in this cycle of abandonment and captivity. The child who went home imagined the ordeal was now over; the parents would realise how it was and so there would be no return. This was rarely consciously stated but it felt like rescue. The child may or may not have complained about the situation. Once again finding the words to do so is difficult for some children. Others complained and were met with the parents' rationalisations, which included such phrases as: 'It will be OK when you are there'; 'I used to feel like that too but you get used to it.'

For most children it is exciting to return home for a month each at Christmas and Easter, and for three months in the summer. Then for some it may be devastating to be returned to the school at the beginning of the new term. The dread of the return may loom over much of the vacation. A terrible feeling of gloom descends when packing begins for the next term. Some children are re-traumatised each time they return to the school, crying and clinging to their mother at the separation. Most finally adapt to this pattern; it becomes part of the resignation in the face of their powerlessness.

There are, however, lasting repercussions to this repetition of loss. It unconsciously replays in adult relationships, particularly in a marriage or lifelong partnership. It manifests in anticipation of rejection and fear of abandonment by later attachment figures. It is rarely conscious. The beloved has the power to leave at any time, and this sense of impermanence may colour behaviour and lead to emotional withdrawal.

Rose – trauma four – the return to school

Rose knew that after the brief respite of the first school holiday she would have to return to the school. She described a fantasy that she shared with her younger sister: Rose imagined her parents taking her back to the school but then, instead of staying in the school, she would secrete herself in the boot of the car unseen. Oblivious to this, her parents would drive back home. Then, still unseen, she would creep out of the car and into the cupboard under the stairs in her parents' house. Her sister would smuggle food to her and so she would live.

Such a fantasy shows just how unhappy a child may be, even in an ordinary school. The adults in this school were not abusive in any overt sense, but Rose had no sense that they cared about her. This fantasy is another example of retreat. Rose was trying to shrink so that she would fit into a tiny place, hidden away where she could reside, secretly and safely. It was preferable to live in a cupboard rather than return to school. This fantasy has a counterpart in her psychological reality. She reduced the space she inhabited, in a psychological sense, to a very small space that would make no ripples. When she was afraid or lonely at school she was not really there.

Narrative and memory

In psychotherapy the task is to create meaning from apparently incomprehensible unhappiness. Rose did not at first give credence to the depth of significance of the broken attachments and traumatic captivity of her story. Even as she recounted the stories there was little emotion; it was as if she did not really believe them. It was only as analysis deepened that the story changed to an emotionally congruent narrative.

Rose began to understand that the incidents that she had recounted had been traumatic. Separated from the life around her, Rose had watched from the attic room as others lived their lives. Her innocent play had led to humiliating punishment. In her bid for freedom she had been thwarted and left with the threat of a police cell. In the mental cupboard under the stairs, she hid away from the world. These memories and the associated images had led to psychological encapsulation. There was nowhere to go but inwards; it was a symbolic retreat into an unborn state, a womb-like place where, not living her own life, she would be hidden and safe. Rose's initial sense of living in a tiny place in the back of her head seemed to be linked to these word pictures. Rose began to consider that it was possible that the origins of her sense of feeling distanced from her own life might reside in these tales.

Time

It was as if Rose's life was on hold and time stood still. The rupture in the life story of the child in a boarding school is typical of the effects of captivity. Captivity disrupts the sense of time.[21] Imprisoned in boarding school, the child lives suspended in timelessness, longing to return home but powerless to do so, often counting the days until the end of her sentence. The loss of liberty means that there is also a loss of traditional family markers of the passing of time. Anniversaries punctuate the story of a life, but when family birthdays occur during term time there is no celebration and so they are unacknowledged. For some children, even their own birthdays passed by unmarked if they took place during term time.

A child depends on the memories carried by, and shared with, attachment figures to reflect a sense of continuity of being and of belonging to a community. Shared memories and the stories attached to them are indicators of intimate family connection. Without these shared memories the child is separated from the continuity of his or her young existence. It is therefore hardly surprising that when as an adult he or she comes to tell the tale, it may lack a narrative flow. This may be why it is sometimes difficult for the ex-boarder to remember the sequence of events.

Rose drew another picture to try to show the sense she had of living in the back of her head. The feeling was difficult to describe; it seemed as if she was still a captive in that attic room. At home she painted a picture of the way it felt to be living as a tiny glimmer in the back of her head. She brought it in to her next session. The feeling was graphically depicted.

Figure 10.2 The Attic Room.

Here, painted on a small piece of paper, is a black arrow-shaped building in a dark forest. This darkest area is barely discernible in this reproduction. On the right at the top of the building is one source of yellow light, here shown as a white triangle. This was her sense of herself.

Post-traumatic stress and dissociation

Rose's sense feeling distant from her own life is a classic symptom of dissociation. Whilst Rose did not have the sudden flashbacks characteristic of PTSD, she felt unreal and as if she were not living her own life. That is a feature of post-traumatic stress.

In the case of imprisonment, there is an absence of loving relationships. Associated with this, there is no one with whom the child feels she can be appropriately angry. There is no one to blame. It is common for a child to experience a sense of impotent rage at times but, in her captivity, Rose had no outlet for anger. She could not even think that she was angry with her parents. After all, this must be in her best interest. In common with many other captives in boarding school, there was no way to express anger. Art, music and drama may offer ways of expressing such split-off emotions. Sport is another – but for those who did not have these opportunities or were not good at sport, that outlet was thwarted. Another way of expressing such feelings is becoming a bully, but Rose was not a bully. Thus the child may turn their anger inwards; this is often the case for girls, whose punishments we have seen are based on humiliation. Such punishments can lead to self-blame and in extreme case self-abuse.

Bettelheim analysed the psychology of his fellow inmates imprisoned by the Nazis in concentrations camps. He suggests that turning aggression inward kept the prisoner out of conflict with the SS but led to 'increased masochistic, passive-dependent and childlike attitudes'.[22] Erving Goffman analysed the ways that inmates learn to adapt to and so live in institutions. When discussing prisons and psychiatric hospitals, he gave us the term the *total institution*. As inmates adapt to the inevitable routine of the prison and realise the hopelessness of fighting the system, they give up and apparently comply. In the process of giving up autonomy, an aspect of the self is relinquished to the institution.[23] In her personal account, *The Last Asylum*, Barbara Taylor gives a sense of the community of a psychiatric hospital and the ways in which this too is a form of imprisonment, as well as respite.[24] Children in boarding school have a similar experience; they apparently adapt to the system whilst keeping a part of the self hidden and so protected.

Conclusion

In boarding school the child is imprisoned for a significant part of his or her childhood. In most cases there are no bars, but the child is nonetheless powerless to escape. Some ex-boarders, like Rose, tell stories of having run away only to be returned to the school. Many – especially in girls' schools – were shamed in the process. A few ran away, and their parents understood and did not return them, but they are a small minority.

In this and the previous two chapters, I have identified the sequence of events that contribute to the trauma. We have seen the selective amnesia that sometimes occurs in relation to this wound and how the losses amount to a form of bereavement. In addition to this, for some children there is the shocking realisation that they are deprived of liberty. The powerlessness is compounded by its repetition when the child returns to the school each term. This trio of traumatic events completes the psychological rupture, creating a dissociated state which becomes part of Boarding School Syndrome.

Notes

1. Herman, J. (1992/1997) *Trauma and Recovery: The Aftermath of Violence From Domestic Abuse to Political Terror*, New York: Basic Books, p. 33.
2. Van der Kolk, B. A., (1996) 'Trauma and memory', in *Traumatic Stress*, Van der Kolk, B. A., McFarlane, A. C., & Weisaeth, L. (eds), London: Guilford Press. p. 283.
3. Boarding Schools Association (2013) www.boarding.org.uk/.
4. Pasternak, A. (2013) 'Boarding school – it's a glorified sleepover', *The Telegraph* (13 February) www.telegraph.co.uk/education/9074666/Boarding-school-its-a-glorified-sleepover.html.
5. *Mark Lawson Talks To . . .* (2013) John le Carre interview broadcast on BBC Four, 18 November.
6. Fry, S. (2004) *Moab Is My Washpot*, London: Arrow Books, p. 413.
7. Okely, J. (1996) *Own or Other Culture*, London: Routledge.
8. Ibid.
9. Herman (1992/1997), op. cit., p. 74.
10. Ibid., p. 27.
11. American Psychiatric Association. (2013). *Diagnostic and Statistical Manual of Mental Disorders*, fifth edition, Washington, DC: American Psychiatric Association, p. 272.
12. Williams, S. (2013) 'What's it like to go away to school at 8?' *The Sunday Times Magazine* (31 August).
13. Murray Parkes, C. (1972) *Bereavement: Studies of Grief in Adult Life*, Harmondsworth: Penguin Books.
14. Schaverien, J. (2002) *The Dying Patient in Psychotherapy: Desire, Dreams and Individuation*, New York: Palgrave Macmillan, pp. 85–86.
15. Okely (1996), op. cit.
16. Herman (1992/1997), op. cit., p. 74.
17. Ibid., pp. 74–75.
18. *The Making of Them* (1994) Directed by Colin Luke (film). Broadcast on BBC 4 http://youtube/2uRr77vju8U.
19. This was described in the case of Caldecott School, where boys were made to feel special by those who sexually abused them. Brown, A., & Bennett, 'Pupils break silence over prep school paedophiles', and Norfolk, A., 'A life ruined by Caldecott paedophile', both in *The Times* (19 December 2013).
20. Herman (1992/1997), op. cit., p. 75.
21. Ibid., p. 89.
22. Bettelheim, B. (1960/1986) *The Informed Heart*, London: Peregrine Books, p. 131.
23. Goffman, E. (1961/1991) *Asylums: Essays on the Social Situation of Mental Patients and Other Inmates*, Harmondsworth, Penguin Social Sciences.
24. Taylor, B. (2014) *The Last Asylum*, London: Penguin, Hamish Hamilton.

Chapter 11

Children of Empire

Exile: a person who lives away from their native country, either from choice or compulsion.
The New Oxford Dictionary of English[1]

> But Delhi: New Delhi! Isn't it splendid? If only I hadn't got to go to school ... The railway station, like other architectural monuments of the British Raj, was a mixture of tawdry provincialism and Imperial domesticity, which even in retrospect can evoke in me nostalgic feelings of great poignancy. I came in time to believe that these feelings were the substitute for what others called 'homesickness'. But I had no home for which I could feel sick – only people and things. Thus, when I found myself alone in the playground of the Preparatory School in England where I kissed my mother a dry-eyed goodbye, I could see, above the hedge which separated me from her and the road which was the boundary of the wide world itself, her hat go bobbing up and down like some curiously wrought millinery cake carried on a wave of green hedge. And then it was gone. Numbed, Stupefied, I found myself staring into a bright, alert face.
>
> Wilfred Bion[2]

In this brief passage the psychoanalyst Wilfred Bion captures, with minimal drama, a sense of the loss of the place from which he came – then, the abrupt moment of bereavement of the child who does not know where his mother has gone. Now Bion was a child in exile, 'numbed and stupefied', left to the mercy of other similar boys, but slightly older, one with the 'alert face'. Like the other children from abroad whom I will consider in this chapter, he was now homeless.

The homeless child

Writing of the homeless state as an aspect of the creation of Boarding School Syndrome, I wrote, 'For those whose parents live abroad the child is effectively homeless.'[3] In this chapter I will develop this point.

Sophie is 29. She sits in the chair, in floods of tears. She is a professional woman but in this moment she is also a small girl, crying profusely, as she recounts her experience in a boarding school to which she was taken by her parents when she was 12. Her father was in the army and posted around the world, mostly in European countries, so in order that she had a good education it was decided that she should stay in the UK at school. Now she is talking about how alone she felt then and later, at University how ill-equipped she was emotionally for being alone in the adult world. She was devastated by the loss of her mother and still misses her. She feels vulnerable and finds it very difficult to cope in her job.

The tradition of boarding in school has been common practice for centuries. However, in considering the psychological impact, there has been little differentiation of the impact on children from diverse backgrounds who came together in these schools. For children who continued to reside in their home country, the sense of abandonment was often overwhelming. Consider then the losses suffered by those who travelled from their homes in other parts of the world. Children whose parents lived in the UK usually maintained a link with their home; most were visited at half terms and returned home in the holidays; those from abroad often had neither of these experiences.

Many from this background began boarding as young as 5 or 6. Sophie did not begin boarding until she was 12. Her parents were in the army and lived abroad, moving home every two years. Prior to boarding school Sophie moved with them and never stayed in schools long enough to make lasting friendships or to feel a sense of belonging. Her home became her parents and sister. Then, when she was boarding, during half terms and the shorter school holidays she would stay either at school or with relatives. In the longer holidays she would join her parents, staying with relatives in the UK or travelling to where they were living at the time. A consequence of their transient life was that, in their absence, Sophie could not picture her parents in a place called 'home'. She had no mental picture of where in the world her mother was, and this meant that she was homeless. This initial loss is compounded by its repetition: as the pattern of term time at school and holidays at home becomes established, the child is unable to settle in either place. Even as an adult, Sophie lived in a state of psychological exile.

Children whose early years were spent in Asia, Africa or other countries of the British Empire suffered additional losses. Francis Grier movingly conveys the nuances of this grief. Many of the young children sent from these countries to boarding school at 8 had been raised by servants drawn from the local community, and these became their first significant attachment figures. Often they would speak to the child in their own language, and so the child may have learned the local language before English. English was 'reserved for formal conversation with their parents and was often spoken with more difficulty'.[4] Therefore, when that child moved to Britain, he or she might find the language strange, as well as the culture. The children looked Western but they were acculturated to their foreign homeland. Added to the strangeness was the often permanent loss of this first attachment figure. Jane Gardam in her novel *Old Filth* gives a vivid portrayal of this.[5]

The mention in psychotherapy of 'the servant who looked after me' or my 'Ayah' or 'Nanny' often belies the importance of this person in the child's early life. When the child went away to school these servants may have been dismissed and so, in some cases, were never seen again. Therefore the traumatic losses incurred by those who travelled from the British Empire included, in addition to their family, the whole environment to which they were accustomed.

Children of exotic locations

David, now in his late fifties, had been 7 when he lost his home, his family and the servant who cared for him. In the first session he described this immense rupture.

David had been born in the UK and as a baby had moved with his parents and older brother to an island in the Caribbean, where he grew up. He described it vividly: everything was brightly coloured, the sun always shone, he never wore shoes, and he was free to come and go as he pleased. This was his home. Then, when he was 7 years old, suddenly all that changed when his parents brought him and his brother to prep school in England. Described to him as 'home', England felt very far from home – inhospitable, drab and grey. He felt cold, a sensation previously unknown to him. After a few days staying with his parents in his grandparents' house, he was taken to a small preparatory school. His parents bade him farewell and disappeared from his life, returning to their sunny island home. The boy left at the school felt abandoned. He and his brother were separated to live in different schoolhouses and so rarely saw each other. (This was a common practice in the prep schools of the day and therefore having a sibling in the school made little difference to the sense of isolation.) He could not have articulated it in this way, but the losses were multiple. He lost his parents, but possibly most significant was the combined loss of the Caribbean woman who had cared for him and the familiar sunshine. The rupture in this child's life was traumatic. However, this was presented to him as a normal course of events. What was not recognised was that, although Britain was his parents' home, this cold country was not his home. Grier vividly conveys these sensory deprivations:

> [These children] . . . lost whichever country they came from, separated from the sensual world in which they had been unconsciously immersed: sounds, sights, light and smells. From their point of view, a grimly Spartan boarding school in a rainy, grey northern European country often formed a brutal, unthinkable contrast.[6]

Children arriving in a boarding school peopled by strangers are alienated. They may cry at first. The children anticipate the familiar caring response which has up till now been the response to tears. However, the response – if there is one – is not as before. Grier writes: 'even well-meaning, affectionate and concerned adults would still be the "wrong" ones, from the child's perspective' and that is the same with 'a genuinely concerned older boy. . . . [He] would still be "the wrong boy", so his efforts at succour would typically be rebuffed.'[7] In this state children soon learn that crying is useless. It brings no rewards and it often brings censure. There was no opportunity for proper mourning of the people and places so profoundly missed. Thus the grief was repressed and eventually lost to conscious awareness.

When working with adults in psychotherapy we attend to the particulars of their childhood losses and, if there is trauma, differentiate its layers. Sophie and David were from different generations but, despite the obvious differences, they were both sent to school from abroad and were essentially homeless for a significant part of their childhood. Sophie, raised by her parents in Europe, had different losses from David, who was raised by a nanny in the Caribbean. These two exemplify stories told to me by many others, both within the consulting room and in interviews.

The tradition of sending 'home'

In the early centuries of the British Empire, boarding schools offered a solution to some very real problems. The popularity of the public schools was in part due to the wealth created by Empire, as we saw in Chapter 2, but in addition to the aspirations of the middle classes, there was necessity. Many men were posted abroad and their wives usually accompanied them. They took up roles in the government of British colonies or were sent by the Church as missionaries; others were employed in British companies, the military or the diplomatic service. This posed the problem of what to do with their families. Brendon, in her extensive research for the *Children of the Raj*, found evidence that the fear of diseases, which were rife in these hot climates, played a major part in the often painful decisions made by parents to send their children 'home'.[8] Children were particularly susceptible to infection. In addition, in many of these outposts, there was a lack of available education.

Therefore it was primarily for their protection that children were 'sent home' to be looked after by extended family. Most attended boarding schools sometimes subsidised by the employer, but parents funded others. For many parents, especially mothers, letting their children go was a huge sacrifice. In the patriarchal culture of the time there were few other options. Few could afford to travel these great distances regularly, so they knew they would not see their children for many years. Brendon describes how children, sometimes aged no more than 3 or 4, but more often at around 7 or 8, were sent 'back home'. This entailed long and frequently hazardous boat journeys across the world. Sometimes their mother or an ayah accompanied them, but many travelled alone, overseen only by the staff of the shipping company. It was not uncommon for children to become ill or even die during the course of the journey.[9] Thus, in the late eighteenth century, the tradition of sending children 'back home' to boarding schools became established. Some parents kept their daughters with them whilst their sons were sent to the UK. The life of one such daughter is well documented in the autobiography of Pearl Buck, whose American missionary parents lived in China. This gives a real sense of the hazards endured by families living in foreign lands.

Pearl Buck, who became a prolific author and Nobel Prize winner, was born in 1892.[10] The daughter of missionary parents from the midwestern USA, she was born and raised in China. Her family story is an example of the dilemmas faced by missionary parents. Pearl was the fifth child of seven born to her parents in China. Three of her siblings died before she was born and her younger brother died in infancy. Pearl, her eldest brother and a younger sister survived. As Hilary Spurling, her biographer, puts it:

> The siblings who surrounded Pearl in [her] early memories were dreamlike. . . . Her older sisters, Maude and Edith, and her brother Arthur had all died young in the course of six years from dysentery, cholera and malaria, respectively. Edgar, the oldest, ten years of age when Pearl was born, stayed long enough to teach her to walk, but a year or two later he was gone too.[11]

Edgar survived but, at the age of 10, he was sent to the USA to be educated and she did not see him again until he was 20. This family's loss of several children from disease was not unusual at the time. Therefore it is not surprising that, to protect them, children were sent home to the country of their parents' origin. It is evident that for these families boarding schools served an important purpose; as well as educating the children, they looked after them for most of the year.

Pearl and her sister, who was six years younger, were not sent home but stayed with their parents. Consequently they settled where their parents were settled and moved with them when they had to leave their homes. This was often under terrifying circumstances. As a small child, Pearl wandered alone, making friends amongst the local population, becoming fluent in their dialect and culture, so that for the rest of her life she felt more Chinese than American. Her life's work grew out of her understanding of the two cultures and this enabled her to write articles and stories that created a bridge between East and the West. She introduced the real life of the ordinary Chinese people, with whom she had lived, to an international audience. Her best-known novel, *The Good Earth*, was published in 1931 and greeted with worldwide acclaim, winning its author a Pulitzer Prize in 1932.[12] In 1938 Pearl Buck became the first American woman to win the Nobel Prize for literature (the second was Toni Morrison in 1993).[13] Throughout her life Pearl Buck continued to bring her understanding of China to the Western world.

Her parents, with all the problems that beset them, were always a presence in her life. It is perhaps worth speculating that Pearl – who remained close to her mother, despite all the terror and anxiety of living the precarious life of missionaries in China at that time – faired better than her brother, who was sent to the USA at 10. She did not have to deny the language or the culture in which she grew up. Her identification with the ordinary Chinese people, developed during her childhood, contributed to the depth of her writings and the international acclaim they later attained.

The alienated child

Once they arrived in Britain, the children who were sent home were entrusted to the care of a guardian appointed by their parents. This might be an unmarried sibling of one of the parents, a distant relative or a friend. It was something of a lottery because the experience of the child depended on how the appointed guardians viewed their task. Whilst some children were well cared for, others – girls as well as boys – whose appointed guardians resented them were treated with disdain, disregard or even, in some cases, cruelty. There were some children who had nowhere else to go, and so spent their vacations in their boarding schools, living there for years at a time with little or no contact with their parents or any other relatives.[14]

This tradition continued into the twentieth century. Today, in the twenty-first century, children of the British military, diplomats and those working for companies abroad are still sent 'home' to school. Today the threat of ill health is rarely the reason and the emphasis is on the stability of their education. Well-meaning parents seek the best education possible for their children without the constant disruption of having to move from school to school as the parents' jobs demand. The landscape is changing and, as the demand for boarding from British families wanes, a new group has emerged from the wider global community. Children come to the UK from their homes in Africa, China, Japan, Russia, Ukraine, India and other countries where parents aspire to a traditional British education.[15] These children from abroad are not 'sent home', because they are not of British origin, rather they are 'sent away'. Many are ill-equipped emotionally to make the transition. The loss of their parents is sometimes compounded, at first, by their lack of fluent English. Eventually, as they become immersed in the language and culture, some lose contact with their parents. In some cases the parents do not speak English and this emphasises the dislocation. The pressure on these young people is immense, as they carry the weight of the expectations of parents who do not understand the system. Some are expected to achieve no less than 100 per cent in their examinations and there is tremendous shame associated with anything less. The disruption to the sense of well-being and psychological health of these children is considerable.

There is little question that the schools have become kinder places and beatings are no longer an acceptable method of discipline. Today, understanding from genuinely caring teachers and counsellors is an important part of their pastoral care. Many children adapt well, especially those who first attend a boarding school at the age of 13. However, a number of children still suffer greatly from the separation from their families and loss of their home. The transition in culture and the long distance from home evokes sometimes prolonged homesickness, which we will now call by its proper name: mourning. A boarding school may provide a caring environment but it cannot provide individual attachment figures to foster the reciprocity of emotional intimacy.

Local nannies and servants

In this chapter we see the immensity of the lifelong effects of the loss of home. Sophie, who grew up in European countries and was raised mainly by her mother, had moved so often that she had no sense of a place called 'home'. As Bion indicates, in the passage with which we began this chapter: 'I had no home for which I could feel sick – only people and things.'[16] David did have a sense of a place called 'home' but he was culturally, as well as physically, dislocated from it at an early age. In common with many others, he never again had intimate contact with his parents; for him people could never again be relied on. Moreover, he permanently lost the colourful world in which he had spent his first years and, most significantly, the family servant who had been his primary attachment figure.

Cathy Kaplinsky gives a very moving account of the lifelong effects of the bond formed by one child and the woman who cared for him.[17] She recounts the moving story of a friend of hers, an exiled white South African man. It begins with a recurring dream he had of a little black boy of about 4 years old playing on a beach in a particular area of South Africa. He was mystified by this dream until he came to realise that this was where, as a child, he had spent summers between the ages of 3 and 7. His mother was distant and at times unkind to him. It was Rosie, a Xhosa servant of the family, who took care of him and who loved him unconditionally during these years. This memory had remained unconscious until between the ages of 35 and 40 he had this dream repeatedly. The dream led him to begin to understand his lifelong unconscious attachment to Rosie and the land where she lived. He came to realise that the boy in the dream was himself as a child, and that he had longed to be Rosie's child. Raised in white Cape Town, with its racist attitudes, there was no way he could consciously own this attachment. He is quoted:

> I was subject at home and at school to extremely strong racist conditioning. I simply could not own a Xhosa woman as my mother. It would have been unthinkable in the world in which I grew up. All the black part of me that had come into being in the Ciskei became inadmissible.[18]

Forty years later, he returned to South Africa and visited Rosie, and thanked her for the love she gave him. He wrote:

> She knew perfectly well how important it had been. . . . I share all the usual reasons for hating apartheid but I have my own additional one . . . it prevented me from owning the most important part of my childhood by making it inadmissible. I could not own the central Black part of myself. I don't have the dream anymore. It must be because I can own the reality.[19]

This is one man's story. It is telling that Rosie had never forgotten him. Whilst the little children who were nurtured by local women were wrenched from their carers, those carers too were affected. Their part of the story is seldom told, so it is refreshing that, in Kaplinsky's paper, we get a real sense of Rosie. Similarly in the story of Pearl Buck we get a sense of the importance of Wang Amah to the whole family.[20] Often the local women were a great support to the lonely mothers of the children who went to boarding schools. Their roles were often unsung. When eventually the families moved on, presumably emotional losses were incurred for the adults as well as the children. Many mothers struggled but felt that it was their role to support their husbands in their work for the Empire.

In the early years children are dependent on those who care for them and it can feel very unsafe to lose such a primary attachment figure. Parents may minimise the loss of a nanny or servant, perhaps not noticing the significance of the bond or thinking it is better not to talk about it. If it is not discussed children have no way to process the loss, no words to help understand. In the absence of adult intervention, children are unable to symbolise. They lack the ability to transform unprocessed emotion into words, and so they are unable to metabolise the experience. Thus, such deep losses become unconscious and only, much later, surface in psychotherapy or, in the case of Kaplinsky's friend, in dreams.

Marriage and the idealisation of women

With this in mind I turn again to David and his transition from the Caribbean to a British prep school. David came into analysis in profound distress after the break-up of his marriage. In his fifties and a successful businessman, he was deeply depressed without understanding why. He had seen a counsellor regularly for the past year and had formed a significant attachment to her. This had been a limited contract and, although it seemed that this had been made clear from the start, when it ended it felt to him as if, quite suddenly, she had told him that she could no longer see him. For David this was devastating because it confirmed what he already knew, that women were unreliable. Although he was not conscious of it, this desertion had reawakened the anguish of his abandonment at school more than forty years previously and the associated permanent loss of his mother and nanny. He told of being brought to school in the UK and of the loss of his counsellor in the same session. Thus, unconsciously, he put together these two losses. The transference to the counsellor was multifaceted, as is often the case with such early, disrupted attachments.

However, David was no longer a helpless victim. He was now an adult and his story was tempered with the misogyny of one who had been betrayed. This is an unconscious reaction in some men who have experienced their abandonment as total. It became evident in his discourse that whilst idealising the counsellor he felt persecuted by his ex-wife. For a while when he talked of her, he appeared consumed with hate. He was in the grip of two poles of experience: on one hand idealisation and on the other denigration of women, which is an unconscious pattern very common in Boarding School Syndrome. Unless it becomes conscious this influences relationships in later life, with women being idealised and then powerfully denigrated. Previously I wrote about this in relation to boarding school:

> It is not uncommon for boys who are sent to boarding school at an early age to yearn for an idealised mother. The separation is a rupture that came too early. Later, in adolescence, separation from the internalised mother . . . is not possible because there has been too little actual closeness. From then on all women seem tantalising; offering the hope of the idealised love object but also the constant threat of abandonment. This contributes to a pattern of women being idealised and then denigrated – loved and hated.[21]

This was how it was for David. He desired and hated women in equal measure. He longed for a close intimate relationship but knew that women always let him down, so he would find ways to leave them first, emotionally if not actually. The problem with the counsellor was that she had left him, and this replayed his greatest fear.

It became evident that this pattern had led to the breakdown of the most important adult relationship of his life, his marriage. He had married young and had clung to his wife, who seemed to offer salvation. She came from a big family, which welcomed him in. However, his idealisation meant that he only later began to know her. He was distressed to discover that sometimes she became angry, which he immediately took as personal rejection. He could not tolerate uncertainty or her changes in mood, so he withdrew or else savagely attacked her verbally, feeling that, as he put it, 'she was asking for it.' It is likely that she was indeed 'asking for "something"'. Perhaps without putting it into words, she was actually asking for a relationship, one in which she was recognised as a person who also had needs. This was doomed to fail because she was, in the end, not the ideal mother/lover that he craved. There was, of course, also her contribution to this dynamic. It is likely that, at first, she was attracted by David's vulnerability, only later experiencing his withdrawal when she tried to get emotionally close.

Misogyny characterised by both fear and hatred of women is often hidden behind the idealisation of them. At the same time as appearing socially confident, the ex-boarder may find intimate engagement threatening. This is well known in couples' psychotherapy where one partner, often the man, attended boarding school and is unable to talk about his feelings. He may make deeply dependent relationships and then suddenly emotionally or actually abandon the loved person. The partner may experience this cutting off from emotional need as a violent attack or abrupt rejection. This often replays in the transference and may lead to the sudden termination of analysis when the rage associated with dependency begins to surface.[22] [23]

This was the process in David's marriage. Grier theorises this from the point of view of a couples' therapist. He describes a couple where both were affected by boarding school. The man was sent from abroad to school at a young age, displaying all the idealisation and fear of intimacy that we are discussing. At the same time his wife had envied her brothers who went to boarding school, while she remained at home. Thus both were impacted by this tradition and envied the other. The problem is, as Grier points out, 'a man with this background may develop serious inhibitions in loving and trusting a woman, intimately and sexually.' As a couples' therapist, he confirms the point that 'the idealisation of women, is accompanied by a distancing or avoidance of them in practice, usually unconscious, usually denied.' He also points out that there is another group: 'men who flit from idealised woman to idealised woman in a series of intensely invested erotic encounters but flee the woman when the first sign of any ambivalence emerges'.[24] This is an outcome of a childhood where those love objects of infancy and early childhood were irrevocably lost. It is important that this was not due to an unavoidable situation, but it was their parents' choice to send them away. The boy, too soon expected to be a man, may never fully catch up; a part of him remains forever a 'lost boy' as in *Peter Pan*, James Barrie's attuned metaphor for boarding school.[25]

The encapsulated self

The child in this lonely situation has to protect him- or herself and does so through withdrawal from emotional reactions. This is the 'encapsulation of the self', which occurs, as it did with David (and with Theo in Chapters 4–7), through an unconscious form of splitting.[26] In order to keep the parents good, the child has to do violence to his own psyche. This is similar to what Duffell has called 'the strategic survival personality',[27] which I see as more conscious and therefore more likely to be available to be recalled later. This is when the child consciously works out that in order to get on in the environment he or she has to be strategic. One of my respondents, who had been subject to anti-Semitic bullying in his boarding school, put it thus: 'I realised what was needed; I had to behave in certain ways. I had to play the game their way and keep my true feelings hidden.' This is strategic thinking, often from a very young person, and it may continue to affect relationships in later life.

It would be logical for the child in this situation to conclude that his parents hate him; how else is a child supposed to make sense of such a violent separation from all that is familiar? This is the double bind in which the child is trapped. As Duffell has pointed out: 'If my parents love me they would not send me away – therefore this must be good for me.' The corollary is a kind of unconscious rationale that keeps the parents good: 'If I don't like it and my parents have invested so much in it, I must be bad.'[28] This is very typical of the type of emotional tangle of psychological splitting described by Klein and of which Grier writes with regard to the child in boarding school. The child has to employ the defences of 'denial, splitting, omnipotence and even mania'. In order to survive, he has to forego the normal 'fluctuations between envy, jealousy, triumph, greed, happiness, sadness and contentment,' experienced by a child in a family.[29]

The child in boarding school is tense and alert but lacks words to express the emotional impact of the experience. A whole new language associated with the culture of the school has to be learned but without an adult to mediate. For children whose parents live abroad this may be intensified because they are left with strangers in the holidays. There really is no respite, sometimes for years at a time. Parents who stayed in the country would only be permitted occasional brief visits once or twice a term and so there was rarely any point in their staying. Today parents are permitted contact with their children by mobile phone and email, and more regular visits are permitted. Even so there are those for whom the loss, physical separation from their homes, their loved ones and pets cannot be remedied by these methods.

Revenge – split off grief

One lasting effect of this split is that the grief, when it is contacted in psychotherapy, produces different behaviour in women and men. With some women, such as Sophie, the tears flow profusely and so mourning may occur. With others, women as well as men, tears are fiercely held at bay and so it is very difficult to contact the grief, and mourn. It is more common for men, especially those who were abused at school, to dream of revenge that would turn the tables on the abuser. This vengeful attitude may serve them well in the world of business where ruthlessness may be useful and adaptive.

David was vengeful on two counts. When he left his prep school, he had attended a well-known public school. There he was bullied because he was seen as different. In the summer holidays David returned to his Caribbean home. There he spent each summer running barefoot in the sunshine and, on his return, his skin was deeply tanned. David was of white British origin but he was taunted with abuse from other boys because of the colour of his skin. He was targeted because he was different: he came from a faraway place, beyond the experience of most of his peers. Boys in boarding schools will often attack difference for fear of being singled out for their own vulnerabilities. They hide their feelings and, through projection, attack the child less able to hide theirs.

From David's point of view, the brutal beatings he received from a sadistic teacher were much worse. David's fantasies of revenge involved finding this man and killing him. The teacher was already dead but David would have taken great pleasure in retribution. Those who have been maltreated as children often dream of revenge and in imagination return, as adults, to turn the tables on their abuser (as we saw with Theo). Sometimes such suffering is tempered by friendships and the companionship of the peer group at school, but often a vigilant stance is automatic when meeting men even in later life. This can play out in work situations where fear and vigilance may get in the way of working relationships.

Sophie – homelessness and mourning

Finally I return to Sophie, with whom the chapter began, the young woman speechless with tears. The loss of her mother had left Sophie vulnerable and, with little sense of an internalised good parent, she found it difficult to regulate her own affect. Sophie was a successful professional but emotionally she was still very young. The losses and events connected with her school experience had broken her and she felt life was not worth living.

It was not only boarding school: prior to this, as we saw, she had changed schools every two years as her parents had moved country. Thus she had never been able to maintain peer friendships. So when she went to boarding school she was ill-equipped to befriend other girls. This continued into her adult life. When she first came into analysis, Sophie was isolated. She had few friends and just waited for companionship until her mother returned to the country. At first her anger was split off and she had no idea that her self-destructive behaviours, such as cutting herself and wanting to end her life, were related to her anger. Her anger manifested itself at work, where she found it almost impossible to relate to her senior colleagues. It was much later that she was able to confront her anger with her parents and make the connection with the situation at work.

It took a number of years of painful analysis to unpack her story and grieve for her losses. For the first year she found it difficult to stop crying; she mourned the childhood she had missed. Then, as the grief abated, her rage came to the fore. The hatred became conscious and Sophie moved from the powerless position of the child to become an agent in her own life. She began to make friendships and changed her job. This was a long and agonising process that took immense courage. Eventually she met a man with whom to share her life, and soon after this she left analysis. Sophie was now in a position to embark on an intimate relationship, with all the ups and downs that that entails.

It is notable that both Sophie and David had siblings in this country. Sophie's younger sister went to a different school and she was therefore out of contact during the term times. In the vacations they would be together with relatives or friends of their parents, but they never developed a close relationship. David's older brother was in the same school but two years ahead of him. As already mentioned they were separated and living in different schoolhouses, so they rarely saw each other. David's experience of the school was very different from that of his brother, who David believed was not bullied. This points out how divisive such schools are with sibling relationships. Rarely are siblings encouraged to keep in contact with each other emotionally. Clearly psychological understanding was minimal – but perhaps it was more intentional than that. Perhaps the aim was to break emotional ties in order to produce the ruthless men whose position in the world would be untrammelled by their emotional attachments. They could then grow up able to send their children away to boarding school as well as take decisions to send their men to war or whatever the patriarchy demanded of them.

Conclusion

Sophie was homeless from 12 years of age when she lost her mother, father and sister. Because her parents moved so often, she did not have an internalised image of a place called home. David too was emotionally homeless, since at the age of 7 he lost the warm climate of the Caribbean as well as his parents and his nanny, so he too was homeless as a child. This emotional sense of exile continues into adult life and often emerges to consciousness as depression in those who are otherwise successful. Like David, the child raised in a hot climate, often with a local nanny, was culturally, as well as actually dislocated from all that was home to him or her. Many never again contact their parents emotionally.

Notes

1 Pearsall, J., & Hanks, P. (eds) (2001) *The New Oxford Dictionary of English*, Oxford: Oxford University Press, p. 644.
2 Bion, W. R. (1982) *The Long Weekend 1897–1919, Part of a Life*, London: Karnac Books, p. 33.
3 Schaverien, J. (2011a) 'Boarding School Syndrome: Broken attachments a hidden trauma', *British Journal of Psychotherapy* 17 (2), p. 141.
4 Grier, F. (2013) 'The hidden trauma of the young boarding school child as seen through the lens of adult couple therapy', in *Enduring Trauma Through the Life Cycle*, McGinley, E. & Varchevker, A. (eds), London: Karnac Books, p. 150.
5 Gardam, J. (2004/2005) *Old Filth*, London: Abacus.
6 Grier (2013), op. cit., p. 150.
7 Ibid.
8 Brendon, V. (2005/2006) *Children of the Raj*, Phoenix: Orion.
9 Ibid., pp. 68–93.
10 Spurling, H. (2010) *Burying the Bones: Pearl Buck in China*, London: Profile Books.
11 Ibid., p. 1.
12 Buck, P. S. (1931/2005) *The Good Earth*, London: Simon & Schuster UK Ltd.
13 Spurling (2010), op. cit., p. 214.
14 Brendon (2005/2006), op. cit.
15 The Independent Schools Council (ISC) census of 2013 reports that at the time there were 25,912 non-British pupils whose parents live overseas. Overseas pupils made up 5.1 per cent of the total ISC population; Lockhart, R. E., Gilpin, A., & Jasiocha, E. (2013) *ISC Census*, London: Independent Schools Council www.isc.co.uk/Resources/Independent%20Schools%20Council/Research%20Archive/Annual%20Census/2013_annualcensus_isc.pdf, p. 14.
16 Bion (1982), op. cit., p. 33.
17 Kaplinsky, C. (2008) 'Shifting shadows: Shaping dynamics in the cultural unconscious', *Journal of Analytical Psychology* 53 (2), pp. 189–207.
18 Ibid., 191.
19 Ibid.
20 Spurling (2010), op.cit.
21 Schaverien, J. (2002) *The Dying Patient in Psychotherapy: Desire, Dreams and Individuation*, New York: Palgrave Macmillan, p. 26.
22 Schaverien (2011a) op. cit., p. 140.
23 Schaverien, J. (2006) 'Men who leave too soon: Reflections on the erotic transference and countertransference', in *Gender, Countertransference and the Erotic Transference*, Schaverien, J. (ed), London: Routledge, pp. 15–31.
24 Grier (2013), op. cit., p. 155.
25 Barrie, J. M. (1904/2010) *Peter Pan*, London: Puffin Classics.
26 Schaverien (2011a) op. cit.
27 Duffell, N. (2000) *The Making of Them*, London: Lone Arrow Press, p. 10.
28 Ibid. p. 140.
29 Grier (2013), op. cit., p. 152.

Chapter 12

Homesickness
Eating and sleeping

> Homesickness . . . that terrible piercing loneliness of small children cast out from their homes . . . is without question the most important single aspect of public school education; yet because it was the most painful it is the memory most usually repressed. But it is the unexpressed longing for their mothers and nannies, the comfort and safety of home, which defines the other deprivations.
>
> Jonathan Gathorne-Hardy[1]

With this quote I set the scene for this chapter, which is about homesickness and two locations in which it is most acutely felt, the dining room and dormitory. The places where children eat and sleep are the most profound reminders of loss. These non-educational locations in the school are where grief may emerge with sometimes overwhelming intensity. Homesickness, as we have seen, is for the exiled child, a form of suppressed mourning. The subject of the close-up focus of this chapter is children, their bodies, and their developmental and emotional needs.

Homesickness

The term *homesickness* encompasses complex symptoms of unprocessed grief. It is a sickness that occurs in response to loss of home. Consequently, many children are emotionally wounded (traumatised), exiled (homeless) and bereaved (grieving). The rupture in their primary attachments is devastating for some young children. Following that, the unremitting nature of the experience dawns with the realisation that their parents are not returning. It may take a few days or weeks to begin to accept this awesome fact and to adapt to the change in the circumstances of their daily living. For many children being suddenly expected to eat and sleep in unfamiliar circumstances, surrounded by strangers, is alarming. Whether they have been raised as only children or in large families, children are often totally overwhelmed by the sheer number of other people with whom they are now expected to live.

The state of loss at this time is often unspeakable. In Bion's words, the child may be 'numbed and stupefied'.[2] Children in such a state are unable to make sense of the experience. The explanation sometimes given by adults is that this is 'homesickness', which is often followed by the reassurance that it will pass. Roald Dahl gives a more honest account:

> I was homesick during the whole of my first term at St Peter's. Homesickness is a bit like seasickness. You don't know how awful it is until you get it, and when you do, it hits you right in the top if the stomach and you want to die. The only comfort is that both homesickness and seasickness are instantly curable. The first goes away the moment you walk out of the school grounds and the second is forgotten as soon as the ship enters port.[3]

Homesickness is not just a thing of the past, to which a more recent observation – not from a child, but from an adult witness – testifies. Patrick Kaye worked as a GP in a major public school for eighteen years, retiring in the middle of the first decade of the twenty-first century. Kaye observed homesickness as underlying many of the ailments presented in the school medical services. He came to realise that some children were unconsciously somatising: they were literally sick because they were missing their homes.[4] Without words to say it, the body finds a way of expressing distress.[5][6] Homesickness might therefore be viewed as a healthy and adaptive expression of loss. There may be considerable relief from the pain if another person understands it. Children intuitively know this and seek out the adult whose job it is to know about 'sickness'; they consult the school doctor. However, the subtle implications underlying the presenting symptom may be missed by less perceptive doctors than Kaye. Sadly, if it is not understood, the wound is concealed and the pain deepens.

Intimate care and the child's body

Despite their apparently privileged status, children in boarding school may suffer a number of material privations related to the most basic human needs of nourishment and rest. The well-documented significance of emotional attachment for the security of the developing child is evident in the simple everyday bodily contact with familiar people. The shared space children inhabit is made up of many subtle and unremarked elements of ordinary loving contact with their families. The gaze, the touch, familiar smells, food and sounds of home all create a subliminal sense of belonging. Thus, even when home life is not ideal, being sent away to live in school is a rupture in the continuity of the life of the child.

As we have already seen, there are some children for whom school is preferable: those whose home is intolerably unstable or abusive find refuge in school. For them, too, there is inevitably an adjustment period. Housed with multiple others, the child lives in a strange state: alone and yet never alone, lonely and yet always in the company of others. This affects embodied awareness and, with little space for reverie, the imaginative life of the child may also suffer.

Children who start at prep school at 7 or 8 are still developmentally sensitive. It is premature to leave home at this age, before they are fully equipped to manage their own bodily needs. Emotional development is a gradual process, which is mediated by the mother or other primary carer. From infancy the mother or, in the more affluent homes the nanny, will oversee the child's bodily welfare as well as fostering their psychological emergence. In boarding school this gradual and mostly unremarked developmental path is suddenly disrupted.

The pattern has been well documented, but in this context a little attention to the theory helps in understanding the seriousness of the rupture. In the early 1950s Michael Fordham proposed that in infancy there was a nascent self, present from the very beginning of life. This was a revolutionary idea at that time and it was based on early infant observation. Prior to this, babies had been seen as unformed until shaped by their environment. Fordham introduced the theory of integration and deintegration. He observed that the infant self is an integrated entity, present from the start. He observed that infants when awake elicit what they need by evoking a response from their carers. Infants move from the integrated state out towards the environment, which he called *deintegrating*. They are active in eliciting the required response from their carer. Infants usually feed willingly but at times turn away and refuse to feed or fall sleep, thus returning to the integrated state. In sleep they assimilate and digest, physically and emotionally. The attuned carer will respond accordingly and permit the infant to take what is needed and then withdraw to sleep, rest or dream.[7]

Daniel Stern and his team in the USA independently observed similar patterns. Conducting extensive research based on filming infants interacting with their mothers, Stern and the Boston Process of Change Study Group demonstrated how influential is the infant in her or his own care. They demonstrated failures in these patterns of attachment and how they impinge on the development of the infant.[8][9] In this regard, Tronick discussed the mother-infant relationship as co-created and he made links with this interplay and that of the analytic dyad.[10] In the UK, Gerhardt and Woodhead are among researchers who have contributed to this understanding.[11][12] Research based at the Anna Freud Centre in London has been influential in disseminating understanding of the importance of this reciprocal relationship. As a result there are national early intervention programmes.[13] The child in boarding school is not an infant, but understanding developed from this research contributes to consideration of older children as well.

The developmental pattern continues and changes as babies grow and they begin to experiment with solid food. Initially food is sampled, tasted, spat out, moved around the plate or thrown away. This testing is vital and eventually leads to the establishment of an eating pattern in which personal preferences are expressed. These are the first gestures of independence. Later, as language is acquired, words are added. This continues throughout childhood as the relationship to food is formed. In a family, parents soon learn their child's likes and dislikes. The recognition of their individual tastes differentiates one child in a family from another, gradually building a sense of autonomy. For example, 'Johnny doesn't like peas' or 'Jenny hates bananas.' These words symbolise much more than at first appears; they recognise the individuality of children and also assert their right to discriminate.

Therefore the research into child development is highly significant in considering the child living in a boarding school who feels homesick. It is particularly relevant in relation to food. This early pattern, the rhythm of feeding and resting, carries with it the seeds of autonomy and so may continue into later life. These developmental and relational processes continue in modified form from infancy into latency and are fertile ground for the development of creative play and imagination. The rupture that occurs when children are prematurely separated from their carers may distort this growth. Children abandoned at an early age, in a strange institution, where the rules are unknown, are tense and on guard and so have little opportunity for genuine reverie. There is no space for integration, and deintegration is to an institution rather than a person.

Independence is also acquired by the development of bodily control. It is only gradually that children come to respond to signals from their bladder or bowel. Infants are dependent on adults to mediate these processes but, as children grow, they often proudly begin to manage these for themselves. There are inevitably accidents but, if these are handled sensitively, the adult is needed less and less. As children mature, it is only in distressing situations or if they are sick that help is temporarily needed. For children living at home the parent is still there to assist, setting them back on the path of autonomy. These developmental processes may be relatively easily managed in a familiar environment – but for some children, away from home, eating, sleeping and toileting may be distressing. They may feel neglected.

Instead of the usual pattern, where only gradually does the young child mature enough to leave the parental shelter, children in a boarding school have to fully manage their own body for twenty-four hours a day, every day. The absence of help from someone who loves them is keenly felt. From cleaning teeth to managing the bladder and bowels, the child is now alone, merely one in a group of children. I have heard from women who, as children in boarding school, were troubled by some bodily discomfort or pain. If it was to do with the genital area, such as cystitis, they were too embarrassed to discuss it with their carers and so they bore it alone. They received no treatment and no reassurance. This is an unremarked consequence of the sudden and premature loss of their home.

Significantly, this is also the abrupt and irrevocable loss of the childhood state. The status of being a child, with a unique place in a family group, is suddenly ended. So, as well as people and places, children lose their role, their sense of themselves as people who belong in a family group. Children of whatever age have to prematurely appear grown up. Part of this is the imperative not to express feelings, such as sadness, with tears. Therefore, it may well be that 'feeling sick' is the only way small children have of expressing the discomfort of their distress.

Overwhelmed with many physical manifestations of grief, something has to happen psychologically for the child to survive, and indeed it does. This is where the 'soul murder' that Theo described comes into play (see Chapter 5, Figure 5.10). As he said, this would be recognised by other ex-boarders. This is because there is no alternative: children learn to live cut off from their internal emotional turmoil. Homesickness is thus an important component in the creation of Boarding School Syndrome. The term might well encompass many forms of feeling sick: sick with fear, sick with grief, and sick with loneliness and loss. It is not uncommon for the repressed distress to emerge in symptoms such as bed-wetting and vomiting. If tears are not permitted, other bodily excretions may take their place; the child may be sick, or wet or soil themselves as a distorted expression of the banned tears of grief. These may express what cannot be put into words. This may come into stark focus in the dormitory.

The dormitory

The dormitory is where a child sleeps. It is the place that is meant to be safe, but it is where the new arrivals secretly cry under the bedcovers. Many feel unprotected in their dormitory and their bed is not a refuge. As Theo put it, 'It was just somewhere you slept.' The lonely tears of the first few nights are an expression of distress often shared by others in the same dormitory. However, each child is alone in their misery, each with their particular set of losses and private grief.

This may be accompanied by other distressing events. It is not uncommon to hear tales of the child having taken a treasured possession to school only to have it stolen or deliberately destroyed. This usually happens in the dormitory when there is no adult witness. For example, the beloved Teddy is often powerfully invested as a transitional object from home[14] (for a small child a toy may be magically experienced as animate). So to witness it being ripped apart by other children, for their amusement, can be quite devastating. When the child is small, it is almost like watching your pet being hurt. This means that the child soon learns to apply the unspoken maxim: 'If I have nothing, I have nothing to lose.' Thus it is that attachment to home, symbolised by objects, is not possible nor does the child feel safe and relaxed when sleeping. The need for safety goes deep into the shadows, where it is hidden even from the child himself, behind a façade of not caring. It may remain there until, as an adult, he or she seeks psychotherapy. This is often the point when the emotional impact of this struggle is recalled.

Even in the most advanced prep schools the lack of personal support for bodily needs will be felt acutely. Because there is no parental support, children in boarding schools worry about being sick and about getting to the toilet in time. In some boys' schools, lavatories had no doors, so there were no self-contained cubicles where the child could manage their body in private. At 6, 7 or even 8 years old, a child may appear autonomous – but if they become ill, or in some other way vulnerable, there is a need for temporary regression to intimate care. Without this support, and especially if lapses occur, the child may feel neglected. Their anxiety may intensify. It is not uncommon for children who have previously been dry at night to find themselves involuntarily wetting their beds.

George Orwell describes the shame induced by this humiliating regression. When he started at his prep school, St Cyprians, he regressed to wetting the bed. This was viewed as a disgusting crime for which the cure was a beating. He explains how as a child he was well aware it was frowned upon, but he was unable to stop. Each night he would fervently pray: 'Please God, do not let me wet my bed, Oh, Please God do not let me wet my bed!' But this made little difference.[15]

Orwell was 8, and he conveys the agony and shame of the inability to control this thing that happened. He was beaten with the intention of curing him, but of course bed-wetting is involuntary and he could not just decide to stop. I have heard of such incidents from people from all different generations. Punishment merely adds to the child's terror and confusion. The shame of the child made to wash his or her own sheets and bedclothes, night after night, is common and humiliating. The body of the child signals emotional distress but if there is no one attuned to the signals they are missed. A child who reverts to bed-wetting in such circumstances is expressing profound suffering. This is serious neglect at a formative time. Thus the child may eventually learn to ignore her or his own needs and desires. This is a factor in the formation of Boarding School Syndrome; the child learns that her or his real self is unacceptable. It is safest to keep hidden.

The dining room

The dormitory is one site of tension for the child new to the institution; another is the dining room. Initially, in the dining room, instead of parents, siblings and familiar food, there are masses of anonymous unfamiliar adults and children, and strange food. Even if the food is good it will at first be alien and this may emphasise the loss of home. Mary Stack, who went to boarding school at the age of 10, describes her first impression of the dining room: 'From that first evening I remember the dark wood-panelled dining hall, smelling of creosote and ink, and eating cold beef and beetroot salad to a background hubbub of excited chat.'[16]

These few words convey a huge emotional event. It is not difficult to imagine the sense of bewilderment children might feel, surrounded by bigger children, in a situation of such alienating chaos. They may well feel physically sick; there may be no other words to express the sense of terror of abandonment to this apparently crazy circus. No matter how good the food, eating in these unfamiliar circumstances would have been daunting.

It was years later that Stack's mother was to confess that she herself had been taken out of this same school because she had a 'nervous breakdown'; she could not bear 'the clatter of knives and forks' in that same dining room.[17] So, as a small child, Stack's mother had escaped the school by expressing her distress convincingly enough for it to be understood and given a comprehensible label: 'a nervous breakdown'. Her escape came with a price, a diagnosis that rendered her as weak. One might wonder if the breakdown that became her 'get out of gaol card' also marked her, for life, as vulnerable. Then, later, tradition outweighed intuitive sensibilities and she sent her own daughter to the same school. It is likely that this mother subjugated her own understanding to comply with the patriarchal imperative of the time. There was nothing untoward in the situation, as described by Stack, no cruel teachers and no bullying children – merely the state of abandonment to chaos which has been remembered for a lifetime. Appetite may be permanently distorted by this anxiety-provoking early trauma and, in some schools, it was made worse because of the rules governing the consumption of food.

Hunger and greed

The emotional hunger of the child deprived of home is exacerbated when actual physical hunger is also involved. Inadequate rations of food, or of love, create a yearning or an insatiable desire. The child who was hungry at school may grow up with a fierce appetite, but may consume food without tasting it. It is similar with love, because the child who was deprived of love at a formative stage may grow into an adult who craves love but does not trust it. This may result in the forming of intensely dependent relationships or possibly a series of unfulfilling ones, where seduction takes place and then the ex-boarder withdraws for fear of abandonment. Because these are unconscious processes it is rare that the source of this hunger is recognised. Originating in the hunger caused by inadequate rations in school or, in the constant yearning for the lost mother, this hunger is not an adult desire but it is historical. Thus this deprivation has lasting impact.

Orwell gives a vivid account of how it felt to be permanently hungry in a boarding school with meagre rations:

> The food was not only bad, it was also insufficient . . . I remember the lengths we would go in order to steal food. On a number of occasions I remember creeping down at two or three o'clock in the morning through what seemed like miles of pitch dark stairways and passages – barefooted, stopping to listen after each step, paralysed with about equal fear of Sambo (the head master) and ghosts and burglars – to steal stale bread from the pantry.[18]

Orwell was not alone in experiencing such hunger in his prep school. Dahl gives a similar account when he explains the uses of the tuck box:

> An English school in those days was a money making business owned by the Headmaster. It suited him therefore to give the boys as little food as possible himself and to encourage the parents in various cunning ways to feed their offspring by parcel post from home.[19]

Dahl's mother complied and sent regular food parcels for her son. Both of these men attended boarding schools in the early part of the twentieth century. However, we cannot take comfort from the thought that this was the long-distant past. In interviews and psychotherapy practice I have heard numerous similar accounts from men and women who attended boarding schools in the late twentieth century. Many of these schools were in the UK, but others were in countries as diverse as Africa, India, Australia and New Zealand. From different generations, these children too were driven to just such lengths as Orwell by the gnawing hunger left by the inadequate rations in their boarding schools.

There is more to this restricted diet than the economic advantages to the headmaster, described by Dahl. There is also a tradition whereby a man who had learned as boy to accept Spartan living conditions was considered able to meet whatever challenges came his way in later life. If we remember that Classical Greek was a major influence in public schools, well into the twentieth century, perhaps it is not fanciful to consider Sparta to have been the model.[20] We saw in Chapter 2 that this Spartan attitude led men who had suffered as boys to reify that suffering and assert that it had indeed made men of them. There was an unspoken camaraderie as they embarked on military service or the challenges of working in the far-flung reaches of the Empire with stoicism. They were unlikely to meet trials that they had not been prepared for. The lack of food, accompanied by beatings suffered at the hands of their mentors and tormentors, stood them in good stead for any future privations they might encounter. They were psychologically armoured against complaining of lack of food or creature comforts. In addition to this, the general understanding of the time (convenient for such headmasters) was that the libido of adolescent boys might be kept in check by a less-than-adequate diet combined with sporting activity.[21] [22]

In girls' schools it is unlikely that Sparta was the model, but girls also suffered such deprivation with regards to food. Hunger was not an issue in all schools, even in the early days, and the situation has changed so that today children in most boarding schools are adequately fed. It is likely that they would soon make it known if they were not. However, some psychotherapy clients now in their middle years had experiences comparable to those of Orwell and Dahl. The psychological aftermath of such early hardships is still evident.

Hunger and greed in the twentieth century

For some, this deprivation has permanently affected their appetites. Examples of two men who experienced hunger in different schools in the 1970s and 1980s illustrate this point. This early Spartan existence had distorted both their attitudes to food and still affected their emotional well-being. Neither of them enjoyed food; it was merely functional, serving the necessary purpose of fuelling the body.

Theo, whom we met in Part 2, attended prep school in the 1970s from the ages of 8 to 13. He recalled always being hungry. The food was of very poor quality, and it was his understanding that the meat they ate had been condemned as unsuitable for human consumption. It was full of veins and gristle. The mass outbreaks of food poisoning that were common amongst the boys seems to confirm that he may have been right about this. There was never enough food. He recalled how stale bread was served up – until it was gone, fresh bread was not served.

This, along with bullying by the staff, breeds a tough and provocative exterior presentation. The vulnerable homesick child has to be clothed in a suit of armour equal to the situation in which he now lives. This has long-term psychological repercussions. In Theo's case, the long-term effect was that food was not important to him. As an adult, he was bemused by the sensual pleasure that his wife and children appeared to derive from eating a variety of different dishes. He admitted he thought this an absurd indulgence: for him, food was merely fuel. He was also completely intolerant of his own emotional and physical needs; he was able to override any physical weakness and deny himself compassion. Therefore he would work like a machine, whether the task in which he was engaged was related to physical exertion or office work. He could not permit himself rest; he was driven. If a job needed doing, he would do it at huge cost to himself. We came to understand that this was rooted in the early denial of his sensual needs at school. This is one of the most common fundamental results of long boarding school existence. To most people who attended boarding school, it is quite alien that other people indulge themselves. One woman commented that she had noticed that in contrast to her family she could never take time to luxuriate in a hot bath or to pamper herself. This was, she realised, because in her boarding school she had always had to get her bath over quickly so that others could have their turn. For many this pattern of behaviour continues into adult life.

Anton had been at a different school from Theo, but there the food was also inadequate. This was a decade later and the outcome was possibly more extreme. Anton had attended two prep schools in the early 1980s from the age of 6 until he was 13, and then he attended public school from 13 to 17. He remembered his first prep school as relatively benign but subsequent schools as locations of various forms of bullying. He recalled his public school as a prison in which he was always hungry. He said with a genuine sense of outrage, 'and my parents were paying for it too!' Like others in this situation, Anton learned to eat very fast because if he did not do so, other boys would steal his food. With no member of staff in evidence to oversee the behaviour, and no one with whom to discuss this injustice, he was forced to fend for himself. He did this throughout his childhood, coping as best he could. Thus his appetite and desires were suppressed. He suffered extreme bullying from the age of 8, when he went to his second prep school, and this continued throughout his childhood. As a consequence, as an adult Anton still ate very fast and preferred to do so alone. Enjoyment of food is a sensual pleasure for which a certain amount of space and relaxed reverie is necessary. It can be dangerous, in school, to admit to pleasure: it has to be concealed, even from oneself, because it is tantamount to admitting to vulnerability. If Anton had been seen to enjoy his food, he would have been exposed to further bullying. If he had shown that he cared that his food was stolen, the bullies would have been gratified by his disappointment. It is safer not to be seen to enjoy any of it because then you have nothing to lose.

Force feeding

In the past, in most schools it was forbidden to leave the table until the food on the plate was consumed. Even if the child found the food unpalatable, it had to be eaten. Andrew Motion describes how unfinished food from the previous meal was served again at the following meal.[23] Many of my respondents told similar stories. There were times when the school rules were cruelly intrusive. In carrying these out to the letter, the staff were culpable. We have seen that when left to experiment with food, children gradually establish their personal preferences; such rules violently disallow the child's exploration.

Several people interviewed recalled this kind of treatment. Others recalled dreading a certain dish that was served regularly each week or finding it impossible to eat a particular meat or vegetable. One person remembered living in fear each Friday, in the knowledge that she would have to sit there until the reviled fish was eaten. Genuine revulsion for certain foods is involuntary and being made to eat them can be devastating. It is invasive, overriding the child's autonomy; whether staff or prefects enforce the rule, it is bullying. To be obliged to eat repulsive foods, or to finish what is on a plate when no longer hungry, is disturbing of body boundaries.

Sickness and food

This type of treatment was not limited to boys' schools. Girls too suffered such deprivation. Convents and seminaries are often considered to be amongst the best schools educationally, and this seems to be borne out by many of those who have attended them. However, some of these institutions have been responsible for some of the worst injustices and sadistic practices. It seems that religious institutions are no protection from cruelty.

The food in Nina's convent school in the 1970s, to which she went when she was 11, was completely inadequate. In addition, the children were not well supervised. Rather like Anton and Stack, Nina described meal times as noisy and competitive. She said: 'On the rare occasions that the food tasted good, fellow pupils stole it from our plates and, when the food was bad, which was frequently the case, it was dumped onto our plates by others.' She was small and thin, and she would never steal from others. So, as she puts it, she usually ended up with the bad things on her plate and never any good things. The bad things she described included mouldy bread and cold solidified porridge. She would be chastised for not finishing her food and she was always being sick because it was impossible to keep this vile stuff down. This was made worse as she was made to, as she put it: 're-eat her food'.

Forcing children to eat their own vomit seems to be something of a tradition. Brendon quotes Henry Longhurst, who attended the same school as Orwell during the World War I. He was so revolted by the vile food provided in his prep school that 'he was sick into his pewter bowl, only to be made to eat it up.'[24] A similar tale was told by A. N. Wilson, a journalist who writes of the prep school he attended in the 1970s, where the headmaster sexually abused him: 'In the dining room . . . Barbara (the wife of this headmaster) was force-feeding porridge to one of the wetter (weaker) boys who was crying and crying, and then threw up in his bowl. She told him to eat it up.'[25] This is child abuse, but the staff overseeing such cruelty would perhaps have another name for it. These are only some of the many stories of ill treatment relating to food that have been told to me by more than one person.

Another woman recalled how she often felt sick at meal times and later this developed into a phobia of vomiting. She dreaded having to get out of bed at night to find the toilets, because it meant a journey down a dark corridor where she would imagine all sorts of terrors. Thus we see that sickness was a significant part of the continuing trauma of boarding schools.

In Nina's tale of the dining table we saw, as well as bullying by other children, neglect by the staff. They were in loco parentis but permitted cruelty within the student group and perpetrated it themselves. Neglect is commonly cited by adults remembering their time as children in the boarding schools of the not-so-distant past. Their bodily as well as emotional needs were often neglected. As one person put it: 'The care was fine if we were really ill. Then we were taken to the sanatorium. For relatively minor illnesses – headaches or colds – there was no help.' There was no one in the school to mediate and care for or reassure the child. To be aged 6 alone and feeling ill is devastating and has lasting repercussions.

Conclusion

The role of a parent or primary caretaker is to look after children, caring for their body and then helping them take over that care themselves. It is also to be present to witness and explain experiences to young children. It is to treat the child with compassion. In the absence of this care children may feel lost, and – although many people recover – the trauma of these events may remain lodged in the vague memories of the past, often discounted until analysis begins.

The term *homesickness* is inadequate to describe the loss of all this. The adult who grew up in the boarding school setting may need mirroring and help in naming the details of the experience encompassed by the term. The distress needs to be seen for what it is in each case.

Notes

1 Gathorne-Hardy, J. (1977) *The Public School Phenomenon, 597–1977*, London: Hodder & Stoughton, pp. 181–182.
2 Bion, W. R. (1982) *The Long Weekend 1897–1919, Part of a Life*, London: Karnac Books, p. 33.
3 Dahl, R. (1984) *Boy: Tales of Childhood*, London: Puffin Books, p. 93.
4 Kaye, P. (2005) *Homesickness*, MA thesis, The Tavistock Institute for Human Relations.
5 Van der Kolk, B. A. (1994) 'The body keeps the score: Memory and the evolving psychobiology of posttraumatic stress', *Harvard Review of Psychiatry* 1 (5), pp. 253–265.

6 Rothschild, B. (2000) *The Body Remembers: The Psychophysiology of Trauma and Trauma Treatment*, London, W.W. Norton & Co.
7 Fordham, M. (1985) *Explorations Into the Self*, London: Karnac Books, pp. 31–32, 50.
8 Stern, D. N. (1985) *The Interpersonal World of the Infant*, New York: Basic Books.
9 Stern, D. N. *et al.* (1998) 'Non-interpretive mechanisms in psychoanalytic therapy: The "something more" than interpretation' *The International Journal of Psychoanalysis* 79, pp. 903–921.
10 Tronick, E. Z. (2003) 'Of course all relationships are unique: How co-creative processes generate unique mother-infant and patient-therapist relationships', *Psychoanalytic Inquiry* 23, pp. 473–491.
11 Gerhardt, S. (2004) *Why Love Matters*, London: Routledge.
12 Woodhead, J. (2004), ' "Dialectical process" and "constructive method": Micro-analysis of relational process in an example from parent-infant psychotherapy', *Journal of Analytical Psychology* 49, pp. 143–160.
13 The Parent Infant Project is an outreach facility started at the Anna Freud Centre in London. There are now centres in several parts of the country including Oxford (OXPIP) and Northampton (NORPIP).
14 Winnicott, D. W. (1971) *Playing and Reality*, Harmondsworth: Penguin.
15 Orwell, G. (1947/2003) *Such, Such Were the Joys*, London: Penguin, p. 1.
16 Stack, M. (2008) 'The making of her: My boarding school experience', *Attachment* 2 (3), p. 322.
17 Ibid.
18 Orwell (1947/2003), op. cit., pp. 23–24.
19 Dahl (1984), op. cit., p. 77.
20 Powell, A. (2013b) 'Sparta boarding school of evil genius', talk given 26 September, Bath Royal Literary and Scientific Institution.
21 Gathorne-Hardy (1977), op. cit., pp. 144–155.
22 Hickson, A. (1996) *The Poisoned Bowl: Sex and the Public School*, London, Gerald Duckworth & Co Ltd, p. 22.
23 Motion, A. (2006) *In the Blood: A Memoir of My Childhood*, London: Faber & Faber, p. 108.
24 Henry Longhurst, quoted in Brendon, V. (2009) *Prep School Children: A Class Apart Over Two Centuries*, London: Continuum, p. 83.
25 Wilson, A. N. (2014) 'Scarred for life by boarding school sadists: How A. N. Wilson was deluged with similar horror stories after revealing his abuse at hands of paedophile head', *Mail Online* (17 May) www.dailymail.co.uk/news/article-2630951/Scarred-life-boarding-school-sadists-How-A-N-Wilson-deluged-similar-horror-stories-revealing-abuse-hands-paedophile-head.html.

Part IV

The boarding school body

Chapter 13

The armoured self
Masculinity, leathers and the lash

The public school child

So far we have been considering the latency child. We turn now to public schools and so to adolescence. Adolescence is a formative time in which all kinds of intimate changes take place in the bodies and emotions of young people. Children in boarding school have to cope with this, as with so much else, without parental care. In order to address this, in this chapter I will attend to some common experiences of boys and the creation of a certain form of masculinity. The next chapter will focus on girls.

At 13 most boys leave their prep school and go on to public school.[1] Despite the Spartan systems and hunger, of which we read in Chapter 12, the child may have adapted to their prep school. As they progress through the school, children eventually gain status, becoming the biggest (and so most prominent) members of the school community. The position of individual children is also established by their strengths, as well as weaknesses, in the school curriculum. Some never feel part of the school and never gain recognition within it, but many attain respect for their achievements, as well as for their seniority.

At 13 all this changes: established groups break up and the children separate, going on to different public schools. In these schools others, new to boarding, join them. They all start school as the youngest, least powerful children in the school. For some it is daunting to be surrounded again by strange and much bigger children. Those who have previously boarded may have an advantage because, although they are unfamiliar with the new school, they are used to living without their families. Moreover, the boys who attended boarding prep school understand the system. Those for whom boarding is a new experience are less equipped to manage; they will miss their homes.[2]

I have established that boarding is traumatic for the very young child, but it can be similarly distressing for children who first board in adolescence. They are developmentally more mature than the prep school child but still they suffer the untimely loss of attachment figures. Older children too need parental care and love. Moreover, they are establishing their sexual identity and gender role.

Therefore loss of home, of familiar adults and appropriate physical contact will be felt acutely for many 13 year olds. As a result they too suffer a period of bereavement.

Many present-day boarding schools are mixed sex, but separation along gender lines was ubiquitous in the past. Therefore many of today's ex-boarders in psychotherapy were raised in single-sex schools. This inevitably created a psychological split between attributes deemed masculine and those considered feminine.[3] As a result of social expectations of gender role, boys' and girls' schools were rather different in their ethos.

The old boy network and false masculinity

An armoured form of masculinity may be created in boys' schools by the unspoken expectation that the little boy behave and dress 'like a man'. A layer of armour is needed for those who suffer bodily violations such as beatings. A boy who is beaten soon learns that crying is not an option. The tradition demands that the boy hide his emotional reactions to distress. Crying is taboo – traditionally permitted for girls, but scorned in boys – and so boys' feelings are hidden even from themselves. One man said that in five years in his public school, he never remembered a boy crying ever, even after a beating. This produces the famous 'stiff upper lip' of the British establishment. It also creates a false sense of masculinity, an image that men are hard and do not show emotion even under duress. This proves to the world and so to themselves that they are not like girls and women, who are permitted to cry. The implication is that real men never show weakness. This is a form of masculinity with an unspoken imperative that no one must break rank. The edifice will crumble if one cries; they will betray the others and all will be exposed as not masters of their own emotions.

It is important to remember that there are positives that come out of the public school experience. It is evident that for some men, despite the beatings they suffered as boys, there is a strong allegiance to their schools. Some dedicated teachers are remembered with affection. Often these are the teachers who were excellent at encouraging the young and fostering their potential. One inspiring teacher can have a huge impact in nurturing the talents of children, making a tremendous difference to their boarding school experience and later life interests.

Institutionally condoned bullying

The 13 year old, new to the school, may meet senior boys who had themselves been the smallest boys in the school only two or three years earlier. The annual cycle means that, as one group of sixth formers leave, the next generation inherits the school. As Chandos has pointed out, these older boys now assume a mantle of entitlement.[4] They have a sense of self-importance, assuming the role of transmitting the school traditions. Some are accorded the status of law enforcers through the prefect system; others merely assume it as a perk of seniority. In

Jason's school it was part of the pedagogical philosophy that boys should learn to be subject to authority and, when they became seniors, to wield authority – hence the fagging system and the fact that prefects were allowed (even encouraged) to use formalised corporal punishment.

Jason told a story which exemplifies this. Until he was 12 he had attended a day school in the South African city where he grew up. Then, at 13, he was sent to a school in another part of that country. Modelled on the traditional British public school, his school was a twelve-hour train journey from his home. He made this first day-long journey to the school alone. A city boy, Jason was understandably disorientated when he arrived at the school, which was located in the middle of unfamiliar countryside, miles from any city. This was where he would live for the next five years.

Jason left the train with one or two other boys, none of whom knew each other. There was nothing happening, as most of the students and staff had not yet arrived. So, leaving his bags, he wandered aimlessly, familiarising himself with the outside spaces. Seeing a lovely patch of rich green grass (clearly a rarity in his African home) he strolled casually on to it. Very soon a senior boy, who to him looked very big, called out to him telling him to get off. He had no idea that he had strayed onto the grass of the rugby pitch, which was one of the sanctified places of the school. The first-fifteen rugby team were the only people ever allowed on this pitch.

This older boy was a prefect and, in a very reasonable tone, explained to Jason that there were penalties for such a violation of the unspoken rules of the school. He offered to beat him as a punishment, there and then. He explained this was the best plan, to get the crime and its retribution out of the way. He took Jason to his study and indicated that he should bend over a chair and proceeded to beat him. This was Jason's first day at this school and he had unwittingly violated a rule of which he was ignorant. The older boy felt entitled to enforce the rule and meted out the punishment without any apparent compunction.

In Chapter 10 we saw that it is common for school rules and traditions to be learned only when they have been violated; Jason's experience exemplifies this. It would be reasonable to expect the school rules to be explained to the child so that he could choose to avoid contravening them, but this was not the way of such schools. Clearly the older boy, as prefect, felt sanctioned by some higher authority to implement the penalty. The effect of this irrational treatment on a child new to the school creates confusion. Jason was 13, not 6 or 8, but he was alone in a strange environment, a vast distance from his home. In this vulnerable state he was humiliated and made all too aware of his powerlessness. He could not leave. There was nowhere to go; he just had to get on with it.

This incident was a violation of the boy's bodily integrity. It would have been appropriate for the adult telling this story to express outrage but it was told with resigned humour. It was well known that this sort of treatment happened. Complaints were rare because there was no authority to which the child could appeal. The lack of adult supervision contributed to this. It is the sort of incident to which children were often subject. Children know such treatment is wrong but they have no option but to comply. This distorts the psyche, as Herman writes:

> The child ... must find a way to preserve a sense of trust in people who are untrustworthy, safety in a situation that is unsafe, control in a situation that is terrifyingly unpredictable, power in a situation of helplessness ... She must compensate for the failures of adult care and protection with the only means at her disposal, an immature system of psychological defenses.[5]

Herman was discussing the child trapped in an abusive domestic relationship, but she could have been discussing children in boarding school. They, too, have to learn strategies for survival. They, too, may have to trust in people who are untrustworthy, and they often feel unsafe and powerless. As a result of experiences like Jason's, as well as those of others recounted throughout the book, some children become fiercely angry. They may form a protective veneer so that they appear to be fine when they are unconsciously seething.

Leathers and the lash

The unpredictability of the punishments, both formal (school rules) and informal (bullying), has a psychological impact. Children have to defend themselves against future insults to their psychological and physical integrity. Such ill treatments often multiply, and so the child forms an outer psychological shell which apparently protects his helplessness from exposure. Developing in this system, the vulnerable self becomes hidden in favour of the defended 'masculine' performance, which we are recognising as an aspect of Boarding School Syndrome. Armoured, his feelings are hidden even from himself.

The accumulation of such experiences prepares the boy to become a man who, whilst apparently playing by the rules, may also be an angry rebel. Boys are encouraged to eschew the reflective concerns of emotionality and vulnerability. These are often deemed feminine attributes, and so shunned in boys' schools. Some boys find ways of making school life bearable or even enjoyable by engaging in sport, military cadets, team games and other physical challenges. Children who enjoy these activities are deemed to be doing well. Indeed, these aspects of school life give boys an opportunity to excel.

It is similar for those who achieve academic success: they too may become respected in their chosen subject. Creative teachers are often responsible for ensuring that children enjoy their experience in the school by fostering their aptitude for a particular subject. Children who have the benefit of these benign role models often go on to do well later. However, there are casualties along the way. Some children never find their niche, fail to attain status within the student group and are unnoticed by the staff. Some are mocked for their academic interests or because they do not fit in in some other way. For example, Jewish boys often experienced the prevailing anti-Semitism of the British upper classes at the schools in the twentieth century.[6][7]

Liberation

Even successful boys cling to the hope that growing up will bring escape. For some it does, in the form of attaining puberty. As the child develops physically, he may find that his stature enables him to defend himself or to excel at sport. Within the school he may at last be able to cease perpetual vigilance. Then, leaving school, there is the eventual release from the childhood of imprisonment. Suddenly children find themselves liberated. The lack of structure may leave some confused, whilst others throw themselves into excesses such as sex, alcohol and drug use –and, in some cases, abuse.

It is not unusual for ex-boarders to have a particular relationship to danger. Attaining adult status and a legal license to drive usually occurs around the time of leaving school. It seems to signify the freedom craved during the years of incarceration. The young man can choose his own risks. This may take the form of speed, motor racing or extreme sports, such as mountain climbing. Driving sports cars or motorbikes is common. Of course, this is common with young men whether or not they attended boarding school, but we are looking at particular aspects of the phenomenon connected with boarding, and one of these is escape.

In these observations I am informed by a number of clients, as well as respondents to my interviews. The lash of school discipline (often literally administered), combined with indiscipline (bullying), creates a psychological suit of armour. A child who has been physically beaten or threatened, or who has witnessed others being beaten, assumes an impenetrable exterior whereby he will not react even when hurt. This has its physical counterpart, which is often unconscious. Thus it may be that, when the opportunity arises, some may encase themselves in the protective equipment of their chosen sport. For example, those who engage in fencing are well defended with protective clothing and masks. It is similar with motorbike equipment: leathers, boots and helmets offer an outer skin and, simultaneously, a potent image. The young man thus clad is protected, speedy, and both visible and invisible. As with the trusty steed of old, there is a relationship between man and machine. Roald Dahl describes the thrill of secretly owning a motorbike during his last year at school:

> Without the slightest regret I said goodbye to Repton forever and rode back to Kent on my motorbike. This splendid machine was a 500cc Ariel which I had bought the year before for eighteen pounds, and during my last term at Repton I kept it secretly in a garage along the Willington road about two miles away. On Sundays I used to walk to the garage and disguise myself in helmet, goggles, old raincoat and rubber waders and ride all over Derbyshire. *It was fun roaring through Repton itself with nobody knowing who you were, swishing past the masters walking in the street and circling round the dangerous supercilious School Boazers out for their Sunday strolls.* [Italics added]. I tremble to think what would have happened to me had I been caught, but I wasn't caught. So on the last day of term I zoomed joyfully away and left school behind me forever and ever. I was not quite eighteen.[8]

The liberation after imprisonment is evident in this description. Dahl conveys the delight in the power of the machine and the satisfaction of anonymous revenge on the bullies. The motorbike offers the perfect getaway vehicle. Dahl is not alone in this. Again, although this was a long time ago, it is still relevant today. The story of one of my clients, Anton, illustrates the gradual construction of the armoured boarding school personality. It shows how eventually motorbikes became his psychological 'get-away vehicle'.

Anton's story: The lash and other boys

When the motorbike is unconsciously used as a get-away vehicle it can be extremely dangerous. This was the case with Anton. Anton's story illustrates the gradual construction of Boarding School Syndrome. We will trace his story from the initial traumatic bereavement of prep school to bullying in the student group, in both his prep and public schools. Bullying had blighted his school life until he became physically mature enough to prevent it. His love of speed and motorbikes had been a significant factor in bringing Anton into psychotherapy.

In school Anton had acquired a much-needed unconscious, defensive structure, which was now not easy to relinquish. Anton was a 35-year-old married man, with one young child. He had approached his GP suffering from unexplained depression and was referred to me for psychotherapy. Anton had been employed in a number of different jobs over the years but now he was self-employed. It became evident, as he recounted his employment history, that despite his success in a number of international companies, he had encountered workplace bullying in several of them. Unable to tolerate his 'unreasonable' employers, he had set up his own small business.

Anton had been married for seven years. Since the birth of his son six years earlier he had insisted that he and his wife sleep in separate rooms, an arrangement which suited him. In boarding school he had shared a dormitory in which he had never been able to relax because of the bullies. Now, free of school, he could choose to sleep in a space of his own; understandably his wife was unhappy about this arrangement. His boarding school experience was also reflected in his eating pattern. At the school dinner table he had been compelled to consume his food rapidly, lest other children stole it. Now he ate fast and was unable to enjoy the leisurely, companionable meals that his wife craved.

Motorbikes

Recently Anton had given up riding motorbikes, which had been his release since leaving his public school. He had been a member of a group which travelled the countryside in convoy at weekends, covering vast distances at great speed. His wife had enjoyed this too until their child was born, but then she gave it up. Anton continued to enjoy the thrill of the extreme risks he took on the open road. He would dodge between cars at dangerous speeds, competing with members of his group to arrive at a certain destination first. He felt immensely powerful, masked and anonymous in his leathers and helmet.

However, he was sharply confronted with the risks he was taking after two of his group had been injured and one killed in separate accidents over a relatively short period. Now a father, Anton began to become concerned about his own safety. Then one day, after overtaking when it was barely safe, he realised that it was only a matter of time before he too was killed or seriously injured. It was not long after this that he gave up motorbikes completely. He realised that he could not ride them safely. As a father he was beginning to realise that his life meant something to other people.

The creation of Boarding School Syndrome 1 – the threshold memory

Eventually we were able to trace the creation of this risk-taking personality back to the multiple experiences of bullying at his boarding schools. The psychological carapace he had acquired had served a necessary purpose whilst he was at school, but now it was redundant and obstructing his ability to live his life. As usual the first day at prep school was remembered as significant. Like so many of the others we have been considering in this book, this 'threshold moment' had been a traumatic event.

Anton was 6 years old when he was taken to his prep school by his parents and accompanied by his little sister. This was exciting, a very grown-up event for which there had been much preparation. He described how his arrival was confusing because there were so many people, teachers and other boys milling around. But it was OK because his parents were with him – and then he suddenly realised with horror that they, and his sister, were back in their car. Uncomprehending, he saw the wheels of the car turning and understood that they were driving away without him. They had not said goodbye. (As an adult he was to discuss this with his parents and was told that they thought that it would upset him if they said goodbye.) The bottom fell out of his world. Now he realised what it meant to be left at school. He felt alone in the world, deserted by his family.

Unlike those who suffer from amnesia, Anton recalled this moment as if it were yesterday. This day was seared into his memory and he was very distressed as he recounted it. I have discussed some aspects of Anton's story elsewhere.[9] I return to it, in this chapter, in order to look in depth at the lasting effects of bullying on an apparently successful ex-boarder. It might be thought that when the child leaves school he leaves behind all the childish experiences, including bullying, but it is not so simple. The effects of bullying and abuse shape the personality, and this continues to have implications in adult life.

Anton was the eldest of two children; his younger sister had been born when he was 5 years old. After the birth of his sister, his mother found his temper tantrums impossible to manage. It was therefore decided that boarding school would be good for him. It was a family tradition to send children to prep school, but usually at 8. Anton had accepted his parents' version of events: he had been a 'difficult child' so they had decided it would be good for him to go early, even though he was just 6. He had concluded that this was because he was bad and felt rejected. When I suggested that he might have been jealous of his sister, it came as something of a surprise to him. Sometimes it is not boarding school alone that has a negative impact, but the story the child is told associated with it. For Anton it had seemed that school was a punishment; he was banished for his badness rather than understood for being distressed at the birth of a sibling. This had continued to be his unconscious sense of it and therefore he felt the bullying was part of the same thing. He was bad, so what could he expect?

After reporting this history he talked about his current work and home life for several sessions. It was only when I asked him more about his school that he began to recount the many cruel incidents of bullying he had suffered. It had started in his earliest days at prep school and continued into his public school life, until he grew physically strong enough to prevent it. At first he dismissed the bullying as merely the type of initiation to which boys were subjected. However, as he became aware that I took these incidents very seriously, he began to do so himself. Then he told me the following story from his first days at prep school, where he was left in the care of strange adults. However, it was not the adults who mistreated him.

One late evening, very soon after he arrived, an older boy appeared to befriend him. He took him by the hand and said they were going for a walk. Innocently Anton allowed himself to be led out into the dark night, a long walk from the school. Then the older boy told him he was going to kill him. Anton was terrified. The boy told him that his parents were not there and no one would hear if he cried out. Having duly frightened the child, he stopped. Then he told him he was only joking and led him, still by the hand, back to the school. Anton was unable to tell anyone what had happened.

This is a case of what may happen in a student group when supervision is inadequate. It is a story of innocence abused. It reveals the trusting nature of a small child exposed to someone only a year or two older. A casual witness might consider that nothing very much had happened; there was no dramatic assault and no physical damage. However, the psychological effects of this incident had lasted nearly thirty years. Anton was in middle age and yet I was the first person he had ever told of this experience. This secret terror penetrated deep into his psyche and here remained unprocessed, unintegrated and unspeakable. His bodily integrity – indeed his very survival – was threatened. Such a trauma haunts the person unconsciously and taints their perception of the world.

Anton's experience highlights one problem: even if staff members are kind, the child is exposed to the impulses of other children for many hours in the day and (even worse) in the night. These children themselves are very young and may have little sense of the impact of their behaviour. Both of these prep school boys were unprotected. At their young age they should have been monitored. It is likely that the perpetrator as well as the victim was in the grip of terrifying fantasies. The distinction between fantasy and reality, between symbolic thought and action, was not yet formed in either of their young minds.

Initially we might blame the older boy as a sadistic abuser. However, he was also a small boy and he was out of control. He, too, was exposed because he could perpetrate an act that adults would have prevented had they known. This was negligence on behalf of the adults; clearly it was a failure in the duty of care. Inevitably this happens when the children are more numerous than the staff available.

Consider the older boy: we might hypothetically assume that he had been left in this school a year or two previously. He would therefore recognise Anton's insecurity. Appearing to take charge of the smaller boy might alleviate his own insecurity and prove to him that he was no longer the youngest. It is possible that he regarded this as a joke, but it is likely to have had a more sinister, if unconscious, psychological motive. By terrifying Anton, it is probable that he was sadistically externalising his own fear. Seeing it reflected in another, he could feel powerful, so in control of his own terrors. Then, in rescuing the younger boy, he could soothe himself and feel benign. One might speculate whether he felt guilt; if so there would be no one to whom to confess and to mediate his own rage and (probably terrifying) sadistic fantasies. Thus the psychology of the bully is intimately entwined with that of the victim.

However, our concern is the lasting impact of his behaviour on Anton. For Anton 'the terrible thing' had happened. For Anton this was no longer an unformed fear: he knew now just how vulnerable he was. His trust had been violently shattered. There were no words for what he had experienced and no one to tell. In order to survive, in cases like this, a hidden compartment in the self is acquired where such experiences are locked away. This type of dissociation is a common response to trauma (as we have seen in Chapter 8) and it is common with people who have suffered sexual abuse as children.[10][11] This was indeed a traumatic event in this child's life: Anton had learned that he could depend on no one. Initially his primary attachments were broken, and subsequently he was offered the potential friendship of an older boy, only to realise that he was at his mercy. He was 6 years old, abandoned, without loving care. Some sort of unconscious defensive structure was needed to protect the trusting vulnerable boy from further assaults.

The creation of Boarding School Syndrome 2—body armour

This defensive structure was further needed when Anton changed schools at 13. In his public school other boys soon picked on him and bullied him mercilessly until he grew too big for them to do so. The many horrifying tales of bullying included violent physical assaults by older boys with boiling water. These were the type of abuses described in Chapter 2. They were comparable with those so vividly described in the novel *Tom Brown's School Days*, which was based on Rugby

School in the nineteenth century.[12] The effect of this physical bullying on creating the armoured presentation of Boarding School Syndrome is significant.

The child exposed to such bullying is unprotected. Again, adults should have known – it was their job to protect him. The role of parents is to protect their child's physical welfare to create a safe circle, usually a family, in which the child can develop and be safe. A child in boarding school also has a right to be protected and, in the absence of the parents, this is the duty of care of the school staff. These people are in loco parentis; that is, the parents trust them to care for their child. When this fails, as it clearly did in Anton's case, there is no option but for the child to unconsciously assume this function for himself as best he can. He is immature and can only approximate such self-care with a brittle exterior presentation. Thus a form of psychological armour is acquired whereby the child seems impervious. Emotionally the true self shrinks into a tiny sphere where it is no longer known. This is why it is so difficult for the ex-boarder to have intimate relationships in adult life. Deep within is the hidden vulnerable child who trusts no one. The outer presentation is a tough invincible masculine image.

Anton participated in sports that built his muscles and eventually he became a black belt in karate. He found that he could command respect because of his physical size. An able and respected sportsman, he now became a protector to younger boys. If he saw a boy being bullied, he would intervene. Now, as an adult, he continued to relish his physical size, knowing that no one would dare to challenge him. He would regard men in public places and assess their physical strength. He knew he now had the physical power to take on all comers; moreover, he could protect his family. They were permitted to be vulnerable; he was not. Thus he was equipped with a physicality that echoed his psychological armour. However, it was not easy to get close to him emotionally, as his wife realised; he never talked about his feelings. Motorbikes had symbolised this sense of invincibility. Armoured, he could fly past cars and other motorcyclists, feeling like the fastest and most powerful thing on the road.

However, his sense of invincibility had broken down. Becoming a father meant that, emotionally, he was less sure of his indestructability. His own child was now attaining the age when Anton had been sent away and this confronted him with how young he had been. His unconditional love for his child helped him to contact his disbelief; he could not imagine how his parents could have sent him to school at the same age. A sense of compassion for himself now emerged through identification with his own child.

It may not be boarding school alone but a combination of that and the home environment that sets a boy up for being bullied. It emerged over time that his mother had an unpredictable temper and, prior to the birth of his sister, when they were alone, she would frighten Anton with irrational behaviour and unjust punishments. It also indicates that his mother might have been relieved to send him away and let others care for him. This led him to feel bad about himself before he started school. Possibly this bullying at home may have predisposed him to being bullied at school.

Boarding School Syndrome and bullying in the present

Anton continued to suffer the after-effects of his schooling. The powerful defence that he had acquired made him virtually unemployable: he could not take orders from anyone. At the school dinner table his food had been stolen and, in bed at night, he never felt safe from the bullies. Thus, once he escaped from school, he revelled in eating at his own pace and sleeping alone where no one could surprise him in the night. He could not bear to take the risk of letting another person close. He did not trust, and this blighted his intimate relationships; his marriage was under threat.

As Anton had protected the younger boys at school from the bullies, he now looked after his loved ones. He was fiercely protective of them. However, he did not expect anyone to look after him. We might understand this in the light of Boarding School Syndrome. The male boarder is trained in a similar way to an officer in the military, to look after his men and to care for others before himself. Consciously, Anton was friendly, kind and thoughtful, but the unconscious opposite of this was that he was also furiously angry. His fear of his own violence kept him isolated; he kept separate to protect those he loved from the perceived danger of getting close to him.

Psychotherapy

Psychotherapy can be like a rehearsal for real life. The therapist is in the privileged position of being empowered to try to approach the difficulties with intimacy. This is a daunting task with someone who has been armoured and invincible for most of his life. Often this behaviour replays in the transference, as it did with Anton. He was at first relieved to be able to confide the stories of traumatic childhood events. This helped him to gradually come to understand why he had always cut off from people who came emotionally close to him. Banished by his parents because of his rage, he continued to feel dangerous in relationships. Bullied by boys at school, he identified with their aggression and anticipated that I would fear him for his power and his size. However, what I saw behind this apparent power was the small boy who had suffered immense hurt.

In common with other ex-boarders, Anton had, in the past, cut himself off suddenly from jobs and from girlfriends. This is a common form of self-harm in Boarding School Syndrome. The person makes a deeply dependent relationship and then severs his emerging tender feelings. Abandoning the loved object is an extreme form of self-abuse; simultaneously it unconsciously expresses rage towards the present lover and those who abandoned him in the past. This replays as psychotherapy begins to become important. Anton expressed his concern about how he would manage when, eventually, psychotherapy ended.

With ex-boarders, the breaks in psychotherapy apparently have little impact at first. The regular pattern of school holidays followed by the return to school arms the ex-boarder with a mechanism for coping with disrupted attachments: he is expert at cutting off. This Anton did for the first two breaks in psychotherapy, telling me that he had been fine. However, after the third break, psychotherapy nearly came to an abrupt end when he left a message informing me that he now needed to stop and work things out for himself. This is a common occurrence when working with Boarding School Syndrome.[13][14][15] Anton could not bear dependency and so he reverted to the previous method of dealing with attachments in his adult life; the impulse was to leave.

It is likely that Anton experienced the feelings that were emerging in the transference as intensely dangerous. The decision to leave was probably motivated by an unconscious need to protect us both from his potential violence. John Steiner writes of the 'patient who is dominated by feelings of resentment and grievance' and suggests that such patients use a form of 'psychic retreat which operates as a defence against anxiety and guilt'.[16] Feelings of 'resentment and grievance' threatened Anton's previous self-image. His defences were breaking down and he was forming an attachment to me. As a result, the sense of injustice and his previously unconscious wish for revenge began to become live in the present. Steiner describes this type of emotional turmoil: 'These patients feel wronged but are unable to express their wish for revenge actively by openly attacking the objects which have wronged them.' Some hold back for fear of retaliation but others are inhibited because of the 'fear that the revenge would be excessive'.[17]

Consciously, Anton was a caring man, but he was beginning to realise that he was violently vengeful. His anger was becoming conscious and he began to realise he was angry with his mother for abandoning him and his sister for replacing him. This anger was replaying in the transference. His impulse to leave was fuelled by conflicted emotions: a desire to make me suffer, as he had, but also the fear that he would wreak some terrible revenge. The 'psychic retreat' to which Steiner refers is an emotional retreat, but with the ex-boarder it can be enacted as a concrete abandonment of the process. Anton was courageous: with encouragement he returned to discuss his decision and eventually agreed to continue.

His return brought the violence of his feelings to the fore; he was terrified of what he might do to me. It became evident that, no longer a victim, he was scared of his own power: now he could be the sadistic abuser. For a while he could not distinguish between his violent fantasies and acting on them; to imagine destruction was to have done it. It took a while for this to become separated out and for him to realise that his hateful fantasies were a form of attachment.

This story is far from unique and only one of many similarly damaging histories that are reported. The deep scars left on the psyche may remain active in the adult, affecting the person's ability to love. The armoured personality is a form of false masculinity, initially created as bravado at a time when the child is too small to defend himself. It then becomes a way of being and influences the way men interact as adults.

The armoured self

It is hardly surprising that boarding schools produce armoured personalities. At the same time as losing everything, the child is attempting to do the 'right thing' and to adapt to an alien system. Within the armour is encapsulated the unconscious emotional life of the person. In boys' schools these are often the attributes split off and rejected as belonging to the feminine in society. They might include love, hate, sadness and erotic sexuality. One of the unspoken rules, clearly conveyed through the ranks of this system, is that boys don't cry. Thus the child soon learns to hide his feelings. The taboo on expressing emotion results in both an inner-world problem and, at a later stage, a social one. This damages the relationship to those attributes deemed feminine in the male psyche. An ambivalent attitude to women may be an external manifestation of this.

Notes

1. Boys' prep schools usually take children from 7 or 8 (sometimes younger) up to 13, when boys take the common entrance examinations. Girls' schools take children as young as 4 and 5 and they usually change schools at either 11 or at 13.
2. Wakeford, J. (1969) *The Cloistered Elite: A Sociological Analysis of the English Public School*, London: Macmillan, pp. 47–48.
3. Peter Lewis traces this split in his semi-autobiographical account; Lewis, P. (1991) 'Mummy matron and the maids: Feminine presence and absence in male institutions 1934–63,' in Roper, M. & Tosh, J. (eds) *Manful Assertions*, London: Taylor & Francis.
4. Chandos, J. (1984) *Boys Together: English Public Schools 1800–1864*, London: Yale University Press, p. 99.
5. Herman, J. (1992/1997) *Trauma and Recovery: The Aftermath of Violence From Domestic Abuse to Political Terror*, New York: Basic Books, p. 96.
6. Raphael, F. (2003) *A Spoilt Boy*, London: Orion. Also see 'Outcast of the sixth', *The Sunday Times*, (9 March 2004), News Review, p. 9.
7. Sacks, O. (2001) *Uncle Tungsten*, London: Picador.
8. Dahl, R. (1984) *Boy: Tales of Childhood*, London: Puffin Books, pp. 167–169.
9. Schaverien, J. (2011a) 'Boarding School Syndrome: Broken attachments a hidden trauma', *British Journal of Psychotherapy* 17 (2), pp. 138–155.
10. Wilkinson, M. (2006) *Coming Into Mind*, London: Routledge.
11. Messler Davies, J., & Frawley, M. G. (1994) *Treating the Adult Survivor of Childhood Sexual Abuse*, New York: Basic Books.
12. Hughes, T. (1857/2013) *Tom Brown's School Days*, Burlingame, California: Collins Classics.
13. Schaverien, J. (2002) *The Dying Patient in Psychotherapy: Desire, Dreams and Individuation*, New York: Palgrave Macmillan.
14. Schaverien, J. (2004) 'Boarding school: The trauma of the "privileged" child', *Journal of Analytical Psychology* 49 (5), pp. 683–705.
15. Schaverien (2011a), op. cit.
16. Steiner, J. (1993) *Psychic Retreats*, London: Routledge, p. 74.
17. Ibid.

Chapter 14

The hidden self
Girls and the tyranny of the dinner table

Although there were many experiences common to girls' and boys' schools, the treatment differed and so resulted in different long-term consequences. In the last two chapters we have seen how inadequate food and sleep as well as unjust physical punishments impact the psychological welfare of children. We observed how, with boys, this might result in the creation of an armoured self and a careless attitude to danger. Girls were trained to hide their emotions too, but in a rather different way. In this chapter the stories of four women from different generations illustrate the creation of the hidden self. This is a kind of internalised oppression arrived at not through overt brutality but through training in selflessness.

Conditions in girls' schools could be as harsh as those already described, but the regime was often less obviously violent. In Chapter 2 we saw how beatings were ubiquitous in boys' schools. Consequently, boys learned to conceal their vulnerability and to project an image of premature masculinity. In Chapter 3 we saw that in girls' schools beatings were far less common and fagging was not part of the culture. Teachers might strike girls and some might be cruelly demeaning but without resorting to the excesses of physical violence meted out to boys. Staff members were sometimes extremely controlling and if they took a dislike to a child could make her school days miserable. Moreover, bullying in the student group could, and often did, plague the child's life. Consequently, like boys, girls also learned to conceal their vulnerability – but, rather than an overtly armoured presentation, they may have appeared to conform to the culture of the school whilst inwardly rebelling.

The expectation of fulfilling the traditional roles of womanhood were inculcated in the girls by the staff and the expectations of their parents. Traditionally, girls were raised in preparation for a life of attending to the needs of others. Whilst being imbued with a culture of service, the environment was often devoid of emotional warmth. The child deprived of personal care developed strategies for coping in a system that was often incomprehensible and permeated with its own form of institutionalised cruelty.

In the early twentieth century many women remained unmarried. There were a number of reasons for this. First, it was a result of the decimation of the male population in World War I, which meant that there was a shortage of young men in that generation. Second, until the mid-twentieth century women were obliged to choose between a career and marriage, and as soon as they married, women teachers had to give up their teaching posts. Third, some women chose the path of academia or school teaching, and so remained single. Amongst these were some very idealistic teachers who were dedicated to the advancement of the education of women. They were altruistic, motivating the girls in their care and eventually bringing about some of the important changes that paved the way for feminist advances of the later part of the twentieth century. They influenced social policy and fought for equal opportunities for girls in education.[1]

Communities of women

One of my informants, Edith, now 85, tells of a school run by such idealistic women teachers. Edith attended the Beacon School in Bridge of Allan, Scotland, from soon after the outbreak of war in September 1939:

> The Beacon may have been recommended because they were used to having girls whose parents were in eastern countries [with her parents she had been living in Haifa, Palestine, soon to become Israel] and if the school had a tradition I think it would be feminist pioneering rather than old traditional. It was started in the 1920s by a group of academic English women from Oxford and Cambridge. The name 'Beacon' was because it was a beacon for the future of educated women who were free to achieve. The Head told our parents and us this at a Speech Day.

Edith reported that only the less-academic girls took domestic science classes, so even in later life, she never enjoyed cooking, always considering it rather a demeaning activity. This school was clearly unusual for its time both in its academic aspirations and deliberate turning away from traditional roles for girls' education. Edith's story gives a sense of how educationally progressive some schools could be in the early to mid-twentieth century. The idealism of the teachers and their enthusiasm for their subjects clearly permeated the school. This, alongside their affection for the girls in their charge, comes across in Edith's vivid pen portrait. She seemed to feel liked by her teachers, as she continued:

> The headmistress was called Miss Buchanan, her sister was Matron (she wore a nurse's uniform with a big handkerchief head dress and we were in awe of her. I thought she was rather ugly but very kind). Miss Buchanan was probably in her forties. I thought she was nice looking with a pale soft skin, a long upper lip, and dark wavy hair. She was kind and we felt we were listened to and understood. Miss Rosemary J. Nichol, a tall, beautiful, very thin woman with sandy hair in a bun and elegant clothes was my housemistress when I moved to the middle school house. She had been a missionary in Africa and was very religious. [All names have been changed.]

The teachers, who had been faced with a choice between marriage – at that time the acceptable place for eros and sexuality – and their professional lives, dedicated their lives to the school. Some women teachers were involved in lesbian partnerships, which had to remain hidden due to the mores of the time. The school may have offered a haven for such relationships, where women could live in close association without having to declare their sexuality. In Edith's school there was such a couple:

> Miss Robertson and Miss Craig lived together and although the words lesbian or homosexual were not, as far as I remember, in our vocabulary, we knew they were sexual partners. They wore Harris Tweed suits, with skirts. Robby's was brown and she managed to look feminine even though both wore shirts and ties and brogues. Robby taught history and was my Form Mistress. She gave me a lifelong interest in history. . . . Craigy, in her green tweeds and short straight black hair, taught Maths and Science and was stern but she too liked me, I think, and was encouraging. I remember all the staff as receptive and felt liked, although they were inaccessible physically in the sense that touching or hugging was unthinkable. We compensated for losing the physicality of family life by turning to each other for love and comfort.

It seems that these teachers were accepted as a couple, so this begs the question of why affection between the girls was considered to be so dangerous.

However, not all teachers were as idealistic as these women, who seem to have produced a high level of education and expectation amongst the girls. In many girls' schools, the education was poor and certainly below the standards of the boys' public schools. The teachers in these schools upheld many of the stereotyped social attitudes to women and this was reflected in their expectations of the girls in their charge.

Dorothy Ruth West was the headmistress of Christ's Hospital girls' school for thirty years, from 1942 to 1972, and her memoir records that period.[2] Christ's Hospital was a charitable school, originally a hospital for orphans and pupils from disadvantaged backgrounds. This changed during the mid-twentieth century, but the nomenclature reveals this hospital tradition. The schoolhouses were called wards and the housemistresses were known as 'wardmistresses'. West reminisced about the school she inherited in 1942, admitting that the school was institutionalised and this was emphasised by the green and dark brown paint with which it was decorated. Each highly organised ward housed thirty-six girls and in each the layout was similar. There were two dormitories, a day room and a study for the use of the sixth-form girls. Here the girls spent their out-of-school hours, doing preparation (homework) in the evenings and letter writing and reading on Sundays. Despite the similarity in layout, each had its own character influenced by the wardmistress (house parent). Each was like a private domain; anyone visiting would ring a doorbell in order to be admitted. When West took over in 1942 friendships between girls in different wards were discouraged and permission had to be obtained to visit a girl in a different ward. According to West, 'this led to a very tight and loyal community of thirty-six girls and the Wardmistress.'[3]

As in other schools, which had similar rules, this may have been a 'tight and loyal community' but the girls' freedom was curtailed. One might speculate about why it was that girls were not permitted to make friends with those in other houses. This rigid control was perhaps a result of the fear of sexuality as it was in boys' schools.[4] Perhaps this was legislation against the emergence of love, intense friendships or lesbian relationships being formed beyond the watchful eye of the wardmistress. Although this was not made explicit it might have been seen as an implicit threat to the order of the community. In this there seems to have been confusion between the ordinary intimate friendships between girls and those expressed physically in sexual encounters.

I am grateful to Denise, a woman who drew my attention to West's book. Denise is now in her seventies. She attended Christ's Hospital School from 1951, when she was 10, until 1958 when she was 17. She lived under the regime of this same headmistress.

Service and the hidden self

In girls' schools in general, girls – whose chief social role was to be wives and mothers of the next generation of men – were taught to subjugate their needs to those of others. This was commonly instilled through service in the school. This ethos of service pervaded the life of the girls when they were not involved in schoolwork. West describes the intimate nature of the chores expected of the girls. Each had her own job in the ward: some cleaned the brass, the taps in the bathrooms and the brass on the front door bell. Others took care of the clothes. There was a hierarchy, at the top of which was the head wardrobe girl. The youngest member of the team had the task of collecting soiled handkerchiefs and counting them for the laundry. Each girl had twelve handkerchiefs and these were kept in a special drawer. When they were returned clean it was the youngest girl's duty to put them away and make sure that two clean handkerchiefs were placed on each person's shelf every week. West tells us that those who had colds were allowed more. The following year the same girl might move on to managing the knickers, then the blouses and night dresses, until eventually she attained the status of head wardrobe girl. The clothes were numbered. This was because each girl was allotted a number, which she kept whilst at the school. In the mornings as girls assembled for prayers their numbers rather than names were signed off. West observes: 'It was not a system I liked, for it seemed so formal, but it was quick and efficient.'[5]

Denise recalls these tasks: 'I was a wardrobe girl but never became head. I stopped at knickers because I kept getting the numbers wrong and I didn't like dealing with dirty knickers.' Others likely shared this reaction. Denise noted that the terms *wards* and *wardmistresses* are reminiscent of members of prison staff, who are usually known as *warders*. Moreover the use of numbers rather than names for the girls may be 'quick and efficient' but it reinforces the impression of this as a form of penitentiary. Numbering children depersonalises them and accentuates the fact that they are neither known nor loved.

There are numerous, subtle ways in which the innate capacity of the child for trust in loving relationships may have been eroded. Often this occurred over time, as a barely discernable diminishing which was hardly noticed by the child herself. It is merely that less support was expected or anticipated; she learned to 'go it alone'. In the absence of a loving connection, children may develop a defensive exterior. Growing to maturity in this bleak setting would disturb the girl's sense of her embodied self. This was compounded because development of her sensuality and sexuality was either ignored or denied.

The idea of femininity imposed on these girls was more like the hard masculinity described in Chapter 13. Like the boys, girls too had to assume a protective shell in order to survive, and they too had to remain hidden. The girls' schools of this time were based on the well-tried and -tested model of the boys' public schools that had preceded them. In the patriarchal society of the time, girls were still being trained to be the wives and mothers of the men who went to build the Empire. Thus the girls' creativity and aliveness remained unseen, often unknown even to themselves, unless they challenged the rules with humour and rebelliousness.

I turn now to a more recent example of the ways in which bullying contributes to the hidden self.

Bullying and initiation

There are many ways in which girls learn to keep emotionally hidden. As we have seen, formal beatings were less common in girls' than in boys' schools, and fagging, which was a legitimised form of bullying, was not part of the tradition. However, informal abuse took place, usually during the evenings and the nights when staff numbers were reduced or no staff were present. At those times children were exposed to the potential cruelty of their peers. Whilst not overtly encouraged, the institution fostered hierarchical and anarchic forms of behaviour amongst the girls.

Philippa had been taken to boarding school in the mid-1960s, when she was 9. She was unusual amongst my respondents in that, for her, the threshold moment was not remembered as an extreme experience of bereavement, nor was it forgotten. Philippa was now 50 and married with three teenage children. The youngest of four girls, she had been impatient to join her sisters at the school, which she knew well from visiting them. The first day she remembers being excited. Upon arriving at the school, she noticed that all the other little girls were crying. Philippa was puzzled; she did not understand why they were upset. This is unusual, and is likely to have been because the transition from home to school was apparently gradual; she had been well prepared.

Philippa enjoyed school, excelling at sport and making lifelong friendships. She considered herself lucky: school had been fun and, unlike others she knew, she had not suffered bullying. Then she started to remember an initiation to which she had been subjected. As Philippa talked, she realised that she had not previously remembered the first-year dormitory, which she shared with ten other girls. She mentioned, in an offhand way, the 'initiation' to which she was subjected in that dormitory: she was stripped naked and then hit with slippers by the other girls. This story was quickly told, without emotion, and Philippa would have passed on to another topic. However, I asked her to pause and think about what she had just told me. As she thought about her 9-year-old self, her demeanour changed; she now began to remember how frightening this had been. Thinking about her own children and how small they were at that age, she began to soften and find some empathy for the child she had been. Philippa had never considered this to be bullying – it was just a normal part of what happened. However, she had never thought of sending her own children away to school. Now she began to appreciate why. She recognised that she had completely blocked the memory of that first-year dormitory, remembering instead her second-year dormitory, which had been much smaller and shared with just two girls whom she liked. Moreover, she was already used to living at school by then.

This is what happens: words such as 'initiation' are attributed to behaviours which would normally be deemed completely unacceptable. Philippa's initiation had been a traumatic event, but for her it was the beginning of becoming accustomed to the ethos of school society. Such institutionalised abuse profoundly affects what the child expects of social relationships. A change in the psychological attitude of the child occurs and a new script is written in which previously shocking behaviours are condoned. The child accepts the rule of the mob. Worse still, members of staff tacitly condone such behaviour, as they apparently ignore it.

Thus, if Philippa's experience were to be reframed in the light of adult perception, she had as a child been exposed to abuse from her peers. This was not the formalised beating given by the prefect in Jason's school, who felt entitled to punish another boy from his superior status (Chapter 13). This was a different form of beating: other children who had themselves probably suffered similar indignities perpetrated this act. They felt a sense of permission to do unspeakable things when teachers were absent. This is the 'Lord of the Flies' mentality, the law of the mob, to which children are exposed in the absence of adult supervision.[6] Philippa was now beginning to take her experiences seriously. She recalled another incident of initiation to which she had been subjected: She was encouraged to climb a tree and then was tied up in it. The other girls were jeering and laughing at her, and she did not understand why. Then they disappeared, leaving her tied up there alone with no one in sight. She had to find a way of getting herself down from the tree, which took time and was very frightening.

This incident was bullying that involved both physical and emotional injury, but it was masquerading as 'initiation'. Thus language distorts the child's perception of right and wrong. To complain about such abuse is to risk the scorn of the group and therefore increase the potential for increased bullying. If it is endured with apparent good humour, the person is then considered a 'good sport' and accepted as one of the group, an 'initiate'. This is how Philippa had coped. She had not admitted, even to herself, the shock and humiliation of being treated in this way. Nor did she admit the fear that the group could turn against her and mete out such punishments at will.

Ignoring pain and shame is a common way of dealing with such incidents, but it also has the effect of subtly eroding the person's attitude to himself or herself. The wounded and vulnerable part of the self remains hidden, safely encapsulated, where its truth is concealed from conscious awareness. This is a common and lasting effect of early trauma (as we saw in Chapter 8). It seems that Philippa did not suffer the pain of separation from her parents as a traumatic bereavement. However, she did suffer from being exposed to bullying in the student group. Glossed over, such an incident is made worse because there is no one in whom to confide, so the child internalises the shame and humiliation.

Philippa's strategies for survival had been humour and, as she put it, 'being naughty'. These had helped deflect from her loneliness and from potential trouble with her peers. It was only now, as an adult, that she realised how her relationship to herself had been affected. As she put it, she had 'spent nine years of her childhood looked after by adults who did not love her'. She had been cheerful, humorous and good at sport, and her vulnerability had been hidden, even from herself. It also remained hidden throughout two analyses. Philippa's first analysis took place in her late twenties at twice a week. Then in her thirties she embarked on analysis for a further five years at three times a week. In neither of these analyses was the trauma of her boarding school experience addressed. It was not until she was in her fifties that a third analysis, at three times a week, brought the suffering of her time at boarding finally and painfully to the fore. This is very common, as already noted. The ex-boarder does not realise the depth of the trauma of such incidents and the analyst may miss it.

Whilst the humour and friendliness of such a woman is different from the hard carapace that students acquire in boys' schools through the beatings they suffer, it is still an outer presentation that hides the inner core of the person. Moreover, it is typical of the way in which Boarding School Syndrome becomes established.

Why did the child not tell?

Here resides one important difference between day and boarding schools: bullying occurs in day schools, but despite the upsetting nature of such events, the child returns home in the evening. For many (although not all) this offers a refuge, a place away from the bully. As already stated, in some homes the chaos and bullying is far worse than that suffered in many boarding schools. However, in many homes, even if the child cannot speak of it, parents notice and are concerned if the child is apparently upset. For the boarder there is no respite and no one to notice.

The instinct may be to tell, but there is no one to listen. This may compound the sense of having been abandoned and contribute to the devastating realisation of being alone in the world.

This raises the question of why, when they saw their parents in the holidays or at weekend exeats, children were unable to tell them of the abuses they suffered. For young children, what happens to them is the norm. Many children rationalised what was happening as normal, even though a part of them recognised it was wrong. Some did try to tell their parents, but it was apparently dismissed with some comment such as, 'Go back and it will be all right' or 'You will get used to it.' Some parents were desensitised by having boarded themselves and they expected their children to survive as they had. There were some parents who did complain to the school and were reassured that steps would be taken over whatever the incident was. In some cases action was taken but the parents were rarely informed.

Children find it difficult to give weight to the gravity of their experiences. They cannot with confidence formulate the treatment they suffered as unjust – often unconsciously they blame themselves. They reason that their parents love them, they are paying a lot of money for this 'privilege' and they think it is good. Therefore, it must be good. The corollary, often unconscious, is, 'I must be bad for not liking it.'[7] There is another dimension, which is the convention that you do not talk and you do not tell tales. This imperative is most strongly imposed by perpetrators of sexual abuse but it was also present in the boarding schools. Children's letters home used to be censored. They would be written at a supervised, appointed time, usually Sunday afternoons. The staff would read the letters and children who complained would be told they could not write this in their letters. Some were made to write another, blander, message. At times letters would be torn up. In one school the offending passages were cut out and the letter sent with those bits missing. One boy who was consistently bullied and unhappy in his school wrote every week to his parents in Africa telling them how unhappy he was and begging them to come and get him. His sister who recounted this story to me was in a school nearby and knew of her brother's distress, but she could do nothing. Brendon gives many examples of such letters written from troubled children to their parents and discusses how the letters were frequently inspected.[8]

Table manners

In order to consider in increasing depth the creation of problematic appetite patterns, we return to the dining room. Nourishment is central for the well being of the child and, as well as physical need, food may be considered for its symbolic value. Food produced with care is generally experienced as good food but, if those preparing it consider it a chore, it may become emotionally as well as physically indigestible.

Girls who were being prepared for the traditional roles of wives and mothers soon learned to place their own needs second to those of others. They were taught to be selfless and self-effacing.[9] However, when children in a school are hungry they do not automatically behave selflessly: as we saw in Chapter 12, some children stole food from others. This type of bullying permanently affected the appetite of children such as Nina and Anton, who as an adult preferred to eat alone. Therefore, some schools tried to legislate against such behaviour by restraining it and invoking strict rules known as 'table manners'. Table manners began with the duty of preparation for meals.

Once again, West sets the scene. Some meals were taken in the ward, and some in the dining room. She describes the laying of dining tables in the wards in preparation for meals. There were two monitors, and one of these was in charge of laying tables. There was clearly precision to this routine. The team involved went into action fifteen minutes before the food was served. They would enter the dining room carrying baskets which contained the cutlery, thirty-six plates and thirty-six glasses. The girls set these out, measuring their exact distance from the edge of the table. Then the meal was brought in by the kitchen staff. At this point girls marched in took their places and said grace before sitting to eat.[10]

Here, food – which intuitively symbolises love and care in many homes – is merely a scheduled duty to be negotiated. The dining room is often stressful and (as we saw from Mary Stack's experience, in Chapter 12) some feared its chaos. The competition for sparse supplies of food meant that patterns of rapid eating might develop which continue into adult life. This overt greedy behaviour was discouraged in girls' schools through a strictly hierarchical arrangement.

Hierarchy at the dinner table

Many ex-boarders have described hierarchical seating arrangements in the dining room. Each school had its own particular way of imposing them. In the school where West was headmistress, seating at meals was arranged according to seniority. Girls usually sat next to the same people for their entire school career.[11]

In Rose's school (Chapter 10), in the 1980s, the dining room was laid out with long tables along which were seated pairs of girls. At the top of the table were the most senior pair of girls; the others then sat in descending order of age. Each week the girls moved down the table. It was the task of the pair at the end to go to the counter and get the food for the others on their table. There was choice, so this meant remembering what everyone wanted to eat. If the wrong thing were presented to the older girls, there was trouble. The whole event was overseen by the headmistress, who would sit on a raised platform with two girls, one on either side of her. It was an honour to be selected to sit with her. Thus the formal hierarchy was reinforced through seniority and perceived favouritism.

It was similar in Philippa's school: the tables were mixed-age groups and girls were moved around every few weeks. Apparent consideration for others was demonstrated through table manners. The unspoken message seems to have been to curb the appetite in favour of others. This was probably intended to be good for social relationships but it was also stressful if the girl was placed beside someone of whom she was in awe. The girls were taught that it is not polite to ask for food so if, for example, a girl wanted the butter she would not say, 'Please pass me the butter.' Instead she would offer it to her neighbour, saying, 'Would you like some butter?' This was the cue for that person, in turn, to offer it to her. However, this did not always work out; sometimes, when there was a particularly fearsome older girl sitting next to her, Philippa did not dare to set this process in motion. Constrained by the convention of table manners she could not ask her neighbour directly to pass the butter and did not dare to offer it to that girl either. This meant that sometimes she went without butter on her bread or milk in her coffee.

This distortion of appetite, as well as communication, was common in girls' schools. Many of those whom I have interviewed shared similar experiences. Instead of a direct request, the desire is couched in terms of the needs of the other. It is disingenuous but perhaps was devised to compensate for the opposite impulse, exemplified by the children who took food from other peoples' plates. In substituting consideration for the other for personal greed, the school seems well intentioned. However, the effect was that the girl learned to subjugate her own needs. This may have affected her appetites as well as later patterns of relating, emotionally and sexually. Everything about the school communicated the unconscious message to curb her desires.

Eating disorders

The girl's own desires were also overruled when she was forced to ingest food that she found unpalatable for whatever reason. Battles over finishing the food served were common. West found this 'a barbaric custom'. She describes how there was sometimes a tussle between the wardmistress and a girl about eating a certain dish. If the girl continued to refuse she was made to take it and eat it in front of the headmistress. West notes that both she and her deputy hated seeing girls being made to eat cold food.[12] Reading this, one is left with the obvious question: if the headmistress considered the custom barbaric, why did she not stop it? Perhaps she was not as powerful as the role might indicate.

If the instillation of table manners was overzealous, or the child was forced to eat food she found inedible, the result might be a disturbed relationship to food. At the most extreme this might result in a serious eating disorder such as bulimia or anorexia. Eating disorders are common in girls' boarding schools, but they are prevalent in girls and young women throughout Western societies.[13] Increasingly, boys and men also suffer from eating disorders although this remains less common.[14] [15] The aetiology is complicated and it would be simplistic to suggest that eating disorders are merely due, in these cases, to living in a boarding school. However, appetite disturbances such as anorexia are often a manifestation of a sense of powerlessness.[16] [17] [18] They are usually a very private affliction, but in boarding schools there are times when they reach epidemic proportions, with girls competing to eat less or be thinner than their peers. They are often a battle for control in a situation where the girl feels powerless, and so living in a school where every aspect of life is regulated may play a part. There will be other factors.

Frequently the girls who suffer in this way are high achievers, apparently happy in school; they make no fuss and so their distress is hidden until the staff or family notices their weight loss. For some of these girls, the loss of their mother or primary carer may be felt most acutely at mealtimes. The manifestation of eating disorders has been observed through many generations.[19][20] In order to bring this up to date, I turn now to my recent analytic practice. In schools, attitudes to food are different now – but still the basic unhappiness of the girl separated from her family may find expression through an eating disorder.

Josephine

Josephine was 16 and still attending a boarding school when she was referred to me for psychotherapy. Her parents lived abroad but returned regularly to this country, where they owned a house not far from the school. In common with other children of the twenty-first century, Josephine was in regular contact with her mother by phone and email, and she was visited and taken home for weekends every few weeks. This was not the 1970s but the second decade of the twenty-first century, and things in boarding schools had improved greatly. The school was mixed sex and its ethos seemed to be kindly and concerned. The house parents were on the whole approachable; there were school counsellors and doctors available. If there were concerns, the child's welfare would be discussed with their parents. In Josephine's school there was a choice of dishes, and snacks were always available in-between meals. But this was no compensation for home. The child's distress was expressed through her attitude to her body and her intake of food was part of that.

Josephine had attended a day school until she was 13. When her parents obtained work in another country, it was decided that it would be best for Josephine to stay in the UK and board. Her older sister had recently left the same school, so she knew it quite well from visiting. At 13 none of the issues described earlier regarding early loss of attachment figures applied in her case, and her parents had treated her respectfully and discussed the decision to board with her. She understood the pragmatic reasons and agreed with them.

The unsymbolised self

Unable to articulate her emotions, Josephine had been deeply affected by the loss of her home and her parents, without at first knowing what was amiss. Like many others who seemed to adapt, she had at first felt lost and missed her parents, but then apparently recovered. It was not the first term but the second when it struck her with some force that she would be living here for a very long time. She was lonely and unhappy, feeling separate from the other girls, with whom she had little in common. She was doing very well academically and part of her thought the school was good for her because of the academic and sporting opportunities it provided. She was also aware of the difficulty it would present for her parents if she let them know she was unhappy. So she internalised her distress – it had no words, no form that could help her understand what was troubling her. Unable to symbolise or speak of her suffering, and not understanding what was wrong with her, the distress became established in embodied form. Her body rebelled.

She started exercising excessively and then gradually reducing her food intake. As a consequence, she felt powerful. Her periods stopped. Emotionally she became frozen. The house parents and the school doctor were concerned about her sharp loss of weight and contacted her parents. As her BMI became dangerously low, numerous approaches had been tried with her. At the point she was referred to me there was a good chance that she would have to leave the school and possibly be admitted to hospital.

Josephine attended for weekly psychotherapy sessions and at first talked very little. I would have to try to guess at how she might be feeling and find ways of talking to her about what I perceived from her presentation. However, gradually she came to trust me and to talk about things apparently unconnected with her weight loss. It emerged that just before her parents had left the country Josephine's maternal grandmother had died. Josephine had been very close to this grandmother and knew her mother had been greatly affected by the loss. However, there had been no acknowledgement of Josephine's bereavement. Questions raised by her first experience of the death of someone close to her had remained unprocessed.

As we continued our meetings, she began to understand how sad she had been. Now she became angry with her parents for sending her away. She was also angry with the school as well as her parents for their high expectations of her academic success. It all felt like a demand, a performance she had to achieve for others. For many months she attended weekly sessions. As her own viewpoint began to emerge, she was able to make the choice to stay at school and finish her course. This was now for herself rather than for anyone else. She talked to her mother about how she was feeling. Although her mother had high expectations, she listened to her point of view with respect. As time passed, the eating disorder ameliorated. With the help of the school doctor her exercise regime became more manageable as she began to understand her metabolism. Significantly, she was permitted to be unhappy and no longer felt she had to be the perfect daughter. Thus she began to express her individuality, to separate psychologically from her parents and so to claim her autonomy. It took another year before she had a period, symbolically permitting her to begin to grow into adulthood as a woman.

In working with young people who are still attending boarding school, particular sensitivity is demanded of the analyst. It is important to be impartial and to see the parents' and teachers' viewpoints, as well as that of the child. It may be enough to witness the distress, providing a space to talk about the young peoples' worries. In finding words for emotional experiences, symbolisation can begin to take place. The distress no longer has to be acted out concretely through the body. The relationship to food often symbolises other deep discomforts or disturbances which need to come to consciousness.

In this chapter we have observed, through witness accounts, the attitudes to food and girls' bodies in schools as they changed through the generations from the 1930s up to today. We see how very much has changed but how some things remain the same. The free and unstructured time when bullying can fill the gap is still significant, as is the traumatic severing of familial ties. I am suggesting that the effects of this rather hidden form of rupture may result in a different manifestation of Boarding School Syndrome in some girls and women. In the next chapter I turn to that most fundamental aspect of the boarding school body: puberty and developing sexuality.

Notes

1 Vicinus, M. (1985) *Independent Women: Work and Community for Single Women 1850–1920*, London: Virago.
2 West, D. R. (1985) *Half to Remember, an Autobiography, With the History of Christ's Hospital School, Hertford as Seen Through the Eyes of the Headmistress 1942–1972*, pamphlet published by Christ's Hospital School.
3 Ibid., p. 31.
4 Hickson, A. (1996) *The Poisoned Bowl: Sex and the Public School*, London: Gerald Duckworth & Co Ltd.
5 West (1985), op. cit., p. 31.
6 Golding, W. (1954) *Lord of the Flies*, London: Penguin.
7 Duffell, N. (2000) *The Making of Them*, London: Lone Arrow Press, p. 140.
8 Brendon, V. (2009) *Prep School Children: A Class Apart Over Two Centuries*, London: Continuum.
9 Okely, J. (1996) *Own or Other Culture*, London: Routledge.
10 West (1985), op. cit.
11 Ibid.
12 Ibid., p. 63.
13 Figures on the numbers of those suffering eating disorders specifically in boarding schools are unavailable. This is an area which merits future research.
14 In Britain, according to the National Institute for Clinical Excellence, 1.6 million people in the UK are affected by and eating disorder of which 11 per cent are male.
15 For a full-length illustrated case study of anorexia in a male patient, see Schaverien, J. (1994) *Desire and the Female Therapist*, London: Routledge.
16 Orbach, S. (1986) *Hunger Strike*, London: Faber & Faber.
17 Chernin, K. (1986) *The Hungry Self*, London: Virago.
18 Lawrence, M. (1984) *The Anorexic Experience*, London: Women's Press.
19 Crisp, A. H. (1980) *Anorexia Nervosa*, London: Grune & Stratton.
20 Crisp, A. H., & Burns, T. (1990) 'Primary anorexia nervosa in the male and female: A comparison of clinical features and prognosis,' in *Males with Eating Disorders*, Andersen, A. E. (ed), London: Routledge.

Chapter 15

Puberty in girls' schools
Love and homosexuality

The accumulated effect of living for years without love is a common and enduring aspect of the psychological impact of boarding. The lack of love, felt so acutely in the first stages of prep school, is noticeable again in relation to the bodily changes that occur during puberty. Young children who lose their homes miss appropriate physical contact and emotional understanding. At puberty this need for caring adults intensifies again, because – even though they are more mature – their bodily changes may be confusing or even in some cases worrying. Intimate care from loving adults enables the development of the sense of an integrated, embodied and emotional self. When this individual attention is lacking, the child may feel at a loss but without realising why.

At school, children are often alone with their bodily changes. There is no trusted adult in whom to confide anxieties about physical problems. It is difficult to manage these changes when living at home, but living in a situation where the only adults are strangers (albeit familiar strangers) can be bewildering at best. At worst it exposes children at this vulnerable stage to potential abuse by adults who may be predatory or merely insensitive. The changes that occur around puberty may affect the person's attitude to their sexuality and relationships in later life. Thus, like latency, this is a crucial time in the life of the child. At the centre of this chapter are more episodes told to me by two of the women from earlier but different generations who were quoted in the last chapter. Both consider their lives to have been blighted by their different experiences in boarding schools.

History of sexuality in girls' schools

Mallory Wober's research in girls' boarding schools of the 1960s has very tentative references to sexuality. He established that there was an expectation of sexual purity. This was part of the ethos of Christian morality on which the schools were founded, alongside the schools' stated aims of training the girls to be wives and mothers.[1] Wober noted that in order to exclude sex from the schools, most girls were fiercely protected against anything male. This meant that boys' schools in the vicinity were out of bounds, except perhaps for formal sixth-form dances. In most cases, the reason for these limits were not explained to the girls. The facts of life were rarely discussed or explained. The existence of masturbation, lesbian attraction or sex in any terms was ignored or completely denied by the authorities.

In the published literature, reference to sexuality in girls' schools is uncommon. The sense is that it was studiously avoided through strictures, discipline and the clothing of which we read in Chapter 3. At the time of the early boarding schools, in the eighteenth century, girls were not supposed to have any sexual feelings at all. However, this was contradicted by the inhibitions and restrictions imposed on them.[2] In girls' schools there was often a taboo on discussion of anything to do with sex. Like boys, girls became interested in sex at puberty – but in the single-sex environment there was little opportunity to do more than fantasise. However, in the single-sex schools the girls, unlike boys, were permitted to dance together as a way of 'learning' ballroom dancing. Denise, who remembers this from the 1950s, hated the school dances but was compelled to take part. She writes:

> I would also like to mention here something I consider a perversion of treatment in general terms. Each year we had a Founder's Day dance to celebrate the founding of the school by Edward VI. For this the staff (all women) would turn up dressed in their best – ball gowns etc. We had only our regular school uniforms to wear. For weeks ahead someone would be assigned to each member of staff to fill up her dance card with girls who would dance with her for that item. The headmistress [D. R. West of whom we read in the last chapter] would sit on the stage of the hall with a girl either side, watching the proceedings. She also had a programme to be filled with names of companions for each dance. Of course, the dances were all ballroom type, and we had to learn them in Gym classes, and then dance sort of 'cheek to cheek'; with our partners. Ugh!
>
> I hated this charade and tried to avoid it by doing something that would elicit the punishment of not attending but I never succeeded and had to turn up at each one and dance with other girls or with a mistress.

Presumably the justification for this was to familiarise the girls with the ballroom dancing etiquette of the time. It seems a rather tragic image – the teachers dressed in their ballgowns with no one to dance with except young girls who found the whole thing distasteful. Reading it in this way it seems to be exploitative too, in that the children enacted the teachers' fantasies. The teachers played the 'female' role, and the girls, who had to fill up their dance cards, were presumably playing the 'male' role. This may have been partly because members of staff were unmarried women at a time when sexual activity in the middle classes was shunned outside marriage. As we saw, women had to choose between their schools and marriage. The teaching profession attracted some lesbian women, as the single-sex communities of that time were places where they could live without censure, but in most cases any love would have remained secret or else unrequited. These dances do not suggest anything of a lesbian nature but more a rehearsal for a traditional heterosexual life. There was often a fear of men and the power they represented. This fuelled the taboos on contact with the community outside the schools and perhaps fostered this charade. In some schools boys were invited in for such school dances, which might have temporarily released the girls from the grasp of the teachers.

Taboo on female sexuality

In girls' schools the taboo on sexuality was, it seems, quite effective. Most girls' activities were rigidly policed, day and night. Even so, in some girls' schools sexual experimentation took place – but any such liaisons were usually hidden. Sexual abuse also happened, but it was less common than in boys' schools. However, sadistic female teachers could and did make the life of some girls miserable. Girls could also be cruel and subject their peers to bullying. The Christian ethos in many of the schools was a constraining element and perhaps contributed to the denial of the girls' developing femininity.

West put forward a rather idiosyncratic personal view in her memoir. She observed changes that came about as girls grew up: 'One of the first signs was the hardening of the girl's jaw when she was about twelve as she lost the rounded contours of her child hood face.' By the time they were 14 or 15 most of the girls were self-disciplined. It was West's view that if they had not attained self-control by the time they were 16, girls might be set on a path of self-destruction.[3]

West's speculation was based on limited psychological understanding, but the tone of these observations is chilling, considering that this woman was in loco parentis. The objectification of the girl, and the apparent lack of empathy, seems to demonstrate the unloving environment in which these girls lived. It seems fairly evident that West, herself an unmarried woman, was a victim of patriarchy. She describes how she took on being headmistress as a young and inexperienced teacher during World War II, with very little psychological or other preparation for the job. The sense given in her autobiography is of a well-meaning but unworldly woman who devoted her life to the girls in her care.

Denise grew up in the school overseen by West and, from the age of 12, her housemistress was a Mrs B., a divorced woman whom Denise believes took a dislike to her and set out to make her life a misery. Denise's description of the abuse perpetrated by this woman gives a sense of the terror of growing up in an institution where people who do not love you can discuss the most intimate details of the body. These are Denise's own words:

> When I was about 13, I thought I should have a bra and I bought one at home and brought it to school. This was against the rules. Only school issue bras were allowed, awful things with elastic that came around to the front and buttoned under the breasts, and also no uplift support of any kind, the seams going North South. We had to sit at meals on our backless benches down the

side of a thirty-six seat table, eighteen each side. The ward mistress would go up and down the line watching us, and she could see the horizontal strap of a commercially bought bra showing through the thin cotton of our clothing in the summer. She noticed mine and I was hauled up after lunch one day for examination. My fault was extreme and I was sent to the bottom of the table to sit among the juniors for a week – a very conspicuous and humiliating punishment in our severely hierarchical society – where I was clearly a sinner since I was a head or so taller than the juniors.

Then I had to present myself for the 'do you need a bra anyway' examination, which entailed going to see her in her room with nothing on above the waist, and wearing a dressing gown. There I had to open my gown and display myself, whereupon she would feel my breasts and tell me if I was sufficiently developed to have a school issue bra. While she was feeling I did mention that there were a few lumpy bits – I think I had normal lumps typical of hormonal changes in a teenager – but Mrs B just sneered and said – quote: 'I suppose you think you have breast cancer.' I did get permission to have a bra but it wasn't much use as I have described.

Here we see clearly the insensitive and intrusive treatment of a girl at this most sensitive time in her life. What was needed was gentle handling of her fear that she might have something wrong with her and an explanation that what was happening was quite natural. Like the prep school children we have seen, this 13 year old also needed someone to speak to her, to mediate her fears in a kindly way. The changes of puberty are bewildering and a loving person is needed to allay the anxiety and answer questions that emerge. Instead she was scorned, shamed and humiliated. This demonstrates how these girls were living in an environment that, far from celebrating their growing femininity, shamed them. It was similar with other aspects of the development of their female bodies, in particular menstruation.

Periods

For girls the onset of their periods is a major life event. Even if it is handled smoothly, known about and expected, it is still a huge transition from one stage of life to another. The practical issues of how to deal with it are often difficult to negotiate. This is without all the mixed feelings that emerge. For a child in a boarding school the onset of their period may be a problematic and embarrassing situation. Once again it is an event where there is no love and no celebration of the transition into adult life that it heralds. It offers the potential for fear, anxiety and humiliation. For example, one woman interviewed recalled that the onset of her periods happened when she was at home and so her mother helped her. She remembered how the girls in school were worried about disposing of the used sanitary products. This can build to giant proportions in the mind of a young girl.

Nina, who attended a convent boarding school, recalled being terrified when her periods started; she did not know what was happening to her. Her mother had died, and no one had thought to prepare her for this big event. She was shocked and horrified to find blood and she thought she had cancer. She was quite unable to tell the nuns and ask for help. Fortunately, she was able to confide in her best friend, who helped her and explained that this was something normal. Clearly it was significant that she had such a friend to whom to turn. Such confiding friendships give some respite in girls' schools, where they are more common than they are in boys' schools.

However, such intimate friendships can be fickle. The pain of rejection if such intense relationships fail is a very particular form of distress in girls' schools. It happens in day schools too, but there the child can get away from the situation and may discuss it with parents when she returns home. Sometimes parents may intervene by talking to teachers on behalf of the child. In boarding school such mediation is rarely possible, even if the child does tell the parents. There are more serious cases where one girl assumes power over another. The, usually younger, girl may feel privileged to have such a friend, especially because she is lonely and hungry for intimate contact. However if, as sometimes happens, the older girl abuses that power, the younger one may find she is living with threats that she can tell no one about. This can blight the life of the girl, who is unable to confide in anyone, for months or even years.

Love and sexuality

We turn again now to Edith, whom we met in the last chapter. She attended the Beacon School where overall the care was good and understanding. However, this changed for her when love became an issue. She writes:

> When I was 11, I became involved in a collective 'pash' for an 'older' girl. She was 14 and called Louise, or Lulu. She was known as a talented pianist and was allowed to practice the piano in the Music Room instead of attending some of her classes. I was by then in the middle school house, which was in a different part of the village. The main building was a large ex-manor house with hilly grounds, where there was a lodge and a new building with the gym and classrooms. Another older girl, Aileen MacDonald, suggested I might like to meet Lulu alone. I don't know how this matchmaking came about, Aileen was my friend but Lulu was someone I wanted to get physically close to. This meeting was to take place in the cloakrooms for the main building where the whole school, I guess about 120 boarders, met on Sunday mornings after Church. There was a rule that we never went to the dorms during the day and on Sundays when we were all together, we had a senior, a middle and a junior sitting-room and we must stay in our respective sitting-rooms before and after lunch. I was thrilled at the chance to be with my beloved and I relished the naughtiness and danger of slipping away from my allotted sitting room to go to an assignation in the basement cloakrooms (which had lavatories but were primarily where we put our coats and outdoor shoes).

There, quite often I recall, I met Lulu and we hugged and kissed and said we loved each other. This was innocent in the sense that no further bodily fondling went on, but it was not innocent in the sense that I felt I was in love.

I assumed all this was a secret escapade. But my experience of adults was rather benign and I was unaware that what I believed to be innocent naughtiness, for which I would be reprimanded at most, would be seriously wicked behaviour to some people. Aileen acted I suppose like a pimp and I think she sometimes watched from afar on Sundays. I suppose she was not so innocent, certainly I was aware that we both felt the excitement of setting up the secret assignations. I think I thought I was Lulu's only love until the heavens dropped on us when, eventually two mothers of daygirls in the Village found incriminating notes their daughters' had hidden. They complained and the staff had to find out what had been going on. I don't remember feeling betrayed by Lulu for writing to other people and presumably meeting them. I worried about how unhappy she would be.

The day I have written into the story I am sending you was one of utter humiliation and fear. I suppose I was a 'witness' and was to be kept isolated when I was taken to the main school where Miss Buchanan (the head mistress) wanted to see me. I waited alone in a room and knew that Lulu and her best friend were in another nearby. Aileen didn't seem to be there. Finally I was called to the Music Room and I remember the scene. Miss Buchanan was seated near the grand piano at the end furthest from the door, the sunny dusty light making a mist around her. Round the room I could see Robby and Craigy and all the other mistresses, plus the mothers of the two day-girls concerned. These two mothers I remember like plump, prosperous, avenging harpies steaming along to make Miss Buchanan do something. I had to walk to Miss Buchanan and sit on the music stool. She was gentle but bravely (I am sure) questioned me about meeting Lulu, and what we did. The room was alert with tension and when I whispered, 'She kissed me' there was a definite sigh and the tension went down.

That was all. I was driven back to the house and the matter was never mentioned again to me by anyone, including my mother. Lulu was not expelled but her career as a musician never eventuated. Thinking about this now she really was a victim of prejudice. She was virtually scorned afterwards, from being popular and musically successful, she became something of an outcast. I never met her again in school and some years later, I heard that she was still living with her parents.

Edith makes the point that the effect of such a single incident can affect the rest of a person's life. She continues:

My lifelong problem with this memory is with the silence after what had been to me an event, which turned the school into a nightmare for me. From being gregarious and popular, I felt so ashamed and guilty about having such unspeakable feelings that I shut down. I think our feelings were not taken seriously and that it was thought better to let the matter be forgotten. There was a way of seeing it: 'pashes' were silly. Girls who indulged in such feelings should realise this, and, that it was because we were in a school for girls only that this sort of thing went on. Boys from the major boys' public schools in the area were shipped in to dances and my mother's sister used to tell me I would soon have lots of lovely boy-friends, as she had when a bit older than me.

This tragic story took place in one of the more educationally enlightened of girls' boarding schools, and it demonstrates how the subtle handling of such sensitive emotions as love could not be dealt with easily – even in a school such as this where, as we saw in Chapter 14, it was accepted that two teachers were partners. This brought to the fore the dreaded spectre of homosexual love.

Homosexuality

In boys' schools too the reaction to homosexuality was often extreme. Headmasters were very worried about it and often went to extremes to prevent it. Hickson, writing mainly of the twentieth century, states that homosexuality was viewed with horror by headmasters and any boys suspected of such liaisons were immediately expelled. Bans on friendships between boys of different ages were in force in most schools, and boys in different houses were forbidden to even acknowledge boys in other houses.[4] This is similar to the ban on girls. No two boys were permitted to be alone together, and any talking in dormitories was forbidden and often enforced by the presence of a member of staff or prefect.

There were still ways around this. Hickson, who interviewed men about their homosexual experiences in school, gives many personal anecdotes to this effect. Homosexuality in boys' schools, whilst drawing opprobrium, was tacitly accepted. Men thus grew up, married and avowedly opposed to any form of homosexuality, whilst secretly engaging homosexual encounters as they had in their schools. Reputations were, and continue to be, risked in meetings with young men in public places. A pattern learned at boarding school is commonly lived out in later years. In order to demonstrate how such an incident as that involving Edith may be more sensitively handled, I give another story, this time from a published account from Stephen Fry.

Stephen Fry's story

The confusions about sexuality are complex, but are so much more so for children who know from an early age that their sexuality does not fit the 'norm'. Even though parents may struggle with acceptance of homosexuality, in most cases the best place for this realisation is at home where children are loved and sheltered. There were teachers in schools in the twentieth century who handled potential bullying around this issue with great skill and sensitivity. Stephen Fry gives a moving example of such a teacher when he describes an incident in the last year at his prep school. I quote it at length here because it gives a sense of how an enlightened teacher can transform a risky situation for a boy into one with a positive outcome.

Fry would have been 12 or 13. A boy who was one of his friends was coming out of the swimming pool and suddenly got a cramp:

> He yowled with pain, flopped forward on to the grass and started to thrash his legs up and down in agony. I was standing close by and so I went and helped him up and then walked him around the pool until the cramp had gone. Fully recovered he streaked away to change and I thought no more about it.[5]

Later that day Fry began to notice he had suddenly become unpopular and boys were shunning him, cutting him and sending him to Coventry. He could not work out what he had done to deserve this. Then a boy passing him in the corridor made a comment that he did not catch. He stopped the boy and eventually got him to repeat what he had said: 'queer'. It took a good deal more threatening behaviour before the boy confessed that everyone was saying this about him because they saw him put his arm around the boy at the pool earlier. He also told him that that boy was mad at him because of it.

Devastated, Fry stumbled away in tears and was found sitting alone by a master who asked why he was upset. Fry recounted the story and the master went on his way. Tearfully, Fry recovered enough to face rejection by his peers in the dining room. He sat down and spaces were made on either side of him as boys moved away. It was halfway through tea that the master in question sounded a gong and made an announcement to the assembled boys.[6] He announced that an act of heroism had been reported. He said: 'I have just heard of a heroic act of kindness that took place by the swimming pool this afternoon.' He went on to describe what had happened and to name the protagonists, suggesting that Fry should be congratulated. He was awarding him merit points as a reward. Then the teacher added, as if as an afterthought:

> It has also come to my ears that some of the younger, sillier boys, who are ignorant about such things, think that putting their arm around a friend in distress is a sign of some sort of perversion. I look to you senior boys, who have a rather more sophisticated understanding of sexual matters, to quash this sort of puerile nonsense. I hope, incidentally that [the boy] has thanked Fry properly for his promptness and consideration.[7]

This remarkable act of understanding and well-timed intervention saved Fry from the possibility of months and maybe even years of subsequent bullying. Unfortunately, such sophisticated understanding was not shown to Edith. These two stories give a sense of the confusion in the student group – and at times in the staff group – regarding sex, love and affection.

In conclusion – the lasting impact of this treatment

I conclude this chapter with quotes from Denise and Edith, who both consider that their later lives have been adversely affected by their experiences at their respective boarding schools. Denise writes:

> These are just a few of the things that happened to me at the hands of someone who was supposed to be in the place of a parent and make up for the lack of parental affection and care. I have lived a life without knowing how to love anything or anybody properly and I think much of this is the result of my teenage experiences with such a woman as Mrs B. When I left, on the last morning as we stood at the dayroom table with 35 others and had final prayers, she turned to me and said, 'You are a broken reed'. In some ways she was right, but she had a great hand in the breaking.

The vindictive cruelty of a statement like this is also prophetic. It makes sure the influence of this figure remains active in the psyche of the girl long after she has left the school. This was abuse of power.

Edith writes of the lasting impact of the experience she described:

> I learned to rationalise and say the problem was the system based on male public school traditions applied to girls. Actually, the Beacon was quite a good haven for many of us who had difficulties with family life, particularly those whose parents were in the Forces or in foreign lands. In those days, being sexual at all as a woman outside engagement or marriage was frowned upon. Preferring one's own sex was assumed to be chaste and to have a 'best friend' showed a girl would be a loving woman to her future man. Sex between women was unimaginable and even nowadays, I find it impossible to reveal inner thoughts on the subject. It was years before I could utter the word 'Lesbian', let alone admit to my early adventures.

I am indebted to both these women for their open discussion of these issues, because otherwise we can only speculate on how damaging boarding schools could be in those early years. Their stories help us in understanding how the schools in the present day have changed. Edith was at school in the 1940s, Denise in the 1950s and Fry in the 1960s–1970s. This is nearly three generations through whose stories we have witnessed the exposure to suffering at that sensitive time in life – adolescence. What was missing for Denise and Edith was a kindly confidante. For Fry, the enlightened teacher made a huge difference in his experience, which may have been profoundly wounding but would have been worse without the teacher's intervention. Perhaps these stories alert psychotherapists to the continuing suffering of people from across the generations who come into analysis unable to articulate the nature of their suffering. It takes a long time to confront and challenge such powerful messages from such a formative time in life.

Postscript

As I was finishing writing this chapter, a woman, now mother of three small children, wrote to me. She had attended a boarding school in the 1980s. Her story confirms that, although we are frequently told things have improved, as each generation grows up and dares to reflect on their experiences, the same stories come to light. She writes:

> I was just reading about your work on boarding schools. It definitely resonates with me. I was sent away as the oldest of three girls in 1980. We were aged 7, 8 and 9. I was separated from my sisters since my age qualified me as a senior at our school. The entire experience was the most traumatic one of my life so far; many of the teachers were bullies. I don't feel vengeful, but I am curious to know if the system attracts or makes bullies, especially among teachers. It was worse for boys. I have sometimes wanted to meet some of these teachers as an adult to ask them what on earth they thought they were doing to vulnerable little people; it concerns me that some are probably still teaching.

She was able to process what had happened to her because she and her sisters often talked about everything that went on whenever they got together in their early adult years. She therefore had witnesses to corroborate her experiences. This makes a difference. The bullying by teachers confirms that there are some things that change, but that small children are vulnerable in the hands of adults who are unknown to the parents. Although Denise's experiences took place long ago, and there are now duvets and teddies in the schools, I wonder how much has really changed.

Notes

1 Wober, M. (1971) *English Girls' Boarding Schools*, London: Allen Lane, the Penguin Press, p. 63.
2 Gathorne-Hardy, J. (1977) *The Public School Phenomenon*, London: Hodder & Stoughton.
3 West, D. R. (1985) *Half to Remember, an Autobiography, With the History of Christ's Hospital School, Hertford as Seen Through the Eyes of the Headmistress 1942–1972*, pamphlet published by Christ's Hospital School, p. 64.
4 Hickson, A. (1996) *The Poisoned Bowl: Sex and the Public School*, London: Gerald Duckworth & Co Ltd, p. 81.
5 Fry, S. (2004) *Moab Is My Washpot*, London: Arrow Books, p. 244.
6 Ibid., pp. 247–248.
7 Ibid., p. 248.

Chapter 16

Boys' sexual activity and sexual abuse

Its lasting impact

In this chapter I will consider the difference between consensual sexual play and the sexual abuse that took place in some boys' boarding schools. Although sexual games and even sexual abuse took place in girls' schools, it seems that it was less prevalent than in boys' schools. This may have been partly because of the strictures of which we have read. When it happened, however, it was no less emotionally damaging than with boys. Here we will examine the long-term psychological consequences of sexualised activity on men who as boys grew to maturity in the institution.

In the press there are increasingly articles bringing to light sexual abuse suffered in boarding schools over the last decades. As I write, in July 2014, a government inquiry has been instigated into historic cases of sexual abuse in British institutions. It will include claims from the increasing number of people coming forward who were abused in boarding schools.[1] Cases have been brought, and as a result some paedophile teachers who were active in boarding schools have recently been convicted.[2] Thus, what was considered a rare and scandalous aberration is now known to have been more common than was previously appreciated. There is an increasing literature in Australia, Canada, New Zealand and the USA of the abuses suffered in the British-style boarding schools in which children of indigenous people were forcibly incarcerated.[3][4][5][6] In 2009 the United Nations commissioned a report on the extent of such enforced separation of indigenous peoples from their communities, worldwide. This revealed such boarding schools in numerous countries, including Asia, Africa, Russia and even Scandinavia.[7] One of the aspects of this trauma is the intergenerational nature of it.[8] The British boarding school situation is clearly different from these cases, because children were not forcibly taken from their parents. However, it is comparable in that children who suffered trauma in British boarding schools may find parenting their own children difficult, and sometimes the trauma is passed on through the generations.

Many of the abuses which we are considering took place in prep schools with the best reputations. Most of these schools deserved their reputation for educational excellence, as is evidenced by the fact that many of those holding office in the British government attended these schools. Other schools misled the parents by giving students a rather second-rate education. Like State schools, some are excellent and others less so. But in boarding schools we now know that, unwittingly, trusting parents have left their young children within a system that exposed them to both physical and emotional harm.

Today children are more closely supervised. However, we cannot be complacent: when children of different ages are unsupervised, the younger ones are vulnerable. There are many schools where the taboos were such that no sexual abuse took place and even homosexual games in the student group were rare. In some schools where excessive beatings were part of the fabric of society, overt homosexual activity was taboo. The rules were such that, as Jason (whom we met in Chapter 13) put it, 'We would never have dared to even contemplate it.' Beatings in boys' schools were ubiquitous until they were made illegal. In State schools beatings were outlawed in 1987, but it took until 1999 for them to be banned in boarding schools in England and Wales. They continued until 2000 in boarding schools in Scotland and 2003 in Northern Ireland.[9] Some boys who were subject to these beatings observed the apparent pleasure their tormentors took in chastising them in this way. It could be argued that these beatings were perverse and, for the perpetrator, as thrilling as the forbidden sex. Although an accepted form of punishment, this was a serious violation of the child's bodily integrity. It was abusive and so numbed the child, perhaps paving the way for submission to other bodily violations, such as sexual ones.

Historical perspective

In the chaos of the early days of the public schools, sexual activities were part of the general chaos and license of the schools. Until the end of the nineteenth century boys shared beds in huge dormitories (as we saw in Chapter 2). Homosexual activities were common, and sometimes these were truly erotic encounters; Gathorne-Hardy gives examples of poetry and art inspired by these early romantic encounters.[10] In girls' schools, as we saw in Chapter 15 the 'pash' was often of a younger girl for an older one. However, in boys' schools it seems that more often this was reversed and the older boys might have a 'pash' on a younger boy.[11] Thus the powerful sexual instincts at puberty and lack of adult supervision could lead to sexual exploitation of the younger by the older boys. This sometimes included rape. This did not mean that all boys in boarding schools were homosexual, but in the absence of women other boys, usually younger, became objects of sexual interest.

The prohibitions of the Victorian age meant that rigid controls to curb sexuality were initiated. Games were introduced in the late nineteenth century. They were seen as character forming by training the body, fostering team spirit and preparing young men for war. It was also hoped that they would sublimate some of the excesses of sexuality.[12] This investment in games, accompanied by prohibitions on overt homosexuality, continued well into the twentieth century. Even so, schools differed in their acceptance of homosexual attachments. Whilst in one school these might be tacitly condoned, in others they were rigorously taboo.[13] Homosexuality was illegal in Britain. It was a criminal offence, carrying a prison sentence, until 1967.[14] This would have added to the perceived dangers of being found out; it may also have added to the excitement. One man interviewed by Gathorne-Hardy admitted that at the school he attended in the 1920s, Haileybury, sex in the school was common. According to him there was a time between supper and prep which was ideal for boys to go to their studies for sex.[15] The bravado of this claim may have belied a more troubling aspect of this permissiveness. One wonders if, as well as giving opportunities for consensual sex, it may have played a part in condoning coercion.

In extreme cases rape and sexual torture may be the result of boys left unsupervised, regulated only by prefects. Even today such cases are occasionally reported in the confidentiality of the analytic setting. However, unless the person chooses to report it or it comes under the aegis of child protection, the analyst cannot speak of it. Abuses therefore may go unreported even in present-day schools. Over the years the tradition has been one of tacit acceptance by staff, who themselves have been subjected to a similar system. This may mean that they turn a 'blind eye' to the abuses that are perpetrated.[16] The magnitude of sexual abuse by paedophile teachers is at last coming to light due to the courage of a number of people, including the journalist Alex Renton.[17]

Puberty

Sexuality was always a problem in boarding schools, but the issues were different in boys' and girls' schools. Children who miss their families, especially the women in their lives – their mothers and nannies – may confuse their desires for intimacy with the sexual. When the child is prepubescent the longing for love finds an object on which to alight, hence the 'pashes' in the girls' schools described in chapters 3 and 15. In boys' boarding schools any form of affection may be interpreted as sexual, even when it is really the yearning for maternal love. In schools, boys create their own social groups. The pressure to grow up is considerable. In this society of children there is no status associated with being young and innocent. Therefore, boys may pretend to be sexual when they are not. The term 'juvenile' is often used by their peers to deride younger boys; the longing for the young matron or a teacher might be termed juvenile and therefore unacceptable. If it is spoken about in lewd terms or interpreted to other boys as sexual interest, then it becomes acceptable. Thus, as a result of peer pressure, premature sexualisation might be fostered in younger boys by older ones.[18]

For many children who go to boarding school in adolescence, the losses are similar to those for the prep school child. It is different, because they are older and at a different developmental stage, but they are still children and need loving care. Adolescents living at home are often quite private but they may choose to talk about their concerns with parents. Thus, as in earlier years, loving adults mediate potential anxieties. The children may sense that they are held in mind and their developing bodies observed, without comment, by parents; unstated approval is communicated through appropriate looks and touch. The adolescent may rebel and pit his strength against the adults; his nascent maturity may be affirmed in the gradual releasing of boundaries. Physicality may be expressed through actual or play fighting, with siblings or parents. This phase can be difficult for all concerned, and in some homes it goes badly awry. However, even when things go wrong, it is the known environment that has failed and the child knows his place in the world. When this developmental phase coincides with the transition from home to public school it can be devastating. The loss of parents and siblings, friends and pets may be felt acutely.

It is likely that the psychologically defensive structures formed in prep school to protect the young child from the insults to his or her emotional life will come into play at this point. In normal development, eating, showering and sleeping in a relaxed manner create a sense of security and are fundamental to health. These activities form the basis for a reflective and caring relationship to the body, self and so, ultimately, to others. Many children in boarding school may have the opposite experience: they are often vigilant, sometimes hungry, with sleep affected by lights out at preordained times. Children living in such a regime may not easily settle into their own bodily rhythms; relaxation, reverie and dreaming are disturbed. If there is the threat of ridicule or abuse in the dormitory this is intensified.

When puberty begins there is often embarrassment and confusion associated with bodily changes. We saw how, for girls, the onset of menstruation can be terrifying, especially if no preparation has been made for it. We have also seen how teachers sometimes subjected adolescent girls to intrusive bodily examinations and how the girls' loving attachments could be cruelly exposed to scrutiny and misunderstanding. Similarly, boys had to manage their bodily and emotional changes alone. Like the girls, boys experienced the lack of privacy, and eating and sleeping en masse. In addition, in many boys' schools, showers were taken communally and the lavatories had no doors. This was so that no private sexual activity should take place in them.

Emerging sexuality may become the dominant psychological theme in the student group, with rumour and suggestion rife. For girls, masturbation leaves no trace and so can be a private activity. For boys, the beginning of sexual maturity may be heralded by wet dreams. If unprepared, the boy may be alarmed at this apparent loss of control. Beginning in the earlier years, the discovery of masturbation may be an exciting private adventure. At puberty it may become addictive for the lonely child, an attempt at self-soothing. If other boys should notice, the shame and ridicule can be mortifying.

Pornography plays a part in the sexual behaviour of boys and in some dormitories the lack of privacy led to abuses. Pornographic magazines could be bought and sold among the student group. Some of the more needy children who sought comfort through masturbation became the object of cruel exploitation. One of my respondents told me of a boy who was mercilessly exploited by older boys. They would sell him pornographic magazines and then punish him for having them.

Sexual activity and sexual abuse

There is an important distinction to be made between sexual activity, which takes place within the student group, and sexual abuse, which is exploitation of the child by an older child or adult. In adolescence, in the absence of loving adults, some comfort-seeking behaviour might become sexualised as warmth is sought with the available other. As a new form of sibling group emerges, mutual sexual experiments may offer solace but may also lead to abuse. The dormitory, often inadequately supervised, is a site of potential sexual activity. Whilst initiating the child into the pleasures of homosexuality, the institution proclaims its dangers. This may lead to confusion about sexual identity and/or sexual orientation that continues into adult life. Christopher Hitchens conveys the chaotic environment in which a large group of adolescent boys dealt with their burgeoning sexuality. He writes of the school he attended:

> There were two ways this hottest of all subjects could 'come up' in an all male school featuring communal showers, communal lavatories, and the ever present threat of an official thrashing on the rear . . . Most boys decided quite early on that, since their penises would evidently give them no rest at all, they would repay the favour by giving their penises no respite in return. The night was loud with the boasts and the groans that resulted from this endless, and fairly evenly matched, single combat between chaps and their cocks. To even the dullest lad, further more it would sometimes occur to think that self-abuse was slightly wasted on the self, and might be better relished in mixed company . . . It was quite possible to arrange a vigorous session of mutual relief without a word being spoken, even without eye contact.[19]

This dryly humorous representation of this behaviour gives a sense of its rather compulsive nature. Whilst this sort of sexual activity was going on in some schools, boys in the same school could mete out cruel punishments to those who were believed to be homosexual.[20] Hitchens qualifies his graphic pen portrait by making this same point:

> It is very important to understand that ninety percent of these enthusiastic participants would have punched you in the throat if you had suggested there was anything homosexual (or 'queer') about what they were doing . . . The unstated excuse was that this is what one did until the so-far unattainable girls became available.[21]

There is a fine line between sexual experiments, in which many growing children participate and which are, in the main, normal and age appropriate, and sexual abuse, which is neither. This is the problem: these rather innocent, if manic, activities may lead to a permissiveness that condones behaviour that is totally inappropriate. It may prepare the child for abuse from an older child or a predatory adult.

Abuse by another child

In some cases mutual masturbation and innocent exploration go on to become abusive. This was the case for a significant minority of children who were subjected to sexual abuse by older boys. The abuse might take many different forms, some of it very obviously assault and others rather more subtle. In some cases it was persistent molestation by one, usually older, boy. Other children experienced rape by one or sometimes a group of boys. Children were most vulnerable in the dormitory at night, when there were few members of staff on duty. Then they were exposed to the sexual experiments of older boys. The prefects were often in charge and these are the times when the youngest children suffered the most. This was the case with Jervis.

When Jervis arrived at his public school in the 1970s, he was 11 and a particularly pretty blond-haired child, so he was singled out for special attention from an older boy. Being special in such schools was usually a poison chalice. The boy for whom he became the object of unwanted attention was the prefect in his dormitory. The prefect, who was 16, arranged for him to be allocated a bed next to his. This meant the younger boy was his plaything, to pick up and drop according to his whim. At night he would approach Jervis and fondle his genitals, disturbing Jervis's sleep with this bewildering sexual assault. This was a regular occurrence. Jervis could never relax; he was always vigilant, waiting for the next time. For the next two years, until the boy finally left the school, Jervis was subjected to sexual touching.

Throughout this period Jervis's sleep was disturbed by anticipatory hyper-vigilance. The psyche as well as the body suffers from such abusive intrusions because there is no time for private reverie. Along with the boy's body, the reverie of sleep and the imaginative life of the dream state were constantly disturbed. Consequently, his fantasy and dream life were impinged upon by this intrusion. Thus it is that sleep difficulties may be common for boys who are sexually abused in the dormitory.

Jervis always knew this was wrong. However, in some cases, it is unclear for the victim if what he experienced even was abuse. This is because a child who is touched inappropriately may not be able to distinguish that from the playful behaviour in the dormitory. Moreover, if the perpetrator is an adult, trusted by parents, how could it be wrong? Thus the child, now adult, is often unsure himself whether or not this constituted abuse. This accounts for the fact that many abuses went unreported.

The move from the preparatory to the public school may offer escape for those bullied or sexually molested. For others it may be the beginning of a period of torment.

The paedophile threat

To be singled out for sexual attention by an older boy was one form of sexual torment; another was the abuse of children by teachers. In some cases a paedophile teacher, or even a group of teachers, took advantage of the children in their care. It could be confusing, and indeed sinister, to be selected to be the object of special favours by a member of the teaching staff. In some cases the paedophile sought out a particular child as his special favourite. It may have been well known amongst the boys in the school that one teacher was a paedophile. Sometimes this behaviour was noticed by other teachers or by matrons, who turned a blind eye.[22]

At his prep school in the 1980s Callum dreaded growing older because he knew that when he grew pubic hair it would be his turn to be chosen by the paedophile teacher. The boys all knew about this teacher who preyed on boys, but they could do nothing. The teacher was not interested in younger boys, but when they reached puberty they would be selected for his unwanted attention.

Callum tried to tell his parents that there was a teacher who was inappropriate with the boys. He desperately wanted to leave, pleading with his parents to let him. However, his parents pacified him with platitudes and appeared not to take his concerns seriously. He was sent back to the school each term. When he reached the dreaded age, his fate followed that of other boys and this teacher subjected him to sexual assaults. It is often the case that parents and adults would not or could not believe this abuse. Partly it was a matter of expediency – but, anyway, how could this be credible? These teachers were often pillars of society outside as well as inside the schools.

There are many such stories, some now in the public arena, such as the courageous men who made the film *Chosen*.[23] Tom Perry and Ian McFadyen, along with two other men from the same school, eventually brought a successful claim to court and watched their former headmaster and tormentor, Peter Wright, and four of his colleagues convicted of sex crimes.[24,25] None of these men had been able to confront the abusers until after their parents' deaths. Children are very loyal, and these men realised that their parents would be adversely affected by learning of such harm to their children. Now they were adults and could speak of it, but it was too late. Their parents could do nothing about it. Alex Renton, who wrote about the abuse he suffered in his prep school, Ashdown House in East Sussex, is unusual in this regard because he told his mother at the time and he now knows action was taken.[26]

The split: Women are for loving – men are for sex

It is common for the pattern learned in school – the split between home life and school life – to continue to be played out in adulthood. One of the ways is in the split between the heterosexual life of marriage and the exciting homosexuality learned in school. One man expressed it vividly when he said: 'Women are for loving and men are for sex.' It is not uncommon for aspects of sexuality to remain split off in this way. As a result, a man may live a life of proclaimed heterosexuality with an overemphatic disavowal of homosexuality. Some men live a publicly heterosexual life but with a secret, parallel life of covert homosexuality.

Until relatively recently, boarding schools were single-sex milieus which cultivated an unnatural separation between men and women. Although many boarding schools today are mixed, many are still single sex.[27] Many of my psychotherapy clients came to maturity in this single-sex culture: at a formative time in their lives, their world was split along gender lines, fostering a 'them and us' culture. Those girls and boys who grew up in such systems knew little of each other, making sex and gender something of a mystery. In boys' boarding schools, women were regarded as a different species and, as sexuality became an increasingly pressing issue, the butt of jokes. Boys became tormented by their desires, combined with the completely unattainable nature of the realisation of them. Pornography was often readily available, providing fuel for masturbation but with no relation to actual girls. Fantasies abounded but the reality of girls in the flesh was confusing and often embarrassing.

Normal developmental confusion about sexuality at adolescence is compounded, in boy's schools, by the implicit message that male is good, strong and desirable; female is other, to be distrusted, denigrated and exploited (sexually and commercially). This is a patriarchal precedent that runs like a fault line through British society. Feminine attributes seen as 'other' and, belonging to this foreign species, were denigrated when perceived in each other. Traits considered feminine such as vulnerability, receptiveness and empathy were eschewed. The single-sex environment fostered unconscious misogyny. Women were seen as foreign, consciously idealised and longed for; they were also (unconsciously) respected, feared and ultimately hated as sirens. The fear that motivated this hatred was that they would seduce the man and then he would again be deserted. Thus the boy, bereaved and abandoned by his mother, may be profoundly affected in later life.

The natural path of individuation is thus distorted. In analysis one of the primary tasks is the unravelling of the person's sexuality, whatever form it may take. This psychological split may be threaded through the personality, often affecting relationships. It may continue in the gendered split between heterosexual home life and the secret, exciting, homosexual life. The male ex-boarder is often split in the following ways:

- A high achiever with no language for emotions;
- An intelligent person with little emotional intelligence;
- A loving person who dare not love;
- A masculine-identified man with early homosexual experiences.

The resulting psychological conflict may be masked until the middle years of life, when the armoured – and often socially successful – personality may break down. This is when the distressed child within the adult may emerge and overwhelm the defensive structures that have until then served so well. The purpose of these splits is therefore to keep consciousness of the pain of the child at bay. Thus the man who lives two parallel, but completely separate, lives is trying to prevent this from coming to consciousness. This unconscious strategy makes him feel safer because no one truly knows him, least of all himself.

At 40, Julian was married and a pillar of the community, but he felt all this might be in jeopardy if his work colleagues were to find out about his secret life. Julian was gay but no one knew this. He took risks, becoming involved with young men with whom he would meet secretly, usually on his travels for work in foreign countries. He came to see me because he was very anxious about being exposed to his wife and, publicly, to his work colleagues, by one of these young men.

The psychological split in boarding school, as we have seen, means that from the time the child is left in prep school he is no longer fully known by his parents. When he is at home, he presents the 'home self', consequently he is only partly known to the family. He plays the game according to the social rules; he passes exams and goes home looking similar to when he left, but he is forever changed. When he returns to school, he is the boy who is known in that community, but his home self is hidden away, secretly grieving. There are many distractions that make it possible to live the 'boarding school self' fully. The home self is forgotten because of the pain associated with it; the 'feminine' traits of vulnerability and distress are cut off. The epithets 'cissy' or 'girl', are terms of abuse that must be avoided at all costs.

The distractions and attractions in the peer group become more interesting at puberty when sexuality becomes involved. The boy now experiments with his peers, is exploited by other boys or teachers, or merely grows up in a secret but wild sense. *Wild* here is to mean not inhibited by those who love and care for him. This was how it had been for Julian. As an adult, Julian's home self was a happily married man. The world saw a perfectly respected couple, known in the community and included in many social events. Privately, all was not well: Julian was not interested in his wife sexually. He had fathered four children (nearly grown up), but the sexual relationship had faded. Now he and his wife lived side by side, amicably, but there was no fire, no passion. Julian's passion was reserved for his 'other self,' which – like its earlier manifestation, 'the boarding school self' – was unknown at home.

For many years Julian's regular but secret adventures with strangers meant that he was unknown at home. He was also not known by these passing acquaintances; he belonged to no one. After one of these brief sexual encounters, he worried that he had been recognised. This had brought him to realise the risks he was taking in clandestine meetings with strangers or near strangers. He was potentially exposed to blackmail. It seemed a relief to be able to talk about this.

In psychotherapy the challenge may be to help the person to be less split and to be known in full. The two aspects of the personality needed space to be known. Julian was living two lives and this was not satisfactory. The split between these two aspects of the self eventually began to come together in psychotherapy. The relief of admitting the double life to another person, who does not judge, is partly in being seen as a whole. At first Julian did not understand that he was seeking the thrill of the sexual excitement to which he had been introduced in school, in part to avoid being whole.

Wives and mothers

Julian's is only one of many such stories. Many women have suffered greatly as a result of having been married to men whom they later found out had been abused as children in their boarding schools. Women have written to me distraught, having found out only after the suicide of the man with whom they had spent their lives that he had been leading a double life: on one hand a married man; on the other, a man who had secret affairs, some with women, others with men. This behaviour is not exclusive to ex-boarders, but the split plays a particular role in the psyche of the ex-boarder. As the man mentioned earlier put it, justifying his rather bland and non-sexual relationship with his wife: 'Women are for love and men for sex.' This is one of the outcomes of the early boarding experience: the man who yearned for the love of his mother, as a small boy, finds a woman to depend on and who will provide the security, he so yearned for in childhood. But now, as an adult, he misses the exciting sexual encounters with his peers and so he seeks them out in illicit meetings with men.

Conclusion

The splits in the personality which are a key element in Boarding School Syndrome replay in adult life. The childhood of each of these men had been distorted by the experiences described. These are only a few examples of the long-term effects of the confusing situation of sexual exploitation that may occur in a boarding school. It barely gets a mention until the child is a middle-aged man, then perhaps, as his own children grow, he begins to realise the significance of what happened to him. The child who becomes pubescent at boarding school does so in an environment of rumour and fear, as well as potential exploitation. It is important to make the point that this did not happen in all boarding schools: sexual abuse is an aberration whenever it occurs. The figures for this are only just emerging, as we read almost weekly in the national press disclosures regarding the abuse suffered in many of the most prestigious boarding schools.

The point is that this abuse is what unsupervised children may be exposed to. There are many forms that abuse may take. Paedophiles come in many guises, from the older boy initiating the younger one into mutual masturbation, to the considered grooming of boys by teachers. Now at last these stories are finding an outlet in the public sphere rather than being confined to the confidential setting of the consulting room. However, let us not console ourselves that this happened long ago and would not occur today. Children today are well protected and there is good pastoral care in most schools, but even so paedophiles may slip through the net. The cases that are coming to light in the press are from many different generations.

Notes

1 As I write, the numbers of case are not known. The landscape is changing as new reports of cases of sexual abuse are coming forward every day.
2 Renton, A. (2014a) 'Abuse in Britain's boarding schools; a personal story,' *The Observer Magazine* (4 May), pp. 31–37.
3 Bradfield, C.R. (2001) 'Residential School Syndrome', *BC Medical Journal* 43 (2), pp. 78–81.
4 Lederman, J. (1999) 'Trauma and healing in aboriginal families and communities', *Native Social Work Journal* 2 (1), pp. 59–90.
5 Lynch, K. (2012) 'Working to heal the wounds of boarding school', *The Native Press* (19 July), pp. 1–3.
6 Buti, A. (2002) 'The removal of aboriginal children: Canada and Australia compared', *University of Western Sydney Law Review* 26 (1) www.austlii.edu.au/au/journals/UWSLRev/2002/2.html.
7 Smith, A. (2009) 'Indigenous peoples and boarding schools: A comparative study', prepared for the United Nations Permanent Forum on Indigenous Issues, eighth session, New York, 18–29 May www.un.org/esa/socdev/unpfii/documents/E_C_19_2009_crp1.pdf. A further report on this was published by the Economic and Social Council of the United Nations following the ninth session in New York, 19–30 April 2010 www.google.co.uk/webhp?sourceid=chrome-instant&ion=1&espv=2&ie=UTF-8#q=indigenous%20peoples%20and%20boarding%20schools.
8 Grounds, L. M. (2011) 'Historical intergenerational trauma and posttraumatic stress disorder: trauma that affects entire cultural groups' http://drlindagrounds.com/2011/historicalintergenerational-trauma.
9 Wikipedia, 'School corporal punishment' http://en.wikipedia.org/wiki/School_corporal_punishment.
10 Gathorne-Hardy, J. (1977) *The Public School Phenomenon*, London, Sydney, Auckland, Toronto: Hodder & Stoughton, p. 167.
11 Hitchens, C. (2011) *Hitch-22: A Memoir*, London: Atlantic Books (an imprint of Grove Atlantic Ltd).
12 Gathorne-Hardy (1977), op. cit., pp. 147–156.
13 Hickson, A. (1996) *The Poisoned Bowl: Sex and the Public School*, London: Gerald Duckworth & Co Ltd.
14 The Sexual Offences Act 1967 decriminalised homosexual acts in private between two men, both of whom had to have attained the age of 21. The Act applied only to England and Wales, and it did not cover the Merchant Navy or the Armed Forces. Homosexuality was decriminalised in Scotland by the Criminal Justice (Scotland) Act 1980 and in Northern Ireland by the Homosexual Offences (Northern Ireland) Order 1982. Source: http://en.wikipedia.org/wiki/Sexual_Offences_Act_1967.
15 Gathorne-Hardy (1977), op. cit., pp. 163–164.
16 This was a factor in the treatment of the men who were interviewed in the documentary film *Chosen* (Broadcast on Channel 4, November http://truevisiontv.com/films/details/97/chosen). It was evident that when the abuse this film documents took place some adults in the Caldicott School knew about it but chose not to report it. In December 2013 Peter Wright was convicted of twelve offences against children when he was headmaster.
17 Renton, A. (2014b) 'The damage boarding schools do,' *The Observer* (20 July).
18 James Taylor, personal communication, 2013.

19 Hitchens (2011), op. cit., p. 89.
20 Gathorne-Hardy (1977), op. cit., p. 163.
21 Hitchens (2011), op. cit., p. 89.
22 *Chosen* (2008), op. cit.
23 Ibid.
24 These abuses took place at Caldecott School, and the convictions were recorded in Brown, D., & Bennett, R. (2013) 'Pupils break silence over prep school paedophiles', *The Times* (19 December).
25 Renton (2014b), op. cit.
26 Ibid.
27 According to Private Schools.co www.privateschools.co/single-sex-schools.asp, the majority of private schools are co-educational. However, of the top twenty UK private schools for 2010, eleven of the twenty were for girls only and eight were for boys, only one was co-educational.

Chapter 17

Boarding School Syndrome
Towards a theory

This final chapter is a conclusion, but it indicates areas for future research and so it is anticipated that it is also a beginning. The term *Boarding School Syndrome* has been proposed and the psychological events that may lead to this distressing condition have been named and described. Thus a theory of Boarding School Syndrome is gradually emerging. There is not merely one single model for working in psychotherapy with this syndrome. Rather, some pointers have been offered that well-qualified analysts and psychotherapists, whatever their institutional affiliation, will have no trouble in identifying.

Analysts and psychotherapists work with diverse early trauma. Mostly they acknowledge that ex-boarders have particular sorts of problems but they rarely realise that these are the result of the life-changing traumatic losses associated with their boarding school experiences.[1] This is evident in articles and clinical discussions where boarding school is often mentioned along with other aspects of a patient's history. Even experienced practitioners may sometimes miss the depth of the wound inflicted by the broken attachments and emotional neglect suffered when the child is sent to boarding school.[2] This is perhaps because it is not easy to believe that something so socially condoned and apparently ordinary as boarding school can be psychologically damaging. What has been described is a set of circumstances that, despite being familiar and so regarded as mundane, are actually also quite extraordinary. This becomes most evident when comparing the British boarding school system with that of other countries. For example, in Scandinavian countries, children are sent to boarding school only as a last resort in cases of extreme need.[3] [4]

Psychotherapy and transference

Ex-boarders may unconsciously play a part in distracting the analyst from the traumatic nature of their boarding school experience. This is because they were raised in the social environment in Britain, which treats this form of education as not merely ordinary but a privilege. As adults, they may disregard their own suffering and so inadvertently mislead the very psychotherapists they engage to help them. As children, the ex-boarders were unable to tell their parents of their suffering. This may replay in analysis, where they may not expect the therapist to take their story seriously; and so they may recount it, but omitting the emotional impact. They may gloss over their suffering with a lightness of language or a well-rehearsed joke. It is hoped that reading this book may cause some ex-boarders to pause, and to desist from trivialising their own suffering. It will perhaps help those embarking on psychotherapy to trust the practitioner with the history that they may not quite believe themselves.

When working with trauma the most disturbing elements may remain unremembered until they emerge, often unexpectedly, into consciousness. Therefore practitioners need to be alert when a new client mentions in passing that they attended a boarding school. It might signal that Boarding School Syndrome is a factor. This does not mean pouncing immediately on the client and demanding to know about their school experience – far from it. It does mean being vigilant, curious and attuned. The impact of boarding school may take time to surface and this cannot be hastened by intrusive questioning. However, neither can it be ignored and left implicit.

The transference in psychotherapy may replay many facets of the boarding school experience. Alongside early family dynamics, which emerge in most analyses, a transference to a teacher or to the whole boarding school edifice may be evoked. However well-intentioned the psychotherapist, he or she may be experienced as cold and abandoning or threatening, or may appear to offer salvation as an idealised parental figure. The risk of re-traumatising the client may mean accepting the role of ally for some time, whilst noting the transference. The moments of meeting[5] may be the strongest therapeutic factors in working with Boarding School Syndrome.

There are two major questions that have arisen from this research that merit further investigation. The first is the enduring power and influence of the 'sibling' groups in boarding schools and how this comes to dominate the British political establishment. The second is a question about mothers: we have read of mothers in tears as they parted with their children. What was it that led women to override their natural instinct to keep their young children close by?

The old school tie and sibling groups

The armoured personality, as we have seen, produces a form of false masculinity in boys. Initially created as bravado at a time when children were too small to defend themselves, it may become a way of being. It may influence the way men, in particular, interact as adults. It seems that this is an area that could fruitfully be explored in further research. How is it that this small elite group of ex-boarders become so politically powerful?

One significant aspect of this is the bonding in the student 'sibling' group, which for some seems to compensate for the loss of family. The sibling group in boarding schools is very important and, in some public schools, lifelong friendships are formed. This is often what the parents pay for. These friendships are central in the 'old boy network' which, in the higher echelons of British society, is a well-known means of social advancement. Men recognise those who shared their school experience and, even when they are not friends, they identify each other by subtle markers. The famous 'old school tie' is both a metaphor for this connection and a literal piece of clothing. Certainly, in the past, it was actually worn by grown men who were proud of the schools from which they came. The accent with which adults who attended the same school as children speak is another subliminal marker. One of my informants recalled, when she was a young woman, visiting a house shared by her friends. She heard a man whom she had never met speaking as he entered the house. Immediately she knew, by his accent, that he had attended the same school as her brother. This type of recognition is significant as men and women identify each other by their accent. Even when they are not personally known to each other, alumni of the same school are identifiable by the way they speak. This has social and political reverberations. For example, in seeking a position of employment preference may be given to someone subliminally recognised as kin.

Therefore the significance of the sibling group continues into adult life. A sense of belonging is maintained, for some, through 'old boys' reunions and through charitable donations to the school. The powerlessness that children at first experience in relation to the rules in boarding school may create a sibling bond. It also may produce people who conform. As the children grow, they take office in the school and learn the system from the inside, becoming pillars of the school establishment, in their turn taking the roles of prefect or head boy. This prepares them well to follow a career in the military, the law or some other highly formalised institution. This is the aim of boarding school and some of its most successful alumni have fitted into these roles with ease.

This sibling group is a factor in the way in which men club together, perpetuating the 'masculine' values that seem to still dominate the corridors of power. The shared values learned in school influence social policy and again lead to questions about the influence of these relatively few elite schools in the country. The sense of entitlement that starts at public school is later strengthened through becoming part of the political establishment. Many members of the current British government constitute such a sibling group, having followed similar paths. Some even attended the same public schools and universities; in many cases, this was Eton followed by Oxford, as Duffell points out.[6] It is remarkable that despite the fact that they are such a minority of the overall population, ex-boarders are still over-represented in influential posts.

There are others who follow rather different paths. The treatment that produces these successful men may also produce people who will never again take orders from authority figures – and so the rebel emerges. These people too are often successful in their professional lives, working freelance, becoming leaders and running successful independent companies. However, there are others, the casualties of the system who may have had little success, remaining sad and unfulfilled; some of these continue to be driven by anger and the desire for revenge. Noting the success of their peers may compound their envy.

Women and sibling groups

Much of what has been said of men applies to women. Women too attend school reunions, and many retain lasting friendships from within their school sibling group. However, it seems there are not the same 'old girls' networks and women traditionally do not have the same access to power as men. This is another question for further research: it may well be that the disparity in their boarding school experiences means that women have different affinities than men.

An ability to relate in a sisterly manner to other women is sometimes evident in psychotherapy. When working with women ex-boarders, as a female analyst, I have observed a sense of 'all girls together'. This is a friendliness which oils the wheels of everyday social interactions. This is the type of behaviour for which boarding schools were designed, an apparent ability to get on with people of all classes and to help others feel at ease. This is part of the compensation of the boarding school sibling group, the rewards of which are so much greater for men than for women.

Conversely, this apparent social ability may work against the best interests of the woman (or man) in psychotherapy, because their suffering may be masked. The analyst may have to resist reciprocating the friendliness in order to take seriously the perceived suffering hidden behind the social presentation. However successful the ex-boarder, as we have seen, it is often in their closest relationships that they may find themselves troubled. It is only as psychotherapy progresses that they begin to trace the source of this to their boarding school experience and eventually to the loss of their mothers at an early age.

Women as mothers

One of the questions with which I began this book was that posed by my own father with regard to his mother: 'If I was so precious why then did she part with me?' This tragic question remains in the air. Why did mothers let their young children go sometimes hundreds of miles away, even across continents? We have read stories of mothers who told their children they did not want to lose them and yet they let them go. The answer to this question lies to some extent in patriarchy and the power relations between women and men.

The developmental path that leads to boarding at an early age originates in early home experiences. Mothers to whom I have spoken have very mixed feelings about the choices with which they were faced when choosing boarding for their children. Until relatively recently women felt that they had to comply with the course set out for them by their husbands or parents. Some women from traditional upper-class families, who themselves had been to boarding school, were merely following the expectation of their class. Often in these families the father and grandparents insisted on boarding. Mothers, often quite young at the time, may not have felt sufficiently confident to resist. Many parents in the military or the diplomatic service have little other option for their children: they move every two years, and their children suffer because they change schools so often that they are unable to sustain a consistent education and friendships. Some mothers to whom I have spoken missed their children deeply but they felt helpless. They truly considered that, given their situation, this was in the best interests of their children. There is little doubt that for some it was. There were women who, distraught at losing their children, turned to alcohol to ameliorate the pain of their loss. However, there were also women who were relieved to delegate childcare. Some informants considered that their mothers were too busy with their social lives to parent their children. As the widowed mother of one of my patients put it, 'Child-rearing is best left to the experts.' With these words she justified sending her children to boarding school at 4 and 6 years of age respectively. I have touched upon these issues in the book, but clearly there are many questions here for further investigation.

Boarding School Syndrome – in conclusion

In conclusion, I will recap some of the ways in which the very 'ordinary' boarding school experience has been reframed. It is my hope that we might see it anew from the perspective of children.

Homesickness

- Homesickness has been reframed as bereavement.
- Mourning is an appropriate grief reaction, following major losses of attachment figures.
- Homesickness is a form of mourning.

Captivity

- The institutional life of some boarders has been reframed as captivity.
- The rules, timetables and a strict regime mean that the child is not at liberty to make little day-to-day decisions.
- Children can leave only when given permission by adults.

Homelessness

- Exile is the state of being of many children in boarding school. The children are effectively homeless, no longer fully belonging at home nor at school.
- The split between the home self and the boarding school self is thus established.
- Children from abroad are doubly exiled because often they have no sense of a place called 'home' to which to return.

The body

- The children's relationship to their bodies is distorted, as normal bodily rhythms are interrupted.

- The lack of appropriate physical contact for a significant part of childhood is a serious deprivation.
- Eating a prescribed diet en masse means that, for some, food may become frightening.
- Hunger and greed become part of a pattern of relating.
- Sleeping times are prescribed. Other children, prefects or staff may interrupt children's sleep.
- For some the bed is not a safe place and so the imaginal world of sleep, reverie and dreaming may be distorted.

Intimacy

- Rules distort loving friendships.
- Sexuality may be distorted by living for years in a single-sex environment.
- Emerging appetites with regard to food, intimate relationships and sexuality may be disturbed by early institutionalisation.

By examining the anatomy of the multiple traumas that some ex-boarders have suffered, I hope to alert practitioners to the very real distress of the boarding school child. This depth analysis may help ex-boarders to identify the origin of certain troubling behaviours and emotions in the present. Facilitating talking about feelings may enhance personal and work relationships. We have seen that Boarding School Syndrome is a symptom of serious psychological distress. It is essential that, as a society, we listen to children and to adult ex-boarders, believe the stories they tell and treat them with the gravity they merit.

Notes

1 Apart from Nick Duffell, who identified the problem in *The Making of Them;* Duffell, N. (2000) *The Making of Them*, London: Lone Arrow Press.
2 Schaverien, J. (2011a) 'Boarding School Syndrome: Broken attachments a hidden trauma', *British Journal of Psychotherapy* 17 (2), pp. 138–155.
3 I became aware of this in 1991when it was pointed out to me by a Dutch colleague. As part of our clinical discourse, I was presenting a client who was an ex-boarder. My colleague had been a hidden child in the Netherlands in World War II. She also worked as a psychotherapist with those who had, as children, survived the Japanese prisoner of war camps. These experiences led her to observe that the British establishment was a group of traumatised people as a result of the practice of sending their children away to school. See Schaverien, J. (2004) 'Boarding school: The trauma of the "privileged" child', *Journal of Analytical Psychology* 49 (5), p. 683.
4 This was also observed by Duffell, whose Danish wife was shocked by the practice; Duffell (2000) *The Making of Them*, p. 10.
5 The moments of meeting were identified by 'The Boston Process of Change Study Group' by Sander, Stern & Tronick, as described in Beebe, B., & Lachmann, F. M. (2002/2005) *Infant Research and Adult Treatment*, London: Analytic Press.
6 Duffell, N. (2014) *Wounded Leaders: British Elitism and the Entitlement Illusion: A Psychohistory*, London: Lone Arrow Press.

Bibliography

Ainsworth, M.D., & Bell, S. M. (1970) 'Attachment, exploration, and separation: Illustrated by one year olds in a strange situation', *Child Development* 41 (1), pp. 49–67.
Ainsworth, M. S. (1989) 'Attachments beyond infancy', *American Psychologist* 44 (4), pp. 709–716.
American Psychiatric Association (1980). *Diagnostic and Statistical Manual of Mental Disorders*, third edition. Washington, DC: American Psychiatric Press.
American Psychiatric Association (2013). *Diagnostic and Statistical Manual of Mental Disorders*, fifth edition, Washington, DC: American Psychiatric Association.
Baron Cohen, S. (2011) *Zero Degrees of Empathy: A New Theory of Human Cruelty*, London: Allen Lane.
Barrie, J.M. (1904/2010) *Peter Pan*, London: Puffin Classics.
Bateman, A., & Fonagy, P. (2013) 'Mentalization-based treatment', *Psychoanalytic Inquiry* 33, pp. 595–613.
Beebe, B., & Lachmann, F. M. (2002/2005) *Infant Research and Adult Treatment*, London: Analytic Press.
Bettelheim, B. (1960/1986) *The Informed Heart*, London: Peregrine Books.
Bion, W.R. (1982) *The Long Weekend 1897–1919, Part of a Life*, London: Karnac Books.
Boarding Schools Association (2013) www.boarding.org.uk/.
Bowlby, J. (1969) *Attachment*, Attachment and Loss, vol. 1, London: Hogarth Press.
Bowlby, J. (1973) *Separation: Anxiety and Anger*, Attachment and Loss, vol. 2, London: Hogarth Press.
Bowlby, J. (1980) *Loss: Sadness and Depression*, Attachment and Loss, vol. 3, London: Hogarth Press.
Bradfield, C.R. (2001) 'Residential School Syndrome', *BC Medical Journal* 43 (2), pp. 78–81.
Brendon, V. (2005/2006) *Children of the Raj*, Phoenix: Orion.
Brendon, V. (2009) *Prep School Children: A Class Apart Over Two Centuries*, London: Continuum.
British Council, The UK boarding school system www.educationuk.org/global/articles/uk-boarding-school-system/.
Buck, P. S. (1931/2005) *The Good Earth*, London: Simon & Schuster UK Ltd.
Buti, A. (2002) 'The removal of aboriginal children: Canada and Australia compared', *University of Western Sydney Law Review* 26 (1) www.austlii.edu.au/au/journals/UWSLRev/2002/2.html.
Casement, P. (2008) *Learning From Life*, London: Routledge.

Chandos, J. (1984) *Boys Together: English Public Schools 1800–1864*, London: Yale University Press.
Chernin, K. (1986) *The Hungry Self*, London: Virago.
Colman, A. M. (2001) *The Oxford Dictionary of Psychology*, Oxford: Oxford University Press.
Crisp, A. H. (1980) *Anorexia Nervosa*, London: Grune & Stratton.
Crisp, A. H., & Burns, T. (1990) 'Primary anorexia nervosa in the male and female: A comparison of clinical features and prognosis,' in *Males with Eating Disorders*, Andersen, A. E. (ed), London: Routledge.
Dahl, R. (1984) *Boy: Tales of Childhood*, London: Puffin Books.
Dickens, C. (1838–1839/1995) *Nicholas Nickleby*, Hertfordshire: Wordsworth Editions Ltd.
Duffell, N. (2000) *The Making of Them*, London: Lone Arrow Press.
Duffell, N. (2011) 'The old school ties', *Therapy Today* 22 (3), pp. 11–15.
Duffell, N. (2014) *Wounded Leaders: British Elitism and the Entitlement Illusion: A Psychohistory*, London: Lone Arrow Press.
Fonagy, P., & Target, M. (2000) 'Playing with reality: iii. The persistence of dual psychic reality in borderline patients', *The International Journal of Psychoanalysis* 81, pp. 853–873.
Fordham, M. (1985) *Explorations Into the Self*, London: Karnac Books.
Freud, A. (1965) *Normality and Pathology in Childhood*, London: Hogarth Press.
Freud, A. (1992) *Ego and Mechanisms of Defense*, London: Hogarth Press.
Freud, S. (1911/1968) 'Notes on an autobiographical account of a case of paranoia', Standard Edition XII. London: Hogarth Press.
Freud, S., (1912) *The Dynamics of the Transference*, Standard Edition XII, London: Hogarth Press.
Freud, S. (1920) *Beyond the Pleasure Principle*, Standard Edition XVIII, London: Hogarth Press.
Freud, S. (1939) *Moses and Monotheism*, Standard Edition XXIII, London: Hogarth Press.
Freud, S. (1964) *New Introductory Lectures on Psycho-analysis*, Standard Edition XXIV, London: Hogarth Press.
Fry, S. (2004) *Moab Is My Washpot*, London: Arrow Books.
Gardam, J. (2004/2005) *Old Filth*, London: Abacus.
Gathorne-Hardy, J. (1977) *The Public School Phenomenon 597–1977*, London: Hodder & Stoughton.
Gerhardt, S. (2004) *Why Love Matters*, London: Routledge.
Goffman, E. (1961/1991) *Asylums: Essays on the Social Situation of Mental Patients and Other Inmates*, Harmondsworth: Penguin Social Sciences.
Golding, W. (1954) *Lord of the Flies*, London: Penguin.
Graves, R. (1929/1960) *Goodbye to All That*, London: Penguin.
Grier, F. (2013) 'The hidden trauma of the young boarding school child as seen through the lens of adult couple therapy', in *Enduring Trauma Through the Life Cycle*, McGinley, E. & Varchevker, A. (eds), London: Karnac Books.
Grounds, L. M. (2011) 'Historical intergenerational trauma and posttraumatic stress disorder: Trauma that affects entire cultural groups' http://drlindagrounds.com/2011/historicalintergenerational-trauma.

Harlow, H. F. (1959) 'Love in infant monkeys', *Scientific American* 200 (6), pp. 64–74.

Herman, J. (1992/1997) *Trauma and Recovery: The Aftermath of Violence From Domestic Abuse to Political Terror*, New York: Basic Books.

Heward, C. (1988) *Making a Man of Him: Parents and Their Sons' Education at an English Public School 1929–1950*, London: Routledge.

Hickson, A. (1996) *The Poisoned Bowl: Sex and the Public School*, London: Gerald Duckworth & Co Ltd.

Hinshelwood, R. D. (2013) *Research on the Couch: Single-Case Studies, Subjectivity and Psychoanalytic Knowledge*, London: Routledge, New Library of Psychoanalysis, 'Beyond the Couch' series.

Hitchens, C. (2011) *Hitch-22: A Memoir*, London: Atlantic Books (an imprint of Grove Atlantic Ltd).

Holmes, J. (1993) *John Bowlby and Attachment Theory*, London: Routledge.

Hughes, T. (1857/2013) *Tom Brown's School Days*, Burlingame, California: Collins Classics.

Jones, E. (1953/1983) *Sigmund Freud Life and Work*, vol. 1, London: Hogarth Press.

Jung, C.G. (1956/1976) *Symbols of Transformation*, Collected Works 5, Princeton: Bollingen.

Jung, C.G. (1969) *Archetypes and the Collective Unconscious*, Collected Works 9, Princeton: Bollingen.

Kalsched, D. (1996) *The Inner World of Trauma*, London: Routledge.

Kaplinsky, C. (2008) 'Shifting shadows: Shaping dynamics in the cultural unconscious', *Journal of Analytical Psychology* 53 (2), pp. 189–207.

Kaye, P. (2005) *Homesickness*, MA thesis, The Tavistock Institute for Human Relations.

Kerstenberg, J. (1985) 'Child survivors of the Holocaust – 40 years later', *Journal of the American Academy of Child Psychiatry* 24, pp. 408–412.

Kipling, R. (1888/1995) *Baa Baa Black Sheep*, London: Penguin.

Klein, M. (1946/1975) 'Notes on some schizoid mechanisms', in *Envy and Gratitude, the Writings of Melanie Klein*, vol. 3, London: Hogarth Press.

Knox, J. (2003) *Archetype, Attachment, Analysis*, New York: Brunner Routledge.

Knox, J. (2011) *Self-Agency in Psychotherapy*, London: W. W. Norton & Co.

Lambert, R. with Millham, S. (1968) *The Hothouse Society*, London: Weidenfeld & Nicholson.

Lanius, R. A., Vermetten, E., & Pain, C. (eds) (2010) *The Impact of Early Life Trauma on Health and Disease: The Hidden Epidemic*, Cambridge: Cambridge University Press.

Lawrence, M. (1984) *The Anorexic Experience*, London: Women's Press.

Lederman, J. (1999) 'Trauma and healing in aboriginal families and communities', *Native Social Work Journal* 2 (1), pp. 59–90.

Lewis, P. (1991) 'Mummy matron and the maids: Feminine presence and absence in male institutions 1934–63,' in Roper, M. & Tosh, J. (eds) *Manful Assertions*, New York: Taylor & Francis.

Leys, R. (2000) *Trauma: A Genealogy*, Chicago: University of Chicago Press.

Lifton, R.J. (1967) *Death in Life: Survivors of Hiroshima*, New York: Simon & Schuster.

Lockhart, R. E., Gilpin, A., & Jasiocha, E. (2013) *ISC Census*, London: Independent Schools Council www.isc.co.uk/Resources/Independent%20Schools%20Council/Research%20 Archive/Annual%20Census/2013_annualcensus_isc.pdf.

May, T. (2009) *The Victorian Public School*, Oxford: The Shire Library.
Macaulay, C. (1763–1783) *The History of England from the Accession of James 1 to That of the Brunswick Line* http://plato.stanford.edu/entries/catharine-macaulay/.
Macaulay, C. (1790) *Letters on Education* http://en.wikipedia.org/wiki/Catharine_Macaulay.
McGilchrist, I. (2009) *The Master and His Emissary*, London: Yale University Press.
McLeod, J. (1994) *Doing Counselling Research*. Thousand Oaks, California: Sage.
Messler Davies, J., & Frawley, M. G. (1994) *Treating the Adult Survivor of Childhood Sexual Abuse*, New York: Basic Books.
Midgely, N. (2006) 'The "inseparable bond between cure and research": Clinical case study as a method of psychoanalytic inquiry', *The Journal of Child Psychotherapy* 32, pp. 122–147.
Motion, A. (2006) *In the Blood: A Memoir of My Childhood*, London: Faber & Faber.
Murray Parkes, C. (1972) *Bereavement: Studies of Grief in Adult Life*, Harmondsworth: Penguin Books.
National Society for the Prevention of Cruelty to Children (2015) www.nspcc.org.uk/Inform/resourcesforprofessionals/lookedafterchildren/introduction_wda88884.html.
Oakley, A. (2011) *A Critical Woman*, London: Bloomsbury Academic.
Okely, J. (1996) *Own or Other Culture*, London: Routledge.
Orbach, S. (1986) *Hunger Strike*, London: Faber & Faber.
Orwell, G. (1947/2003) *Such, Such Were the Joys*, London: Penguin.
Papadopoulos, R. (ed) (2002) *Therapeutic Care for Refugees: No Place Like Home*, London: Karnac Books.
Papadopoulos, R. (2006) 'Refugees and psychological trauma: Psychosocial perspectives' http://isites.harvard.edu/fs/docs/icb.topic920418.files/arc_1_10refandpsych-1.pdf.
Partridge, S. (2007) 'Trauma at the threshold: An eight-year-old goes to boarding school', *Attachment* 1 (3), pp. 310–313.
Partridge, S. (2013) 'Boarding School Syndrome: Disguised attachment-deficit and dissociation reinforced by institutional neglect and abuse', *Attachment* 7 (2), pp. 202–213.
Pearsall, J., & Hanks, P. (eds) (2001) *The New Oxford Dictionary of English*, Oxford: Oxford University Press.
Peel, J., & Ravenscroft, S. (2006) *Margrave of the Marshes*, London: Random House.
Power, A. (2007) 'Discussion of trauma at the threshold: The impact of boarding school on attachment in young children', *Attachment* 1 (3), pp. 313–320.
Power, A. (2013a) 'Early boarding: rich children in care, their adaptation to loss of attachment', *Attachment* 7 (2), pp. 186–201.
Powell, A. (2013b) 'Sparta boarding school of evil genius', talk given 26 September, Bath Royal Literary and Scientific Institution.
Raphael, F. (2003). *A Spoilt Boy*, London: Orion.
Roth, A., & Fonagy, P. (1996) *What Works for Whom? A Critical Review of Psychotherapy Research*, London: Guilford.
Rothschild, B. (2000) *The Body Remembers: The Psychophysiology of Trauma and Trauma Treatment*, London: W. W. Norton & Co.
Sacks, O. (2001) *Uncle Tungsten*, London: Picador.
Sandler, J., Sandler, A. M., & Davies, R. (2000) *Clinical and Observational Psychoanalytic Research Andre Green and David Stern*, London: Karnac Books.
Schatzman, M. (1973) *Soul Murder: Persecution in the Family*, New York: Random House.

Schaverien, J. (1992) *The Revealing Image*, London: Routledge. This edition London: Jessica Kingsley Publishers (1999).
Schaverien, J. (2002) *The Dying Patient in Psychotherapy: Desire, Dreams and Individuation*, New York: Palgrave Macmillan.
Schaverien, J. (2004) 'Boarding school: The trauma of the "privileged" child', *Journal of Analytical Psychology* 49 (5), pp. 683–705.
Schaverien, J. (2006) 'Men who leave too soon: Reflections on the erotic transference and countertransference', in *Gender, Countertransference and the Erotic Transference*, Schaverien, J. (ed), London: Routledge.
Schaverien, J. (2011a) 'Boarding School Syndrome: Broken attachments a hidden trauma', *British Journal of Psychotherapy* 17 (2), pp. 138–155.
Schaverien, J. (2011b) 'Lost for words', *Therapy Today* 22 (3), pp. 18–21.
Schore, A. N. (1994) *Affect Regulation and Origins of the Self*, Hillsdale, New Jersey: Lawrence Erlbaum Associates.
Shengold, L. (1989) *Soul Murder: The Effects of Childhood Abuse and Deprivation*, New York: Fawcett Columbine.
Smith, A. (2009) 'Indigenous peoples and boarding schools: A comparative study', prepared for the United Nations Permanent Forum on Indigenous Issues, eighth session, New York, 18–29 May www.un.org/esa/socdev/unpfii/documents/E_C_19_2009_crp1.pdf.
Spurling, H. (2010) *Burying the Bones: Pearl Buck in China*, London: Profile Books.
Stack, M. (2008) 'The making of her: My boarding school experience', *Attachment* 2 (3), pp. 321–328.
Steiner, J. (1993) *Psychic Retreats*, London: Routledge.
Stern, D. N. (1985) *The Interpersonal World of the Infant*, New York: Basic Books.
Stern, D. N. et al. (1998) 'Non-interpretive mechanisms in psychoanalytic therapy: the "something more" than interpretation', *The International Journal of Psychoanalysis* 79, pp. 903–921.
Taylor, B. (2014) *The Last Asylum*, London: Penguin, Hamish Hamilton.
Tomalin, C. (2011) *Charles Dickens: A Life*, London: Viking.
Trevarthen, C. (2009) 'The intersubjective psychobiology of human meaning: Learning of culture depends on interest for co-operative practical work-and affection for the joyful art of good company', *Psychoanalytic Dialogues* 19, pp. 507–518.
Tronick, E. Z. (2003) 'Of course all relationships are unique: How co-creative processes generate unique mother-infant and patient-therapist relationships', *Psychoanalytic Inquiry* 23, pp. 473–491.
Van der Kolk, B. A. (1994) 'The body keeps the score: Memory and the evolving psychobiology of posttraumatic stress', *Harvard Review of Psychiatry* 1 (5), pp. 253–265.
Van der Kolk, B. A. (1996) 'Trauma and memory', in *Traumatic Stress*, Van der Kolk, B. A., McFarlane, A. C., & Weisaeth, L. (eds), London: Guilford Press.
Van der Kolk, B. A., & d'Andrea, W. (2010) 'Towards a developmental trauma disorder diagnosis for childhood interpersonal trauma', in Lanius, R. A., Vermetten, E., & Pain, C. (eds), *The Impact of Early Life Trauma on Health and Disease: The Hidden Epidemic*, Cambridge: Cambridge University Press.
Van der Kolk, B. A., & Fisler, R. (1995) 'Dissociation and the fragmentary nature of traumatic memories: Background and experimental evidence', *Journal of Traumatic Stress* 8, pp. 505–525.

Van der Kolk, B. A., & Kaddish, W. (1987) 'Amnesia, dissociation and the return of the repressed,' in Van der Kolk, B. (ed), *Psychological Trauma*, Arlington, Virginia: American Psychiatric Press, pp. 173–190.

Van der Kolk, B. A., & McFarlane, A. C. (1996) 'The black hole of trauma' in *Traumatic Stress*, Van der Kolk, B. A., McFarlane, A. C., & Weisaeth, L. (eds), London: Guilford Press, pp. 3–5.

Van Dijken, S. (1998) *John Bowlby: His Early Life*, London: Free Association Books.

Vicinus, M. (1985) *Independent Women: Work and Community for Single Women 1850–1920*, London: Virago.

Wakeford, J. (1969) *The Cloistered Elite: A Sociological Analysis of the English Public School*, London, New York: Macmillan.

Walford, G. (1986) *Life in Public Schools*, London: Methuen.

Watson, N. (1994) *In Hortis Reginae: A History of Queenswood School 1894–1994*, London: James & James.

West, D. R. (1985) *Half to Remember, an Autobiography, With the History of Christ's Hospital School, Hertford as Seen Through the Eyes of the Headmistress 1942–1972*, pamphlet published by Christ's Hospital School.

Wikipedia, 'School corporal punishment' http://en.wikipedia.org/wiki/School_corporal_punishment.

Wilkinson, M. (2006) *Coming Into Mind*, London: Routledge.

Wilkinson, M. (2010) *Changing Minds in Psychotherapy*, London: W. W. Norton & Co.

Winnicott, D. W. (1971) *Playing and Reality*, Harmondsworth: Penguin.

Winnicott, D. W. (1958/1982) *Through Pediatrics to Psychoanalysis*, London: Hogarth Press.

Wober, M. (1971) *English Girls' Boarding Schools*, London: Allen Lane, the Penguin Press.

Wollstonecraft, M. (1792) *The Vindication of the Rights of Women*, Kindle edition, in the public domain.

Woodhead, J. (2004) '"Dialectical process" and "constructive method": Micro-analysis of relational process in an example from parent-infant psychotherapy', *Journal of Analytical Psychology* 49, pp. 143–160.

Articles in the press

Brown, A. M. (2011) 'Does "brusque" and "rude" David Cameron suffer from boarding school syndrome?' (23 June) http://blogs.telegraph.co.uk/news/andrewmcfbrown/100093533/.

Brown, D., & Bennett, R. (2013) 'Pupils break silence over prep school paedophiles', *The Times* (19 December), p. 1.

Englhart, K. (2013) 'Brits warned to beware of "boarding school syndrome"', *Macleans* (23 April).

Lakani, N. (2011) 'Boarding is as damaging as being taken into care, says therapist', *The Independent on Sunday* (24 April).

Leigh, W. (2011) 'Bedlam, bullying and baked beans three times a day', *The Mail* (1 May).

Lynch, K. (2012) 'Working to heal the wounds of boarding school', *The Native Press* (19 July), pp. 1–3.

Marsh, S. (2011) 'Cold, disengaged, and detached: Do you suffer from boarding school syndrome?' *The Times* (23 June).

Monbiot, G. (2012) 'The British boarding school remains a bastion of cruelty', *The Guardian* (16 January) www.theguardian.com/commentisfree/2012/jan/16/boarding-school-bastion-cruelty.

Norfolk, A. (2013) 'A life ruined by Caldecott paedophile', *The Times* (19 December), p. 9.

Pasternak, A. (2013), 'Boarding school – it's a glorified sleepover', *The Telegraph* (13 February) www.telegraph.co.uk/education/9074666/Boarding-school-its-a-glorified-sleepover.html.

Raphael, F. (2004) 'Outcast of the sixth', *The Sunday Times* (9 March), News Review, p. 9.

Renton, A. (2014a) 'Abuse in Britain's boarding schools; a personal story,' *The Observer Magazine* (4 May), pp. 31–37.

Renton, A. (2014b) 'The damage boarding schools do,' *The Observer* (20 July).

Williams, S. (2013) 'What's it like to go away to school at 8?' *The Sunday Times Magazine* (31 August).

Wilson, A. N. (2014) 'Scarred for life by boarding school sadists: How A. N. Wilson was deluged with similar horror stories after revealing his abuse at hands of paedophile head', *Mail Online* (17 May) www.dailymail.co.uk/news/article-2630951/Scarred-life-boarding-school-sadists-How-A-N-Wilson-deluged-similar-horror-stories-revealing-abuse-hands-paedophile-head.html.

Duffell, N. (1990) 'The old school', *The Independent* (1 September).

Radio and television programmes and films

A Renaissance Education: The Schooling of Thomas More's Daughter (2012). Presented by Dr Helen Castor (TV programme). Broadcast on BBC 4 (5 January).

Chosen (2008) Broadcast on Channel 4, November http://truevisiontv.com/films/details/97/chosen.

The Making of Them (1994) Directed by Colin Luke (film). Broadcast on BBC 4 http://youtube/2uRr77vju8U.

Mark Lawson Talks To . . . (2013) John le Carre interview broadcast on BBC 4 (18 November) www.bbc.co.uk/programmes/b00dwcp6.

Leaving home at 8 (2010). Cutting Edge Programme on Channel 4 www.channel4.com/programmes/leaving-home-at-8/episode-guide/series-1/episode-1.

Sport and the British (2012). Presented by Clair Balding. Thirty-part series broadcast on BBC Radio 4.

Young Children in Brief Separation (1971). Five-film series produced by James and Joyce Robertson.

A Two-Year-Old Goes to Hospital (1952). Film produced by James and Joyce Robertson www.youtube.com/watch?v=s14Q-_Bxc_U.

Index

abandonment 83, 102, 108, 120, 137–50, 158, 169–70; anatomy of Boarding School Trauma 137–8; Boarding School Syndrome with dissociative symptoms 140; breaking the rules trauma 142–3; dissociation and the captive child 139; dissociation and post-traumatic stress 149; drawing 144–5; freedom trauma 143–4; grief and mourning 141; imprisonment 138–9; narrative and memory 147; post-traumatic stress and dissociation 149; regime and punishment 142; repetition 145–6; return to school trauma 146–7; time 147–9; trauma in bid for freedom 143–4; trauma in breaking the rules 142–3; trauma in returning to school 146–7; trauma on first day 140

abuse 40, 50, 57, 81, 117, 196–9, 225n16, 226n24; by another child 187, 220–1; and bullying 185; paedophile 221; revenge to abuser 102, 161; self 149, 189; sexual 115, 116, 121, 143, 150n19, 174, 187, 199, 207, 215–24, 225n1

adolescent bodies 179

affect regulation 99, 117

Ainsworth, Mary 128

alienated child 153, 156–7

amnesia 9, 32, 113–24, 137, 150, 185; body remembers 118–21; childhood trauma 116–17; cultural 121; and dissociation 114–16; psychotherapy presentation 118; social pressure to forget 121; witnessing and the narrative function 117–18

anger after summer break 101–2

Anna Freud Centre 166, 175n13

armoured self 179–91; armoured self 190–1; body armour 187–8; bullying in the present 189; institutionally condoned bullying 180–2; leathers and the lash 182; liberation 183–4; old boy network and false masculinity 180; psychotherapy 189–90; public school child 179–80; study of a boy/man who had been bullied 184–91; threshold memory 185–7

Ashley, Francis 22

attachment 6, 7, 10, 41–2, 58, 132, 148, 152, 179, 190; broken 2, 8–9, 99, 125, 128–9, 132, 135, 147, 202, 227; early patterns 114, 166; emotional 127, 162, 165; homosexual 217; primary 2, 114, 117, 122, 157, 158, 164, 187; seeking 134

Attachment 6

Barrie, James: *Peter Pan* 160
Beacon School 193, 209, 213
Beale, Dorothea 35, 36–7, 40
beatings 4, 9, 17, 20, 23, 24–5, 37, 38, 43, 107, 127, 132, 161, 169, 171, 180, 192, 197, 198, 216; *see also* cruelty
Bedford College 35
bereaved child 125–36; actual bereavement 134–5; attachment 128–9; autobiographies of boarding school arrival 129–32; bereavement 132–3; breaking emotional bonds 127–8; mourning 133–4
bereavement: actual 134–5; losses 52, 79, 121, 125, 126, 127, 130, 132–4, 137, 141, 150, 151, 152–4, 155, 180; *see also* bereaved child

Index

Betjeman, John 20
betrayal: and trust 103–4mother 89–90, 91
Bettelheim, B. 116, 149
Bion, Wilfred 9, 129, 151, 157, 165
Blue Stocking Society 34
boarders: enjoyed boarding 4–5; in population 3–4
boarding school self/home self 98
Boarding School Syndrome: clinical method 11; hypothesis 1–2; locked away 81–2; old school tie and sibling groups 228–9; pattern 2, 11; psychotherapy 9–10; psychotherapy and transference 227–8; research method 2–3; review of literature 5–6; towards a theory 227–32; women and sibling groups 230; women as mothers 230–1
bodily needs 166, 168
body 207, 218, 231–2; armour 187–8; expressing distress 165, 169, 203; fuelling 171; girls' bodies 39–40; intimate care and the child's 165–8; lack of food 171; remembers 118–21; restrictions 39; training 216; *see also* abuse; adolescent bodies; beatings; boys' sexual activity and sexual abuse; children's bodies; girl's bodies; hunger and greed; men's bodies; menstruation; puberty in girls' schools; sexual abuse
Boston Process of Change Study Group 166
Bowlby, John 9–10, 132; *Attachment and Loss* 128
boys' boarding schools: accommodations 19–20; brutality 20–1; Clarendon commission 25–8; dormitories and brutality 21–3; grammar school foundations 18–19; grammar schools 18; history 17–31; lessons and sleeping arrangements 19–20; prefects and fagging 23–4; public school reform 25–8; public schools 19; rebellion 24–5; reforms and after 28–9
boys' sexual activity and sexual abuse 215–26; abuse by another child 220–1; historical perspective 216–17; paedophile threat 221; puberty 217–19; sexual activity and sexual abuse 219–20; the split: women are for loving—men are for sex 221–4; wives and mothers 224
breaking the rules trauma 142–3
Brendon, Vyvyen 5, 19, 120, 154, 173, 199; *Children of the Raj* 26, 154

Brougham, Henry 25
Brougham Committee of the House of Commons 26
brutality 20–1; and dormitories 21–3; *see also* abuse; beatings
Buck, Pearl: *The Good Earth* 154–5, 158
bullying 8, 20, 22–3, 172–3, 192; and initiation 196–8; institutionally condoned 180–2; in the present 189; study of a boy/man who had been bullied 184–91; *see also* prefects
Buss, Mary 35, 37

Caldecott School 150n19, 226n24
Cambridge University 36
captive child 137–50; anatomy of Boarding School Trauma 137–8; Boarding School Syndrome with dissociative symptoms 140; breaking the rules trauma 142–3; dissociation 139; dissociation and post-traumatic stress 149; drawing 144–5; freedom trauma 143–4; grief and mourning 141; imprisonment 138–9; narrative and memory 147; post-traumatic stress and dissociation 149; regime and punishment 142; repetition 145–6; return to school trauma 146–7; time 147–9; trauma in bid for freedom 143–4; trauma in breaking the rules 142–3; trauma in returning to school 146–7; trauma on first day 140
Chandos, John 5, 20, 21, 24, 27, 49, 180
Charity Commissioners 26
Charterhouse 22, 26
Cheltenham Ladies College 26, 34, 35, 36, 40
the child *see* alienated child; bereaved child; captive child; children of the British Empire; latency child; looked after children; public school child
children in care 7
children of the British Empire 151–63; alienation 156–7; encapsulated self 160–1; exotic locations 153–4; homeless 151–2; homelessness and mourning 161–2; local nannies and servants 157–8; marriage and the idealisation of women 158–60; revenge 161; tradition of sending 'home' 154–6
children's bodies 218, 231–2
Christ's Hospital 194, 195

Index

Clarendon Commission 25–8
clothing 129; and discipline 206; fencing 183; 'old school tie' 229; *see also* girl's clothing; school uniforms
communities of women 193–5
corporal punishment 17, 181
countertransference 61
couples psychotherapy 2, 159
cruelty 17, 20, 24, 49, 57, 98, 99, 108, 127, 156, 173, 174, 192, 196; vindictive 213; witnessing 104; *see also* beatings; brutality; trauma

Dahl, Roald 52, 129–30, 132, 165, 170–1, 183–4
Davies, Emily 35
day schools 8, 32, 38, 40, 42
death 50, 116, 133; brutality 22; of child 22, 27, 28, 141; of grandparent 126, 203; of parent 125, 134; saints 68
deintegration 166, 167
deportment in girls' schools 39–40; corsets 39, 40; stays 39
developmental trauma (case study part 1) 49–59; boarding school arrival 52–3; confronting women 55–6; dormitory terror 53–4; first break 56; first meeting 50–2; returning to school after summer break 56–8; second session 52–3; transference 54–5
Diagnostic and Statistical Manual of Mental Disorders (DSM) 116, 117, 139
discipline 20, 24, 27, 156, 183; and control in the twentieth century 38–9; discipline and control in the Victorian era 37–8; *see also* corporal punishment; fagging; prefects
disassociation 140, 141, 144; amnesia 114–16; captive child 139; childhood trauma 116, 117, 187; and post-traumatic stress 149
distortion of a boy (case study part 3) 80–93; as adult meeting the boy 85; Boarding School Syndrome feeling of being locked away 81–2; garden in spring 84; the journey 89–90; letter to mother 91–2; looking at pictures 82–3; mother betrayal 89–90, 91; packing 81; rage 85–7; relationships 80–1; regression 90–1; taking care of the boy 87–9; talking to parents 83; tortoise 83–4

dormitories: and brutality 21–3; and despair 76–9; homesickness 168–9; terror 53–4
dream 51, 61, 98, 107, 139, 220; committing murder 104; recurring 55, 95, 157; wet 218
DSM *see Diagnostic and Statistical Manual of Mental Disorders*
Duffell, Nick 6, 10, 160, 229, 232n1, 232n4

eating disorders 201–2, 204nn13–14
The Edinburgh Review 24, 25, 26
Elizabeth I (queen) 33
encapsulated self 160–1
endowed schools 19
Endowed Schools Bill 28
Endowed Schools Commission 35
Eton 18, 20, 21, 22, 25, 26, 28, 60, 229
exeats 49, 72, 77, 199
exotic locations 153–4

fagging 28, 181, 192; and prefects 23–4
fear of sexuality 195
femininity 196, 207, 208; false 43
first day of school trauma 140
floggings 25
food 25, 34, 70–3, 166–7, 169, 184, 199–201, 203–4, 232; eating disorders 201–2; force feeding 173; hunger and greed 170–2; inadequate 192; lack of 171; and sickness 173–4
Fordham, Michael 166
freedom trauma 143–4
Freud, Anna 128; Centre 166
Freud, Sigmund: amnesia 114–15, 117; cultural amnesia 121; defensive measures 53, 119; investigation 2; repressed memories 61; sexual abuse 121; soul murder 73, 104; transference 54
friendships 8, 152, 209, 231; adult 103; boys 211; daygirls 40; girls 41, 194–5; homosexuality 211; lifelong 197, 228–9; loving 232; peers 162, 187; senior girls and teachers 42; sexual encounters 195; sibling groups 230; suffering 161; taboos 42, 207–8
Fry, Stephen 129, 138, 211–13

Gardam, Jane: *Old Filth* 152–3
Gathorne-Hardy, Jonathan 5, 19, 20, 21, 24, 28, 35, 49, 164, 216, 217

Index

Gerhardt, Sue 98, 128, 166
girls and the tyranny of the dinner table 192–204; bullying and initiation 196–8; communities of women 193–5; eating disorders 201–2; hierarchy at the dinner table 200–1; service 195–6; table manners 199–200; unsymbolised self 201–4; why the child does not tell 198–99
girls' boarding schools: accomplishments 34–5; cruelty 9; curriculum 34–5; day vs. boarding schools 40–1; deportment and girl's bodies 39–40; discipline and control in the twentieth century 38–9; discipline and control in the Victorian era 37–8; entitlement and disenfranchisement 32–3; further education 36; headmistresses 36–7; history 32–45; intimacy 41–2; lasting effects of lack of intimacy on marriage 42–3; teachers and their training 35; women's education, history of 33–4
girl's bodies 39–40, 204; *see also* menstruation; periods
girls' clothing 208
Girton College Cambridge 35, 36
grammar school foundations 18–19
grammar schools 18
Graves, Robert: *Goodbye to All That* 9
grief 55, 89, 119, 120, 121, 125, 132, 133, 152, 168; and mourning 141; revenge—split off grief 161; *see also* homesickness
Grier, Francis 6, 152, 153, 159–60

Harrow 24, 26, 28, 29
headmasters 52, 62, 103, 129–30, 131, 132; autonomy 37; brutality 26, 57, 65–6, 97; convicted of abuse 221, 225n16; embezzlement 26; Eton 20; fagging 24; fantasies of retribution against 102; flogging 25; food supply 170, 171; Harrow 24; homosexuality 211; Marlborough 25; public schools 28; reforms 26; Roedean 35; sexual abuse 174; Sherborne 20; tuck box 170; wives 64, 174; *see also* Keate
Headmaster's Conference 28

headmistresses 36–8, 144, 193, 207; Cheltenham Ladies College 35, 36–7; Christ's Hospital School 194, 195; dictator 38; eating disorders 201; hierarchy at dinner table 200; London Collegiate 37; prefects 37; public schools 35; school dance 206; *see also* Beale, Dorothea; Buss, Mary; West, Dorothy Ruth
Henry VI 18
Henry VIII 18
Herman, Judith 49, 50, 53, 57, 80, 105, 116, 117, 121, 137, 139, 142, 143, 182
Heward, Christine 7
Hickson, Alisdare 5, 42, 211
hidden self 192–204; bullying and initiation 196–8; communities of women 193–5; eating disorders 201–2; hierarchy at the dinner table 200–1; service 195–6; table manners 199–200; unsymbolised self 201–4; why the child does not tell 198–99
Holmes, J. 9–10
homelessness 125, 151–2, 231; and mourning 161–2
homesickness 9, 67, 68, 72, 127, 132, 133, 137, 141, 164–75, 231; definition 164–5; dining room 169–70; dormitory 168–9; force feeding 173; hunger and greed 170–1; hunger and greed in the twentieth century 171–2; intimate care and the child's body 165–8; sickness and food 173–4
homosexuality 28, 42, 211, 216–17, 219, 221–2, 225n14; *see also* lesbianism

imprisonment 90, 137, 138–9, 141, 143, 147, 149, 183, 184
Independent School Council (ICS) 3–4, 163n15
initiation 43, 186, 196–8
intimacy 2, 41–2, 126, 135, 189, 217, 232; fear of 159; lasting effects of lack of in marriage 42–3

Journal of Analytical Psychology 6
Jung, C. G. 55, 61, 115
Jungian psychoanalysis 11, 79n7, 98

Kalsched, Donald 53, 113, 115, 119
Kaplinsky, Cathy 157, 158

Kaye, Patrick 165
Keate 20
Kerstenberg, J. 116
Kings School 18
Klein, Melanie 120, 160

Ladies' Academies 34, 36
Lambert, Royston 5, 29
Lanius, R. A. 99
lashing 182, 183
latency child 9, 179
leathers and the lash 182
Leaving Home at 8 134
le Carre, John 138
left side 79n7, 99
lesbianism 194, 195, 206–7
Lewis, George 24, 25
Lewis, Peter 191n3
liberation 40, 64, 183–4
locked away 81–2
London Collegiate for Ladies 35, 37
Longhurst, Henry 173
looked after children 7–8; definition 7
losses 10, 81, 113, 119, 120, 122, 146, 174, 217, 227, 228; abandonment by parents 108, 117, 156, 158, 161–2; attachments 2, 4, 7, 32, 58, 129, 135, 179, 202, 205, 218, 230, 231; bereavement 52, 79, 121, 125, 126, 127, 130, 132–4, 137, 141, 150, 151, 152–4, 155, 180; betrayal 89, 90; home 157, 158, 161, 164, 165, 167, 168, 169; of identity 33; liberty 147
Lovendal-Duffell, Helena 6
Luke, Colin: *The Making of Them* 6, 143

Macaulay, Catharine: *History of England* 34; *Letters on Education* 34
Marlborough 26; Rebellion 24–5
marriage 33, 126, 206; attachments 125; communication 51; and the idealisation of women 158–60; lasting effects of lack of intimacy on 42–3; preparation for 34–5
masculinity 9, 41, 42; false 43, 179, 180, 228; hard 196; premature 192
masturbation 218, 220, 222, 224
McGilchrist, I. 99
memory: loss 113, 114, 115; and narrative 147; threshold 185–7
men's bodies 9
menstruation 39, 208, 218
Merchant Taylors' 26

Montague, Elizabeth 34
More, Margaret 33
More, Thomas 33
mothers: betrayal 89–90, 91; and wives 224; women as 230–1
Motion, Andrew 52, 129, 130–2, 173
mourning 133–4; and homelessness 161–2

nannies and servants 157–8
narrative: and memory 147; and witnessing 117–18
National Society for the Prevention of Cruelty to Children (NSPCC) 7
neuroscience 117; developing brain 94–109; the split 97–101, 221–4
New Society 5
The Nine 26

Oakley, Ann 36
Okely, Judith 10, 32, 33, 38, 39, 40–1, 83, 138: *Own and Other Culture* 5
old boy network and false masculinity 180
old school tie and sibling groups 228–9
Oppenheim, Paul 114
Orwell, George 29–30, 60, 169, 170, 171, 173

packing 81, 82, 146
paedophiles 65, 215, 217, 221, 224–5
Papadopoulos, R. 116
Parent Infant Project 175n13
Parkes, Colin Murray 125, 132–3
Partridge, Simon 6
Peel, John 129
periods 208–9
pornography 218–18, 222
post-summer break 56–8, 146–7
post-traumatic stress disorder (PTSD) 50, 69, 113, 114, 116, 117, 118–19, 139, 149; and dissociation 149
Power, Anne 6
prefects 37–8, 173, 180, 181, 197, 211, 217, 220, 229; and fagging 23–4
preparatory schools 18–19, 151, 153; Maidwell Hall 130
privacy, lack of 218
psyche, mapping the (case study part 2) 60–79; dormitory and despair 76–9; food 70–3; horror 65–6; kindness 75–6; religion 66–7; territory 61–5; soul murder 73–5

psychotherapy: amnesia 118; armoured self 189–90; Boarding School Syndrome 9–10; couples 2, 159; and the hidden trauma 9–10; transference 227–8
puberty, boys 217–19
puberty in girls' schools 205–14; history of sexuality 205–7; homosexuality 211; lasting impact of experiences at a boarding school 213–14; love and sexuality 209–11; periods 208–9; taboo 207–8
public school child 179–80
public schools 9–10, 17–18, 19, 85–6, 154, 172, 184, 186, 220; Beacon School 193, 209, 213; boys 5, 37, 196, 211, 213; brutality 20; bullying 187; Charterhouse 22, 26; Cheltenham Ladies College 26, 34, 35, 36, 40; Christ's Hospital 194, 195; class conscious 29, 37; Classical Greek 171; curriculum 34–5; diet 28; early 54; entitlement 229; Eton 18, 20, 21, 22, 25, 26, 28, 60, 229; fagging 23; fair play 24; friendships 228–9; girls 34; Girton College Cambridge 35, 36; Harrow 24, 26, 28, 29; headmistresses 35; homesickness 164; Kings School 18; Ladies' Academies 34, 36; London Collegiate for Ladies 35, 37; loyalty 29, 180; Marlborough 24–6; Merchant Taylors' 26; The Nine 26; positive experiences 4; reform 25–8; Roedean 34, 35; Rugby School 26, 28, 187–8; sexual activities 216; Shrewsbury 20, 26; South Africa 25, 181; 'stiff upper lip' 180; St Paul's 26; St Peter's School 18, 165; teachers 194; Uppingham Public School 19, 28; Wellington 26; Westminster 21, 26; Winchester 18, 26
punishment: beatings 4, 9, 17, 20, 23, 24–5, 37, 38, 43, 107, 127, 132, 161, 169, 171, 180, 192, 197, 198, 216; corporal 17, 181; floggings 25; lashing 182, 183; and regime 142

Queens College for Women 35

rage 2, 71, 85–7, 102, 189
rebellion 24, 25
regression 57, 69, 77, 80, 90–1, 95, 96, 105; humiliating 169; temporary 168
religion 18, 26, 29, 66–9, 71, 104

repetition 145–6
respite 106–7
returning to school: after summer break 56–8; trauma 146–7
revenge 161
Robertson, James 128
Robertson, Joyce 128
Roedean 34, 35
Rothschild, Babette 57, 119
Rugby School 26, 28, 187–8

Sacks, Oliver 129
Sargent, William 115
Schaverien, Joy: *The Dying Patient in Psychotherapy* 6
Schore, Alan 98; *Affect Regulation and the Development of the Self* 117
school uniforms 40, 85, 142; girls 38, 41, 206
self, armoured *see* armoured self
self, hidden *see* hidden self
self, encapsulated *see* encapsulated self
self abuse 149, 189
sending 'home', tradition of 154–6
Sex Disqualification [Removal] Act 36
sexual abuse 115, 116, 121, 143, 150n19, 174, 187, 199, 207, 215–24, 225n1; *see also* paedophiles
sexual activity/behavior *see* boys' sexual activity and sexual abuse; fear of sexuality; homosexuality; puberty in girls' schools; public schools: sexual activity
Sexual Offences Act 1967 225n14
Sherborne 20
Shrewsbury 20, 26
sibling groups: and old school ties 228–9; and women 230
Smith, Sydney 25
social pressure to forget 121
soul murder 73–5, 104, 168
split 97–101, 221–4
Stack, Mary 6, 169–70, 173, 200
Stern, Daniel 128, 166
Storr, Anthony 29
St Paul's 26
St Peter's School 18, 165
suicide 22, 224

table manners 199–200, 201
Taunton Commission 27–8
Therapy Today 6

threshold memory 185–7
Tom Brown's School Days 9, 187–8
Totnes Grammar School 20
transference 54–5, 56, 90, 101, 158, 159, 189, 190; and psychotherapy 227–8
trauma: anatomy of Boarding School Trauma 137–8; breaking the rules 142–3; childhood amnesia 116–17; definition 114, 141; dissociation and post-traumatic stress 149; on first day 140; freedom 143–4; grief and mourning 141; post-traumatic stress and dissociation Trauma and 149; psychotherapy and the hidden trauma 9–10; *see also* affect regulation; beating; bullying; cruelty; dissociation; post-traumatic stress disorder; regression
trauma and the developing brain (case study part 4) 94–109; anger after summer break 101–2; betrayal and trust 103–4; cellar drawing 105–6; dream 107; end of cellar 107–8; recalling the boy 104–5; respite 106–7; revisiting the school 103; the split 97–101; *see also* developmental trauma
Tronick, E. Z. 166

unsymbolised self 201–4
Uppingham Public School 19, 28

Van der Kolk, Bessel 114, 116, 117, 137
Vaughan, C. J. 24
Vietnam War 116

Wakeford, John 5, 29
Walford, G. 5
Wellington 26
West, Dorothy Ruth 194–5, 200, 201, 206, 207
Westminster 21, 26
William of Wykeham 18
Wilson, A. N. 174
Winchester 18, 26
Winnicott, Donald 128
witnessing and the narrative function 117–18
wives and mothers 224
Wober, Mallory 5, 41, 205
Wollstonecraft, Mary: *The Vindication of the Rights of Women* 34
women as mothers 230–1
women's bodies ; shaming 43
women's education 33–4, 35, 36
women teachers 35, 193, 194
Wood, Charles 22
Woodhead, J. 166
Wootton, Barbara 36
World War I 115, 173, 192
World War II 115, 123n18, 128, 129, 207, 232n3

eBooks
from Taylor & Francis

Helping you to choose the right eBooks for your Library

Add to your library's digital collection today with Taylor & Francis eBooks. We have over 50,000 eBooks in the Humanities, Social Sciences, Behavioural Sciences, Built Environment and Law, from leading imprints, including Routledge, Focal Press and Psychology Press.

Choose from a range of subject packages or create your own!

Benefits for you
- Free MARC records
- COUNTER-compliant usage statistics
- Flexible purchase and pricing options
- All titles DRM-free.

Benefits for your user
- Off-site, anytime access via Athens or referring URL
- Print or copy pages or chapters
- Full content search
- Bookmark, highlight and annotate text
- Access to thousands of pages of quality research at the click of a button.

REQUEST YOUR FREE INSTITUTIONAL TRIAL TODAY

Free Trials Available
We offer free trials to qualifying academic, corporate and government customers.

eCollections

Choose from over 30 subject eCollections, including:

Archaeology	Language Learning
Architecture	Law
Asian Studies	Literature
Business & Management	Media & Communication
Classical Studies	Middle East Studies
Construction	Music
Creative & Media Arts	Philosophy
Criminology & Criminal Justice	Planning
Economics	Politics
Education	Psychology & Mental Health
Energy	Religion
Engineering	Security
English Language & Linguistics	Social Work
Environment & Sustainability	Sociology
Geography	Sport
Health Studies	Theatre & Performance
History	Tourism, Hospitality & Events

For more information, pricing enquiries or to order a free trial, please contact your local sales team:
www.tandfebooks.com/page/sales

www.tandfebooks.com